™

References for the Rest of Us! ®

BESTSELLING BOOK SERIES

Are you intimidated and confused by computers? Do you find that traditional manuals are overloaded with technical details you'll never use? Do your friends and family always call you to fix simple problems on their PCs? Then the *...For Dummies*® computer book series from IDG Books Worldwide is for you.

...For Dummies books are written for those frustrated computer users who know they aren't really dumb but find that PC hardware, software, and indeed the unique vocabulary of computing make them feel helpless. *...For Dummies* books use a lighthearted approach, a down-to-earth style, and even cartoons and humorous icons to dispel computer novices' fears and build their confidence. Lighthearted but not lightweight, these books are a perfect survival guide for anyone forced to use a computer.

> *"I like my copy so much I told friends; now they bought copies."*
>
> — Irene C., Orwell, Ohio

> *"Quick, concise, nontechnical, and humorous."*
>
> — Jay A., Elburn, Illinois

> *"Thanks, I needed this book. Now I can sleep at night."*
>
> — Robin F., British Columbia, Canada

Already, millions of satisfied readers agree. They have made *...For Dummies* books the #1 introductory level computer book series and have written asking for more. So, if you're looking for the most fun and easy way to learn about computers, look to *...For Dummies* books to give you a helping hand.

IDG
BOOKS
WORLDWIDE
®

1/99

VISIO® 5

FOR

DUMMIES®

VISIO® 5 FOR DUMMIES®

by Debbie Walkowski

IDG Books Worldwide, Inc.
An International Data Group Company

Foster City, CA ◆ Chicago, IL ◆ Indianapolis, IN ◆ New York, NY

Visio® 5 For Dummies®

Published by
IDG Books Worldwide, Inc.
An International Data Group Company
919 E. Hillsdale Blvd.
Suite 400
Foster City, CA 94404
www.idgbooks.com (IDG Books Worldwide Web site)
www.dummies.com (Dummies Press Web site)

Library of Congress Catalog Card No.: 99-61893

ISBN: 0-7645-05475

Printed in the United States of America

10 9 8 7 6 5 4 3 2 1

1B/QW/QU/ZZ/IN

Distributed in the United States by IDG Books Worldwide, Inc.

Distributed by CDG Books Canada Inc. for Canada; by Transworld Publishers Limited in the United Kingdom; by IDG Norge Books for Norway; by IDG Sweden Books for Sweden; by Woodslane Pty. Ltd. for Australia; by Woodslane (NZ) Ltd. for New Zealand; by TransQuest Publishers Pte Ltd. for Singapore, Malaysia, Thailand, Indonesia, and Hong Kong; by ICG Muse, Inc. for Japan; by Norma Comunicaciones S.A. for Colombia; by Intersoft for South Africa; by Le Monde en Tique for France; by International Thomson Publishing for Germany, Austria and Switzerland; by Distribuidora Cuspide for Argentina; by Livraria Cultura for Brazil; by Ediciones ZETA S.C.R. Ltda. for Peru; by WS Computer Publishing Corporation, Inc., for the Philippines; by Contemporanea de Ediciones for Venezuela; by Express Computer Distributors for the Caribbean and West Indies; by Micronesia Media Distributor, Inc. for Micronesia; by Grupo Editorial Norma S.A. for Guatemala; by Chips Computadoras S.A. de C.V. for Mexico; by Editorial Norma de Panama S.A. for Panama; by American Bookshops for Finland. Authorized Sales Agent: Anthony Rudkin Associates for the Middle East and North Africa.

For general information on IDG Books Worldwide's books in the U.S., please call our Consumer Customer Service department at 800-762-2974. For reseller information, including discounts and premium sales, please call our Reseller Customer Service department at 800-434-3422.

For information on where to purchase IDG Books Worldwide's books outside the U.S., please contact our International Sales department at 317-596-5530 or fax 317-596-5692.

For consumer information on foreign language translations, please contact our Customer Service department at 1-800-434-3422, fax 317-596-5692, or e-mail rights@idgbooks.com.

For information on licensing foreign or domestic rights, please phone +1-650-655-3109.

For sales inquiries and special prices for bulk quantities, please contact our Sales department at 650-655-3200 or write to the address above.

For information on using IDG Books Worldwide's books in the classroom or for ordering examination copies, please contact our Educational Sales department at 800-434-2086 or fax 317-596-5499.

For press review copies, author interviews, or other publicity information, please contact our Public Relations department at 650-655-3000 or fax 650-655-3299.

For authorization to photocopy items for corporate, personal, or educational use, please contact Copyright Clearance Center, 222 Rosewood Drive, Danvers, MA 01923, or fax 978-750-4470.

About the Author

Debbie Walkowski has had a wide and varied career in the computer industry. Beginning in 1980 when no one even knew what a PC was, Debbie learned about and taught CP/M, now a relic of operating systems. She brought executives and administrators kicking and screaming into the personal computer age, teaching classes about word processors, spreadsheets, and more sophisticated programs as they became available. She sold, taught, and finally settled into writing about computer solutions. She has written documentation for major corporations and has authored 15 books on popular personal computer software including Microsoft Windows, Word, Excel, PowerPoint, Project, Office, Quicken, WordPerfect, and Lotus 1-2-3.

Debbie makes her home in Redmond, Washington where she lives with her husband Frank, eight-year-old son Christopher, and faithful and fluffy dog, Mickey. As if she isn't busy enough writing books, she also runs a clothing design business and stays sane by training vigorously in martial arts.

ABOUT IDG BOOKS WORLDWIDE

Welcome to the world of IDG Books Worldwide.

IDG Books Worldwide, Inc., is a subsidiary of International Data Group, the world's largest publisher of computer-related information and the leading global provider of information services on information technology. IDG was founded more than 30 years ago by Patrick J. McGovern and now employs more than 9,000 people worldwide. IDG publishes more than 290 computer publications in over 75 countries. More than 90 million people read one or more IDG publications each month.

Launched in 1990, IDG Books Worldwide is today the #1 publisher of best-selling computer books in the United States. We are proud to have received eight awards from the Computer Press Association in recognition of editorial excellence and three from Computer Currents' First Annual Readers' Choice Awards. Our best-selling ...For Dummies® series has more than 50 million copies in print with translations in 31 languages. IDG Books Worldwide, through a joint venture with IDG's Hi-Tech Beijing, became the first U.S. publisher to publish a computer book in the People's Republic of China. In record time, IDG Books Worldwide has become the first choice for millions of readers around the world who want to learn how to better manage their businesses.

Our mission is simple: Every one of our books is designed to bring extra value and skill-building instructions to the reader. Our books are written by experts who understand and care about our readers. The knowledge base of our editorial staff comes from years of experience in publishing, education, and journalism — experience we use to produce books to carry us into the new millennium. In short, we care about books, so we attract the best people. We devote special attention to details such as audience, interior design, use of icons, and illustrations. And because we use an efficient process of authoring, editing, and desktop publishing our books electronically, we can spend more time ensuring superior content and less time on the technicalities of making books.

You can count on our commitment to deliver high-quality books at competitive prices on topics you want to read about. At IDG Books Worldwide, we continue in the IDG tradition of delivering quality for more than 30 years. You'll find no better book on a subject than one from IDG Books Worldwide.

John Kilcullen
Chairman and CEO
IDG Books Worldwide, Inc.

Steven Berkowitz
President and Publisher
IDG Books Worldwide, Inc.

*Eighth Annual
Computer Press
Awards ≥ 1992*

*Ninth Annual
Computer Press
Awards ≥ 1993*

*Tenth Annual
Computer Press
Awards ≥ 1994*

*Eleventh Annual
Computer Press
Awards ≥ 1995*

Author's Acknowledgments

Some books are more fun to write than others. The people you get to work with determine that almost entirely (and a good product always helps!). In this case, I had the best of both worlds: a great product and great people — what could be better?

Let me start with the folks at Visio Corporation, a truly top-notch, sophisticated, quality organization. I had the pleasure of learning about this young company four years ago and was highly impressed then. My opinion hasn't changed a bit. Thanks to Stacy Dellas, Corporate Trainer, who was enthusiastic about this project from the beginning and helped us get it off the ground. She was never too busy to talk or answer questions, and she accommodated my every need. And special thanks to Charlie Zaragoza and Lorrin Smith–Bates, Visio's top trainers. They answered many questions for me and were willing to e-mail me from any place in the world! Charlie pulled together "Answers to Ten (Or So) Burning Questions about Visio," presented in The Part of Tens. Another Part of Tens chapter, "Ten of the Best Visio Tips," comes from Charlie's and Lorrin's expertise as Visio trainers.

And now for IDG Books Worldwide, Inc. Thanks to Joyce Pepple, acquisitions editor, who pitched this book internally and made it fly. Thanks to two *terrific* partners, Andrea Boucher, project editor, and Stacey Mickelbart, copy editor. They really know their stuff, and I could never have asked for a more supportive, helpful team. Credit for the quality of this book rests entirely on their shoulders. They had great ideas, offered terrific suggestions, and really kept me calm (especially near the last week of writing when I spent five days in bed with a 104-degree fever!). Thanks also to Jim McCarter, who took the time to painstakingly test every step in this book to ensure its technical accuracy.

Thanks also to Lisa Swayne, who made this opportunity possible. And a special thanks, as always, to my number one supporter and partner, Frank. I could never do half of what I do without him.

Publisher's Acknowledgements

We're proud of this book; please register your comments throught our IDG books Worldwide Online Registration Form located at http://my2cents.dummies.com.

Some of the people who helped bring this book to marke include the following:

Acquisitions, Editorial, and Media Development

Project Editors: Andrea C. Boucher; Stacey Mickelbart

Acquisitions Editor: Joyce Pepple

Copy Editors: Stacey Mickelbart; Rowena Rappaport

Technical Editor: Jim McCarter

Associate Permissions Editor: Carmen Krikorian

Editorial Managers: Rev Mengle; Leah P. Cameron

Media Development Manager: Heather Heath Dismore

Editorial Assistant: Paul E. Kuzmic

Production

Associate Project Coordinator: Maridee Ennis

Layout and Graphics: Angela F. Hunckler, Jane Martin, Lisa Rowell, Brent Savage, Jacque Schneider, Janet Seib

Proofreaders: Kelli Botta, Vicki Broyles, Christine Sabooni, Nancy Price, Rebecca Senninger, Ethel M. Winslow

Indexer: Glassman Indexing Services

Special Help
Darren Meiss; Alison Walthall

General and Administrative

IDG Books Worldwide, Inc: John Kilcullen, CEO; Steven Berkowitz, President and Publisher

IDG Books Technology Publishing: Brenda McLaughlin, Senior Vice President and Group Pubisher

Dummies Technology Press and Dummies Editorial: Diane Graves Steele, Vice President and Associate Publisher, Mary Bednarek, Director of Acquisitions and Product Development; Kristin A. Cocks, Editorial Director

Dummies Trade Press: Kathleen A. Welton, Vice President and Publisher; Kevin Thornton, Acquisitions Manager

IDG Books Production for Dummies Press: Michael R. Britton, Vice President of Production and Creative Services; Cindy L. Phipps, Manager of Project Coordination, Production Proofreading, and Indexing, Kathie S. Schutte, Supervisor of Page Layout; Shelley Lea, Supervisor of Graphics and Design; Debbie J. Gates, Production Systems Specialist; Robert Springer, Supervisor of Proofreading, Debbie Stailey, Special Projects Coordinator; Tony Augsburger, Supervisor of Reprints and Bluelines

Dummies Packaging and Book Design: Patty Page, Manager, Promotions Marketing

◆

The publisher would like to give special thanks to Patrick J. McGovern, without whom this book would not have been possible

◆

Contents at a Glance

Cartoons at a Glance

By Rich Tennant

page 39

page 201

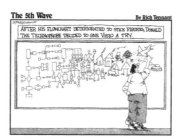

page 7

page 251

page 109

Fax: 978-546-7747 • E-mail: the5wave@tiac.net

Table of Contents

Introduction

●●●

*I*t's 11:45 a.m., and your stomach is telling you that it's time for lunch. As you're putting on your jacket and heading for the door, your phone rings. It's your boss telling you that she needs a really impressive Visio drawing (impressive enough to present to clients) illustrating your organization's logical network, and she needs it by the end of the day today. You immediately break out in a cold sweat. You're not an artist and you've never used Visio before. So much for lunch. You take off your jacket, sit down, fire up Visio, stare blankly at the screen, and wonder where on earth to begin.

Thankfully, this scenario is only hypothetical, but it isn't far-fetched. Bosses make requests like this every day. And if you're not prepared, you may find yourself in a state of panic. So, if you're not an artist and need to create a Visio diagram — anything from software flowcharts to office furniture and fixture layouts — don't worry; this book is for you. *Visio 5 For Dummies* leads you through the process of using Visio in as little time as possible. And believe me, I understand that your time is at a premium; you don't have hours to pore over a new software program and figure it out in-depth. In most cases, you have a rush job to do, and getting it done is your primary concern.

About This Book

This book is for everyone out there who has a job to do. And the job is *not* to learn Visio well enough to teach it; the job is to figure out Visio well enough to create a drawing or diagram, whatever the level of complexity.

With this in mind, *Visio 5 For Dummies* is designed to make you productive as quickly as possible. You'll find good, basic, useful information that helps you accomplish your goals rather than equipping you to write an essay on the history and virtues of Visio. You'll find real-world examples and figures that *show* you how to do something rather than just tell you. You'll find concise step-by-step instructions for accomplishing specific tasks rather than vague "it happens sort of like this" statements.

You can use Visio 5 with Windows 3.1 or higher.

About the Author

I'm probably a lot more like you than you think. I don't live for computers, and I'm not in love with them, either. But I am eternally grateful to have them and appreciate them tremendously because they make my work so much easier.

There was a time (almost 17 years ago?) when I knew next to nothing about computers. I took a job working for a major computer manufacturer and every day thereafter was a learning experience. Much of it was frustrating and humbling, especially in the beginning; but it was rewarding, too. In less than four years, I found myself teaching others how to use software and writing about it. In the last six years I've written 15 books on popular PC software (my degree in technical writing came in handy here).

In all my years working in the computer industry, I've never forgotten how it feels to be a beginner. My goal is (and always has been) to make the process of figuring out new software as painless and enjoyable as possible for the reader.

How to Use This Book

Don't feel you have to sit down and read this book cover to cover! Part I is designed to get you up and running, and Part II gives you the basic tools for creating drawings. From there, pick and choose what you want to read about. If you need help drawing shapes, there's a chapter just for that. If you want to incorporate layers in a diagram, there's a chapter for that, too. And after you've mastered the basics and you consider yourself a die-hard Visio junkie, check out Part IV, which covers creating custom templates, styles, and shapes, and how to share Visio files with data from other programs and vice versa. But, hey — if you never get to the die-hard junkie stage, don't worry about it. You'll still know a whole lot more about Visio than you ever thought you would.

Whatever level Visio user you are, be sure to glance through Part V, The Part of Tens. Here you find answers to common questions, examples of cool Visio wizards and stencils, tips, and ten really cool looking drawings and diagrams that were created using Visio.

Concentrate on these parts

If you've never used Visio, work your way through at least Part I and Part II of this book. These two parts give you the minimal knowledge required to turn out Visio drawings successfully, although not necessarily highly sophisticated drawings. When time permits and you want to know a little more about a particular topic, take a look at Part III.

Skip these parts if you want

If you're new to Visio and you just want to know enough to create simple drawings or diagrams, you can safely skip Part IV, which I have affectionately deemed as the part for die-hard Visio junkies. Clearly, every reader will not become a die-hard. Browse through Part III for the features that you find useful, and glance at Part V for anything interesting that pops out at you.

On the flip side, if you've used Visio before, you can safely skip Parts I and II, which offer basic getting up and running information.

How This Book Is Organized

Visio 5 For Dummies is organized into five distinct parts and an appendix:

Part I: Starting with Visio 5 Basics

This section lays the groundwork for your success with Visio. Every software program has its unique "personality;" Visio is no exception. Here you find conceptual information about Visio, get the Visio terminology down, discover how to recognize and work with what's on the screen, start Visio, save and open files and workspaces, and how to close Visio.

Part II: Creating Basic Drawings

If you're in a hurry, this section teaches you the basics of creating a *simple* drawing. I go over the basic elements of a Visio drawing and how to get them into your drawing. I also show you how to add text and manipulate it, as well as how to work with margins and tabs, indentation, alignment, spacing, and so on. You also see how to manipulate a drawing's *connectors,* the lines that connect one shape to another (they're more than just simple lines, as you'll soon discover). Finally, you get to see your drawings on paper in printed form.

Part III: Customizing Your Work

Here you move into the intermediate features of Visio. Find out how to place shapes precisely on a drawing, create your own shapes, enhance and manipulate shapes, do some more sophisticated stuff with connectors, work with pages and layers, and use wizards to create drawings.

Part IV: For the Die-hard Visio Junkie: Using More Advanced Stuff

Certainly not every user needs to pursue this section! Here I show you how to create custom templates and styles, how to store data in shapes and report on that data, customize shapes using a ShapeSheet spreadsheet, and protect your shapes and drawings from inadvertent changes. You also see how to use Visio drawings with other programs and on the Internet.

Part V: The Part of Tens

One of the most entertaining sections of every *...For Dummies* book, The Part of Tens is a set of various collections, each with ten or so items. In *Visio 5 For Dummies,* you find answers to ten burning questions about Visio, plus check out ten of Visio's coolest wizards and stencils, ten best tips, and ten sample drawings from the makers of Visio.

Appendix

Be sure to check out the appendix, which offers a stencil gallery — a visual tour of stencils included with Visio Standard, Technical, and Professional versions. The appendix is a great reference for finding the shapes that you want.

How This Book Works

Here's a summary of the conventions used in this book:

- ✔ When directions indicate that you type something, for example, "Enter **13** in the size box," the characters you type appear in bold.
- ✔ When I say "click," I mean to click your left mouse button. If you need to right-click, I specify "right-click."
- ✔ When I say "drag," I mean to click and hold the left mouse button as you move the mouse. Release the mouse button when you're done dragging.
- ✔ The term *shortcut menu* refers to the pop-up menus that appear when you right-click on something on the screen. When I want you to select a command from the shortcut menu, directions specify "right-click." (Shortcut menus are not available for all elements in a drawing.)

✔ You can select commands using toolbar buttons, menu commands, or the Alt key. Because toolbar buttons are by far the fastest method, I always list them first, followed by the menu command. (When toolbar buttons aren't available, I list only the menu command.) I specify a menu command by saying "Choose File⇨Save," which means to click on the File menu to open it, and then choose the Save option.

✔ Notice that the F and S are underlined in File and Save. This demonstrates a third way to select commands: with the Alt key. Press Alt+F to open the File menu; then just press S (no Alt) to select the Save option. This is not my preferred method for selecting commands, but if you're a keyboard lover, it can be great. I point them out when they are clearly timesavers.

Icons Used in This Book

The following icons are used in this text to call attention to specific types of information:

The Tip icon indicates information that's likely to save you time if you read it, or information that will make you say to yourself, "Wow, I never knew that!" Be sure to read this stuff.

When you see a Technical Stuff icon, I try to explain in lay terms something that is complicated or bogged down in technical jargon. You won't find too many of them, but when you do, you may want to take a gander.

Definitely pay attention to the Warning icons; they're designed to warn you of impending doom, or at the very least, a possible problem you'd just as soon avoid.

Remember icons are designed as a gentle nudge rather than a blatant slam to the head. In other words, "Remember this — it may be important to you someday!"

I use this funky little icon to point out weird stuff that Visio does every now and then.

Assumptions

I make the assumption that if you're reading this book, you have a reasonable working knowledge of Windows 95, Windows 98, or Windows NT 4.0, as one of these is required to run Visio. For this reason, I don't spend any of your valuable time in Chapter 1 describing how to find your way around Windows or how to work with dialog boxes. If you need to review these concepts, see *Windows 98 For Dummies,* by Andy Rathbone (IDG Books Worldwide, Inc.).

Part I

Starting with
Visio 5 Basics

AFTER HIS FLOWCHART DETERIORATED TO STICK FIGURES, DONALD THE TECHNOPHOBE DECIDED TO GIVE VISIO A TRY.

In this part . . .

So, you gotta learn Visio and you barely even know what it is, huh? Well, this is the place to start. Visio's a whole different animal than any software you've ever seen before, but don't worry — you'll be friends with Visio before this is over! In this part I show you what Visio is and does, how to speak Visio's language, and how to find your way around the screen. I also show you how to print — something you may find very useful if you want to be productive!

Chapter 1

Visio 101

● ●

● ●

*V*isio is truly a unique product! Although Visio is very easy to use, you can benefit from a bit of explanation before you jump right in. This chapter lays a solid foundation for your knowledge of Visio. In this chapter I help you to become familiar with what you see on the screen and to understand conceptually how Visio works.

Getting the Scoop

Close your eyes for a minute and picture the amount of visual information that comes to you in any given day. Magazines, newspapers, reports, television programs, and presentations convey a great deal of information in the form of charts, tables, graphs, diagrams, and technical drawings. You don't typically think of these examples as *art,* but they are graphical, and this is where Visio comes in handy.

In simple terms, Visio is a diagramming tool for business professionals, many of whom are self-confirmed non-artists. Although Visio is often referred to as a *drawing* tool, it really isn't, because it requires no artistic ability. It's more accurate to say that Visio is a tool for creating visual aids. That's comforting, because even in highly analytical, non-art related careers, you may be called upon to create a chart, diagram, or — perish the thought — a *drawing!* If the suggestion of drawing *anything* strikes terror in your heart, Visio can help.

Visio is actually like a grab bag of icons. These icons — or *shapes,* as Visio calls them — represent all sorts of things from computer network components, to office furniture, to boxes on an organization chart. You simply drag the shapes that you want into the drawing area and arrange and connect them the way that you want. You can add text and other graphical elements wherever you like.

Who's using Visio and why?

Visio is designed for anyone who needs a tool for diagramming, illustrating, or charting. It's frequently used by professional people who work in a business setting: operations managers, architects, salespeople, secretaries, financial analysts, software developers, marketing analysts, Web page designers, information technology (IT) consultants, or project managers. It may seem odd that such a diverse group of people can use Visio, but it's true. At some point, many of these professionals may need to create some sort of illustration for their work. Visio supplies all the shapes that you need to create typical business charts and diagrams. Even people with highly developed artistic skills use Visio because Visio's collection of shapes makes diagramming so easy. Why reinvent the wheel if you don't need to?

Examining the four Visio products

Visio doesn't make four distinct flavors of its product just to confuse you. Each one addresses a slightly different audience, although each uses the same core technology. That means that each product's basic operating functions are the same. Regardless of the Visio product that you run, I address the basic functions common to each. The following list gives you a brief description of each:

- **Visio Standard** is designed for mainstream business professionals such as salespeople, general managers, financial analysts, and project and product managers. It includes over 1,300 Standard shapes that help you communicate typical business information in a graphical form.

- **Visio Professional** widens the audience of Standard users to include network managers and designers, database designers, and software developers. Visio Professional gives you the tools to diagram and document things like networks, software, and databases. It includes the 1,300 Standard shapes plus an additional 1,300 Professional shapes.

- **Visio Technical** addresses the needs of professionals in specialized fields like facilities management, engineering (electrical, civil, mechanical, fluid dynamics, and so on), and architecture. You can use its more than 2,500 Technical shapes in combination with the 1,300 Standard shapes to create space plans, schematics, heating, ventilation, and air conditioning (HVAC) designs, and computer-aided design (CAD) drawings.

✔ **Visio Enterprise** builds on Visio Professional. It includes over 14,000 shapes to help you automatically diagram LANs and WANs, databases, and software designs at the highest levels.

Getting Familiar with Visio Lingo

Like all software programs, Visio uses certain unique terminology. You need to be familiar with some of the following terms before you begin creating diagrams and drawings.

✔ **Drag and drop** is the method Visio uses to create drawings. What are you dragging and where are you dropping it, you ask? You drag shapes and you drop them onto a drawing page.

✔ **Shapes** are probably the most important element of Visio. Shapes represent objects of nearly any conceivable kind — office furniture in an office layout diagram, road signs in a directional map, servers in a network diagram, boxes on an organization chart, bars on a comparison chart. Visio contains literally thousands of different shapes. You can draw your own shapes, too, as I show you in Chapter 7.

✔ **Stencils** are the tools Visio uses to organize shapes so that you can find the one you're looking for. A stencil is nothing more than a *collection of related shapes*. If you want to create an office layout diagram, for example, you use the office layout stencil, which includes shapes such as walls, doors, windows, telephone jacks, panels, furniture, plants, and electrical outlets. (Sorry, no reclining chair or big screen TVs are included with this template.) Stencils are displayed in a special window on the left side of the screen so that the shapes are always available while you're working. (Of course, you can minimize the window if it gets in your way.)

Visio makes the distinction between master shapes and instances of shapes. I explain the difference, but my advice is, don't clutter your mind with such hair-splitting detail! Master shapes are the shapes that you see on a stencil. When you drag a shape onto the drawing page, you're copying a master shape onto your drawing page, making it just one instance of that shape. In other words, the master stays on the stencil.

✔ **Templates** are plans for particular types of drawings. When you need to create a document, Visio makes life easy for you by providing templates that define certain characteristics of the drawing so that the drawing is consistent in its properties. For example, when you use a Visio template for a specific type of drawing, Visio automatically opens one or more appropriate stencils, defines the page size and scale of your drawing, and defines appropriate styles for things like text, fills, and lines. Of course, you can change any of these elements, but the point of using a template is to maintain consistency throughout the drawing. After all, your drawing may include several pages, and you want them to look as if they go together.

✔ **Connectors** are lines (or other shapes) that connect one shape to another. You can see perhaps the most common example of a connector on an organization chart. The lines that connect the president to various groups within an organization and the lines that run through an organization are connectors. In Visio, connectors can be very sophisticated, and I show you more about them in Chapter 5, but for now this definition is all you need to remember.

Making your drawings extraordinary

At first glance, it seems Visio is just an ordinary tool used for creating ordinary documents in an ordinary way. The organization chart shown in Figure 1-1 is an example of an ordinary drawing that you can create using Visio. There's nothing particularly fancy or exciting about it; an organization chart is an organization chart. (That said, however, try creating one using a word processor — easier said than done!)

Although you can use Visio to create ordinary documents, the program is anything but ordinary. In its fifth version, Visio has become quite sophisticated in its functionality. The following list describes some of the things that you can do with Visio.

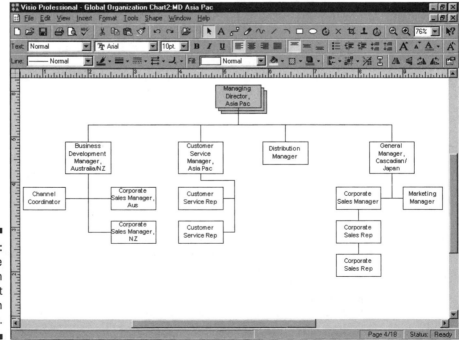

Figure 1-1:
A simple organization chart created in Visio.

- ✔ **Drill down** is a feature that lets you jump quickly from an overview drawing to a detailed drawing, just by double-clicking on a shape. For example, you can draw an overview map of a world-wide computer network and double-click on the name of a city to see a drawing of that city's computer network. This drill-down feature is possible because Visio lets you define a shape's behavior when you double-click on it. See Chapter 12 for more information.

- ✔ **Hyperlinks,** which are so popular on the Internet, are possible in Visio, too. You can jump from a Visio drawing to a different drawing, to a document outside of Visio, or to a location on the Internet. I discuss this feature in more detail in Chapter 12.

- ✔ **Reporting on data** is another sophisticated feature of Visio. What does this function do, exactly? Let me give you an example. Suppose you draw an office layout plan that includes cubicle walls, fixtures, office furniture, and computer equipment. You can store each piece of furniture and office equipment with data such as its inventory number, owner, and current location. The computer equipment shapes can also include data about the manufacturer, hardware configuration, and Internet address assigned to it. From this drawing, you can generate property, inventory, and location reports. See Chapters 12 and 13 for more information on storing and reporting on data in shapes.

Visio also provides impressive interaction with other applications. You can

- ✔ Include data or objects from other programs in your Visio drawings

- ✔ Create charts and diagrams from data stored in other programs

- ✔ Use Visio drawings in Microsoft PowerPoint presentations and vice versa

- ✔ Open Visio from within PowerPoint

- ✔ Use your Visio drawings on the Internet, either as HTML pages or as a part of your Web page

Getting In and Out of Visio

Visio gives you several options for starting up, opening stencils, and saving drawings. In this section I show you options for getting in and out quickly.

Starting Visio

Although you can start a new Visio document from scratch, without any pre-programmed settings, the most practical way to start Visio is with a template (and, in fact, Visio defaults to this method). A template lets you begin a new document with certain preprogrammed settings like the size of the page, a drawing scale, and the types of shapes that you may need to use. If you're creating a business form, for example, starting Visio with the Form Design template is the best idea. This template automatically opens the Forms Shapes stencil and sets your page size to 8-½ x 11 and your drawing scale to 1:1 (drawing size: actual size). The template specifies other settings that you may not notice right away (like a typical point size for text in a form), but you don't need to worry about these settings right now. You can change anything that you don't like later.

Visio stores templates in folders (like Business Diagram, Network Diagram, or Flowchart) based on the type of drawing that you want to create. These folders are stored in the Solutions folder. Don't worry about remembering this when you want to find them; Visio leads you right to the folders when you start the program.

To open Visio using a template, follow these steps.

1. **From your Windows desktop, click Start➪Programs➪Visio (Professional, Standard, Technical, or Enterprise).**

   Visio displays the Choose a Drawing Template dialog box. In the Look In box, notice that Solutions is the selected folder. Templates are stored in this folder.

2. **In the list, double-click on the folder name that represents the type of drawing you want to create.**

   Visio displays the templates in that folder.

3. **Click on the template that you want to use.**

   If you're not sure which one you want, just click on one and you can see a sample of it in the Preview area of the dialog box. After you find a template, click OK.

   Now Visio opens a blank drawing page like the one shown in Figure 1-2. Depending on the template that you choose, one or more stencils are automatically displayed on the left side of the drawing area. (In Figure 1-2, only the Forms Shapes stencil is open.) The drawing area is blank except for a non-printing grid used to position shapes.

Opening additional stencils

If you want to use a shape that's not available on the open stencil, you can open additional stencils at any time. For example, suppose you decide you want to add a mini-calendar to your business form so that your employees can't exclaim "I didn't know there was a meeting today!" A calendar shape is available on the Calendar Shapes stencil. You can only use that shape if the stencil is open.

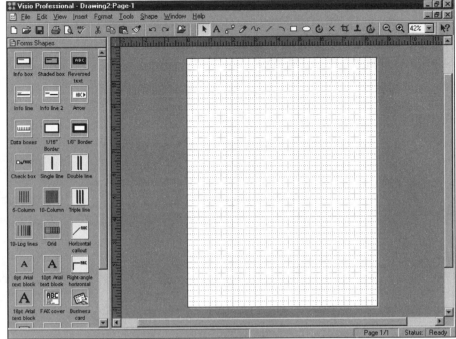

Figure 1-2:
When you open Visio using a template, Visio displays the appropriate stencil(s) to the left of the drawing area.

When you choose File⇨Stencils, Visio displays a submenu. Pay attention to the bottom portion of the submenu, which lists categories of stencils. Notice that each one is followed by an arrow, indicating that there is a submenu for each particular category. For instance, the Flowchart category lists 11 stencils for specific types of flowcharts. If you really want to be impressed by all the choices Visio gives you, take a look at the list of Network Diagram stencils shown in Figure 1-3, which has literally *dozens* of stencils, each for a specific type of network diagram. You can open as many stencils as you want to find the shapes that you need for your drawing.

To open a stencil, use these steps:

1. **Choose File⇨Stencils.**

   Visio displays a submenu listing categories of stencils.

2. **From the submenu, click on a stencil category.**

3. **From the submenu, click on a stencil name.**

   Visio opens the stencil and displays it on the left side of the screen. For more information about arranging stencils, see "Moving and arranging stencils" later in this chapter.

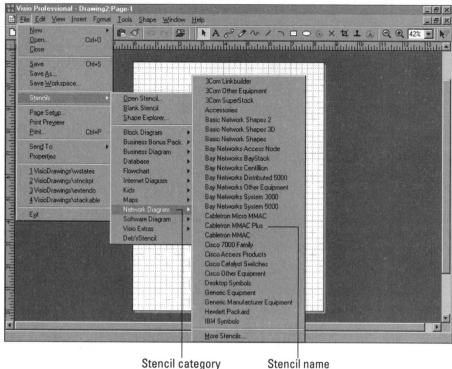

Figure 1-3:
Stencils are
listed first
by category
in the sub-
menu; then
by name.

Stencil category   Stencil name

Saving a drawing

After you spend a lot of time creating a drawing, you'll find it important to save your file. In fact, don't wait until you have finished a drawing; save it frequently from the minute you start creating it.

One great feature of Visio is that during the process of saving a file, Visio displays a Properties dialog box (see Figure 1-4). In this dialog box you can list information about the file that makes it easy for you to find and identify the file later, such as title, subject, author, manager, company, category, keywords, and description. In addition, you can choose whether to save a preview picture, which helps you identify the file in the Open dialog box before you open the file. The preview feature is especially nice because you can often identify a file more quickly visually than by its name. To save a file for the first time, use these steps.

1. **Choose File⇨Save.**

   Visio displays the Save As dialog box shown in Figure 1-4.

2. **In the Save In box, click the folder where you want to store the file.**

   (Click the down arrow to choose a new folder if necessary.)

Figure 1-4:
Type a file
name in the
Save As
dialog box.

3. **Type a name in the File Name box.**

4. **If the .vsd file extension is not selected in the Save As Type box, select it now.**

   .vsd is the file extension Visio uses for all drawings.

5. **Click the Save button.**

   Visio displays the Properties dialog box shown in Figure 1-5.

6. **Fill in as many of the fields as you want in the Summary tab to help you identify the file (all fields are optional).**

7. **To save a preview of the file, click the Draft or Detailed button.**

   (The Draft option saves shapes only, whereas the Detailed option saves all objects in the drawing and therefore increases the file size.)

8. **To conserve file space when saving a Preview, click the First Page Only option.**

9. **Click OK.**

Saving a workspace

Because you can spend a lot of time opening additional stencils and arranging them on the screen, Visio lets you save your screen arrangement along with your drawing. This feature saves you the time you'd spend opening the same file and stencils and arranging them on your screen the next time you want to work. Visio calls this *saving your workspace* and performs this function automatically whenever you save a file (unless you change this option). The check box for this option appears in the lower-right corner of the Save As dialog box (refer to Figure 1-4). To turn off this feature, remove the check from the Workspace box. When you save the file, Visio uses the file name for your drawing with a .vsw file extension (instead of the typical .vsd file extensions for drawings).

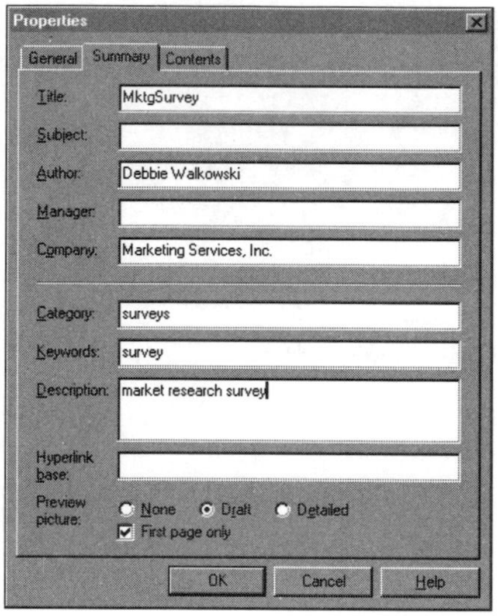

Figure 1-5:
Enter infor-
mation
in the
Properties
dialog box
to help you
identify
your file.

If you have more than one drawing file open and want to save your workspace, you can do this, but you must choose a new file name. Note that
saving a workspace doesn't automatically save changes to each open drawing. Be sure to save changes to each drawing individually.

To save a workspace when you have more than one drawing open, use these
steps:

1. **Choose File➪Save Workspace.**

    Visio opens the Save Workspace dialog box. The default file type in the
    Save File As box is Workspace (.vsw).

2. **In the File Name box, enter a unique file name.**

3. **Click OK.**

Opening a saved drawing or workspace

While you're working in Visio, you can open a saved drawing or workspace at
any time. The file that you open becomes the active drawing (or workspace);
any other drawings that are already open are still open. All open drawings are
listed on the Windows menu. For more information on arranging windows on
your screen, see *Windows 98 For Dummies,* by Andy Rathbone (IDG Books
Worldwide, Inc.).

Use the following steps to open a drawing or workspace.

1. **Choose File➪Open.**

    Visio displays the Open dialog box.

2. **In the Look In box, choose the folder where your file is located.**

3. **In the Files of Type box, choose either All Visio Files (*.vsw*), or a specific file type such as Drawing (*.vsd).**

4. **In the document list, click on the file that you want to open.**

5. **Click OK.**

The bottom of the File menu lists the most recently opened files. Just click a file name to open the file.

If you want to open a saved drawing or workspace and are starting up Visio at the same time, remember that Visio assumes that you want to begin by opening a template. It automatically displays the Choose a Drawing Template dialog box and selects the .vst (template) file extension in the Files of Type box. You can still open non-template files from this dialog box, but you need to change the setting in the Files of Type box to All Visio Files (.vs*) or to a specific file type, such as Drawing (*.vsd). Now Visio can see your other files and display them in the dialog box.

Closing Visio

When you're ready to close Visio, choose File⇨Exit. If you haven't recently saved all open files, Visio prompts you to do so for each file. Choose Yes to save or Cancel to return to Visio without saving the drawing.

Working Onscreen with Visio

A typical Visio working screen looks like the one shown in Figure 1-6. In this figure, the drawing is a simple office layout. The gridded area represents the drawing page. The blank area (it's actually blue on your screen) surrounding the drawing is called the *pasteboard*. The drawing area is bounded by rulers on the top and at the left of the screen, and by scroll bars on the bottom and at the right. The Office Layout stencil, containing flowchart shapes, appears on the left side of the screen. The Visio menu bar appears at the top of the window under the title bar. Beneath the menu bar are three open toolbars: the Standard, Text, and Shapes toolbars. The status bar, which provides information about your drawing, appears along the bottom of the drawing area. Note that one of the shapes in the drawing is selected, so the status bar displays the shape's width, height, and angle.

To zoom in for a closer look at a drawing, press Ctrl+Shift as you click the left mouse button, or click the Zoom In button on the Standard toolbar. (It looks like a magnifying glass with a + inside.) To zoom out, press Ctrl+Shift as you click the right mouse button, or click the Zoom Out button on the Standard toolbar (same magnifying glass, with a – inside). You can also choose a zoom percentage using the Zoom tool right next to these buttons.

Moving and arranging stencils

You can have as many open stencils as you like while you're working. (See the section "Opening additional stencils" earlier in this chapter.) Notice in Figure 1-6 at the top of the open Office Layout stencil that two additional stencils called Basic Shapes and Callouts are open.

The default "docking location" for stencils is on the left side of the screen; however, you have two options for rearranging stencils. You can "float" a stencil so that it appears in a separate window with its own Close and Minimize buttons, or you can switch sides and dock stencils on the right side of the screen. To use either of these options, right-click on the stencil's title bar, then choose either the Float or Switch Sides option from the drop-down menu. In Figure 1-7, one stencil is moved to the right side of the screen while the other remains on the left. You can arrange stencils this way, but notice that it reduces the size of your drawing area.

Minimized stencils

Toolbars   Rulers   Selected shape   Menu bar

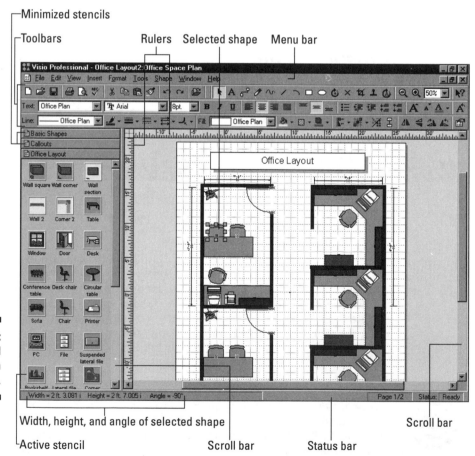

Figure 1-6:
A typical Visio screen layout.

Width, height, and angle of selected shape

Active stencil   Scroll bar   Status bar   Scroll bar

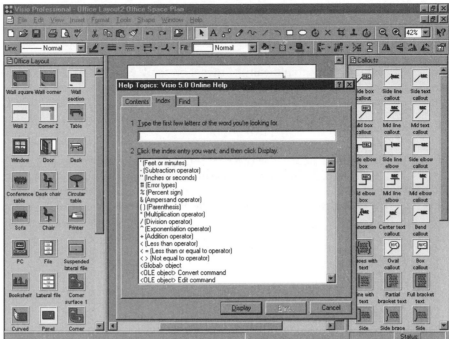

Figure 1-7:
Stencils can
be docked
on either
side of the
screen.

The advantage of floating a stencil window is that you can minimize it by clicking on the Minimize button, or you can move it anywhere you want on the screen. To return a floating stencil to the docking location, drag the title bar to the left side of the screen (or the right if you switched sides). The stencil snaps into place in line with other open stencils.

To close a stencil, right-click the title bar, then choose the Close option from the drop-down menu.

Working with more than one drawing

You can work with more than one drawing at a time. Each open file is listed at the bottom of the Window menu. If you want to view more than one drawing on the screen at the same time, choose Window⇨Tile, or Window⇨Cascade. After all your drawings are open, you can drag a window border to resize it or drag the title bar position to where you want them to appear on the screen.

Displaying and hiding toolbars

Visio has seven toolbars, three of which are displayed automatically when you start the program. The three default toolbars are Standard, Text, and Shape. You can hide any of these, or display View, Page, Web, and Developer toolbars as well. After you begin to recognize the buttons, it's much faster to use the toolbar buttons rather than select the menu commands. I include a lot of these buttons on the Cheat Sheet at the beginning of this book to help you out.

In Figure 1-1 earlier in the chapter, the Standard, Text, and Shape toolbars are displayed. To hide or display other toolbars, use these steps:

1. **Right-click anywhere in the toolbar area.**

   Visio displays a toolbar drop-down menu.

2. **To hide or display a toolbar, click on its name in the list.**

   (Toolbars currently displayed appear with a check mark on the drop-down list.)

3. **To see large toolbar icons, click the Toolbars option and choose Large Icons; then click OK.**

The drop-down menu that appears when you right-click in the toolbar also lets you display or hide the status bar. The status bar is displayed when a check mark appears next to its name.

Checking out the menu(s)

Visio's menu bar contains some typical menus found in almost every Windows application (like File, Edit, and Help). I like to review the contents of each menu because they often contain commands that you may not expect. The following list gives you a brief summary of Visio's menus:

- **File:** Look in the File menu for the typical New, Open, Close, Save, and Print commands. You also find the command for opening stencils, which I discuss in "Getting In and Out of Visio" earlier in this chapter.

- **Edit:** The typical Cut, Copy, Paste, Find, and Replace commands are found on this menu. Unique to Visio are commands for deleting and reordering pages and opening a group (shapes can be grouped to function as one shape).

- **View:** On this menu you find all of the zoom options. In addition, you have options for viewing rulers, grids, guides, and connection points.

- **Insert:** This menu lets you insert a page as well as insert objects such as ClipArt, WordArt, pictures, and graphs from outside of Visio.

- ✓ **Format:** The Format menu contains all the commands that you need to change the look of text, lines, and shapes.

- ✓ **Tools:** On this menu you find all kinds of tools for working with shapes, the drawing page and the drawing itself, Visio's color palette, rulers, grids, and so on.

- ✓ **Shape:** The Shape menu contains commands for sizing, positioning, flipping, rotating, and grouping shapes. You also find commands on this menu for changing the stacking order of shapes.

- ✓ **Window:** This menu lists all open windows and allows you to choose how they're displayed on your screen. You also find special commands for displaying Visio ShapeSheets (tables that describe the properties and characteristics of shapes) and master shapes.

- ✓ **Help:** Visio's help commands are located in this menu. Note that if you have an Internet connection, you can log right on to Visio's Web page here.

Getting help when you need it

As a Windows-compatible program, Visio's help feature works consistently with other Windows applications. To get help on a Visio topic, choose Help➪Visio Help. Visio displays the Help dialog box (shown in Figure 1-8), which contains tabs for Contents, Index, and Find. As the name implies, the Contents tab lists items in a format similar to a table of contents in a book. If you want to look up a topic like you would in the index of a book, choose the Index tab. If you're not sure how to search for what you're looking for, choose the Find tab to help you narrow your search.

Figure 1-8:
Visio's Help
dialog box is
similar to
that of other
Windows-
compatible
programs.

The Help menu has additional features unique to Visio. If you need help working with Visio templates, choose Help⇨Template Help. Visio takes you directly to help topics regarding templates. If you need help working with a particular shape, click on the shape to select it, then choose Help⇨Shape Help. An information box describing how to use the selected shape pops up. Finally, if you want to connect to Visio's home page or other locations on the Internet, choose Help⇨Visio on the Web.

Chapter 2

Hot Off the Press: Printing

. . . .

. . . .

*F*or the most part, printing in Visio is a breeze — not much different than printing from any other Windows application. However, because Visio drawings can sometimes be non-standard sizes, or multiple pages, you need to know about some special printing considerations. In this chapter I show you everything you need to know to print your drawings successfully.

Understanding Printing Terms

Almost every application has some new terminology to learn, and Visio is no exception. When it comes to printing, most of the terminology is logical, so it's easy to remember. You need to understand Visio definitions of the following terms:

- **Drawing page:** Refers to the drawing area that you see on the screen represented in white.

- **Page orientation:** The direction a drawing prints on the paper. When you hold a sheet of paper the *tall* way, the orientation is called *portrait*. When you turn the page a quarter turn so that you're holding it the *wide* way, the orientation is called *landscape*.

- ✔ **Page Setup:** Defines how your drawing page is set up in Visio; that is, its size and orientation. You can change page setup by choosing File⇨Page Setup.

- ✔ **Printed page:** The paper on which you print your drawing.

- ✔ **Printed drawing:** The final result; that is, your drawing as printed on paper by your printer.

- ✔ **Printer Setup:** Defines the page size and orientation that your printer uses when you print. When you're printing with a 1:1 ratio (drawing size: actual size), Page Setup and Printer Setup settings must match in order to print successfully. You change printer setup by choosing File⇨Page Setup⇨Print Setup.

- ✔ **Tile:** When a drawing is too large to print on a single sheet of paper, Visio *tiles,* or breaks up, the drawing into separate pages. Each tile prints on a separate sheet of paper. Visio marks where the drawing will tile with a wide gray line, which is visible in Print Preview (see "Previews: They Aren't Siskel and Ebert!" later in this chapter).

How Printing Works with Visio

When you create a drawing in Visio, the drawing page is represented by the white area in the drawing window. You can see the size of the drawing page by looking at the vertical and horizontal rulers along the edges of the drawing area. You can determine the orientation of the drawing page by whether the page is wider than it is tall (landscape) or taller than it is wide (portrait). Choosing File⇨Page Setup tells you the same information. In Figure 2-1, the drawing is landscape on 8½-x-11-inch paper.

The most important concept to keep in mind when you're printing with a 1:1 ratio for drawing size and actual size: *To print successfully, the settings for your printer must match the settings for the drawing page.* But you're in luck, because when you use a template to create a drawing, Visio takes care of matching these two settings. You can print your drawing correctly just by selecting File⇨Print.

But, suppose that you change something about the drawing — for example, the print orientation. If the template is set for portrait orientation and you change the drawing to landscape, the drawing doesn't print correctly. Likewise, if your drawing is 8½-x-14 inches and your printer is set up to print on 8½-x-11-inch paper, the complete drawing doesn't print. All printer settings must match drawing page settings. To figure out how to make these changes, see "Making Adjustments" later in this chapter.

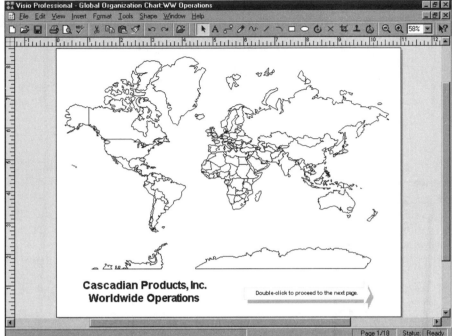

Figure 2-1:
This drawing is landscape orientation, and rulers indicate the drawing page size.

Previews: They Aren't Siskel and Ebert!

Previewing your drawing lets you see how it will look on the printed page. Your drawing probably isn't nearly as exciting as Siskel and Ebert reviews, but it's definitely more important! Figure 2-2 shows how a drawing looks in the Preview window.

Previewing a drawing gives you a chance to see that everything in the drawing is placed exactly where you want it, and to check for the correct placement of shapes, balance, symmetry, readability, and so on. Also, check to see that all shapes fall inside the wide gray lines around the edge of the paper, which indicate the drawing's margins. These page margins are only visible in Preview. Shapes that fall across the margin lines don't print completely.

Previewing a drawing also shows you if your drawing page size and orientation match the same settings for your printer. In Figure 2-3 you can see that the printer is expecting to print on 8½-x-11-inch paper in portrait orientation because that's where the preview displays the margin lines.

Notice in Figure 2-2 and Figure 2-3 that the preview screen has its own toolbar. The first five buttons — New, Open, Save, Print, and Preview — also appear on the Standard toolbar; the remaining buttons are described in Table 2-1.

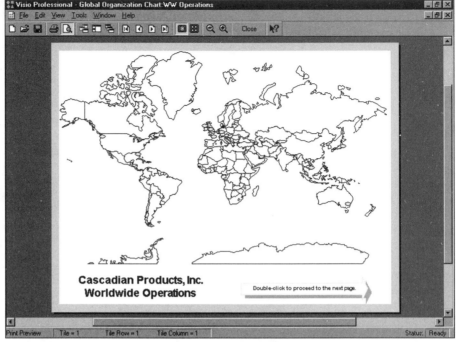

Figure 2-2:
The preview screen shows how your drawing will look when you print it.

Figure 2-3:
This preview shows that the printer settings don't match the drawing settings.

Page break

Table 2-1	Preview Toolbar Buttons
Button	**Function**
	New Window: Opens the active document in a new window.
	Tile Windows: Arranges all open windows like tiles (side by side) so that each one is visible.
	Cascade Windows: Arranges all open windows so that the title bars of each are visible.
	First Tile: When you select the Single Tile option, clicking this button displays the first tile.
	Previous Tile: When you select the Single Tile option, clicking this button displays the tile before the one currently displayed.
	Next Tile: When you select the Single Tile option, clicking this button displays the tile after the one that's currently displayed.
	Last Tile: When you select the Single Tile option, clicking this button displays the last tile.
	Single Tile: Lets you view a single tile at a time in a drawing that's tiled.
	Whole Page: Lets you view all tiles in a drawing at the same time.
	Zoom Out: Reduces your view in the Preview window so that you can see more of the drawing.
	Zoom In: Magnifies your view in the preview window. (You see less of the drawing.)
Close	**Close:** Closes the Preview window and takes you back to Normal drawing view.
	Help: Changes the mouse pointer to a question mark; displays help on the item that you click on.

Preparing Oversize Drawings for Printing

When you create an oversized drawing (that is, larger than the paper in your printer), you can see in a print preview that the drawing doesn't print on a single sheet of paper. Before you can print, Visio *tiles* the drawing, or breaks it into printable pages.

When you have a drawing larger than the largest paper installed in the current printer, your options are

- ✔ **Print at 1:1 ratio for drawing size: actual size** (no reduction) and let Visio tile.

- ✔ **Choose a reduction factor**.(Visio may still tile your drawing if you didn't reduce it enough.)

- ✔ **Tell Visio how many tiles (pages) that you want your drawing to fit on to** both horizontally and vertically, and let Visio choose the reduction factor. (This is especially useful, for example, if you choose one tile in each direction: Visio chooses a reduction factor to fit the drawing on one page.)

In any case, use Print Preview before you print to check that you have the settings (Page and Printer) correct.

One important point: Many templates that ship with Visio set the Drawing page size to "Same as printer." If you want to decouple the drawing size from the printer page size, you must select a specific Drawing page size using File⇨Page Setup.

To determine where these tiles occur, Visio uses the page size and orientation currently set in the Print Setup dialog box. Visio displays gray lines (similar to the margin lines shown in Figure 2-2) on the drawing page to indicate the borders of a tile. You can see how Visio tiles a drawing by clicking the Print Preview button or choosing File⇨Print Preview. Figure 2-4 shows how Visio breaks a very large drawing, like a building floor plan, into more than a dozen tiles on 8½-x-14-inch paper. (Visio does the tiling for you; you can't change where the tiles fall.)

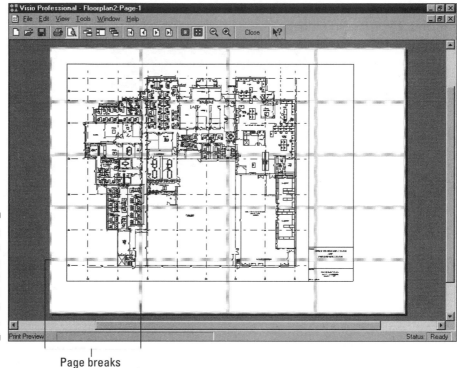

Figure 2-4:
Visio breaks
this drawing
up into more
than a
dozen tiles
for printing.

Page breaks

Making Adjustments

So, when you run into printing problems, how do you solve them? Remember the most important principle of printing with Visio: You have to make your Page Setup and your Print Setup match.

Begin by looking at your drawing in Print Preview. If the drawing looks good to you on the screen (it fits without overflowing, and so on), you probably want to print it with the current settings. Check the rulers to determine the size of the drawing page; then follow these steps:

1. **Choose File⇨Page Setup.**

2. **In the Page Setup dialog box (shown in Figure 2-5), click on the Page Size tab.**

3. **Note the Page Orientation (portrait or landscape) and the Page Size (standard 8½ x 11 or other).**

4. **Click the Print Setup button.**

   Visio displays the dialog box shown in Figure 2-6.

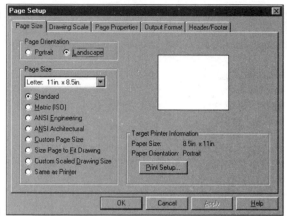

Figure 2-5:
The Page
Size tab in
the Page
Setup dialog
box shows
you the
orientation
and size set-
tings for
your draw-
ing page.

5. **In the Orientation box, choose the same orientation that you noted in the Page Setup dialog box in Step 3.**

6. **In the Size box, choose the same size that you noted in the Page Setup dialog box in Step 3.**

7. **Click OK to return to the Page Setup dialog box.**

8. **Click OK.**

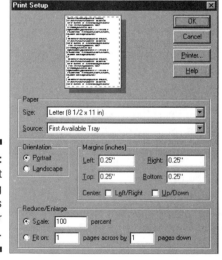

Figure 2-6:
The Print
Setup dialog
box shows
printer
settings.

Changing margin settings

If your drawing doesn't quite fit on the page, you can sometimes tweak the margin settings enough to fit the drawing on the page. Before you consider this option, think about the aesthetic appeal of the drawing. You don't want your drawing to look like you squeezed a Chevy Suburban into a parking space marked for a compact car. If you have room to breathe in your drawing, narrowing the margins may work.

Be aware, however, that many printers can't print within ½ an inch of the edge of the paper (top, bottom, or sides). I recommend that you keep your margins at least ½-inch wide or more. Check your printer's manual to determine your printer's capabilities.

To change margin settings, use these steps:

1. **Choose File⇨Page Setup.**

2. **In the Page Setup dialog box, click on the Page Size tab (refer to Figure 2-5).**

3. **Click the Print Setup button.**

   Visio displays the Print Setup dialog box (refer to Figure 2-6).

4. **In the Margins box, enter new margin measurements in the Left, Right, Top, and Bottom boxes (enter fractions as decimals, such as .5 for ½ inch).**

5. **Click OK to close the Print dialog box.**

6. **Click OK.**

Now that you're back at your drawing, choose View⇨Page Breaks. This command displays the margins as gray lines around the outer edges of the drawing page. Check to make sure that all your drawing shapes fit within the new margins. If the shapes still don't fit on a single drawing page, consider scaling the drawing when you print. See "Reducing and enlarging drawings" later in this chapter.

Centering a drawing

If you create a drawing that doesn't take up an entire page, you may want to center it on the page before you print it. You can do this by selecting all of the shapes on the drawing and moving them manually, but this method isn't very accurate (and is way too time-consuming). Visio makes it easy and exact by providing a command that does it for you. When you choose Tools⇨Center Drawing, Visio automatically centers all shapes in the drawing between the top, bottom, right, and left edges of the paper. When you print the drawing it appears in the center of the page.

Reducing and enlarging drawings

If a drawing is slightly too large to fit on a single page, changing the *print scale* (the reduction or enlargement of the printed drawing), to 90 percent may make it fit on the page and make it look better, too. Conversely, when a drawing is too small — so small that it's difficult to read — you can enlarge the print scale and make it easier to read when you print it.

Keep in mind that the print scale is completely different from the *drawing scale,* which is the size of the actual drawing. I show you how to change the drawing scale in Chapter 6.

To alter the print scale of a drawing, use these steps:

1. **Choose File⇨Open to display your drawing.**
2. **Choose File⇨Page Setup.**
3. **In the Page Setup dialog box, click the Print Setup button (refer to Figure 2-6) to display the Print Setup dialog box.**
4. **In the Reduce/Enlarge section of the Print Setup dialog box, click the Scale option.**

   Enter a number smaller than 100 percent to reduce the printed size of the drawing. Enter a number greater than 100 percent to enlarge the printed size of a drawing.
5. **Click OK to return to the Page Setup dialog box.**
6. **Click OK.**

You may expect your drawing to change on the screen, but it doesn't. This is because you've altered the *print* scale only, not the *drawing* scale. (It's just like reducing or enlarging a page on a photo copier — your original doesn't change; only the copied result changes.) To check that the change will take place when you print, click the Print Preview Tool button or choose File⇨Print Preview. The Print Preview shows you that the printout will be enlarged or reduced by the percentage you specified. Cool, huh? If you need to print the drawing at regular scale, be sure to follow the previous steps to change the percentage back to 100 before you print again.

Another way to scale your drawing is to specify exactly how many pages you want your drawing to fit on. Refer to the drawing in Figure 2-4, which is tiled across more than a dozen 8½-x-14-inch sheets of paper. If you want your drawing to print on less than a dozen sheets, you can tell Visio how many pages across and how many pages down you want the drawing to be printed on. Use these steps:

1. **Choose File⇨Open to display your drawing.**
2. **Choose File⇨Page Setup.**

3. **In the Page Setup dialog box, click the Print Setup button (refer to Figure 2-5) to display the Print Setup dialog box (refer to Figure 2-6).**

4. **In the Reduce/Enlarge section of the Print Setup dialog box, click the Fit On option.**

   Enter the number of pages across and the number of pages down that you want to print on.

5. **Click OK to return to the Page Setup dialog box.**

6. **Click OK.**

   You can see Visio scale your drawing on the screen to fit within the number of pages you specify.

Fitting the drawing on the number of pages you specify doesn't affect the actual scale of the drawing — just the printed copy.

Printing Your Documents

If the settings for your drawing page and your printer match, you're ready to print. Follow these steps:

1. **Choose File⇨Open to display your drawing.**

2. **Choose File⇨Print.**

   Visio displays the Print dialog box shown in Figure 2-7. (Note that your Print dialog box may look slightly different depending on the printer that you're using.)

3. **In the Printer Name box, select the correct printer.**

   (This is only necessary if you have access to more than one printer.)

4. **In the Page Range dialog box, indicate which pages you want to print.**

Figure 2-7:
Use the Print dialog box to specify how you want to print your drawing.

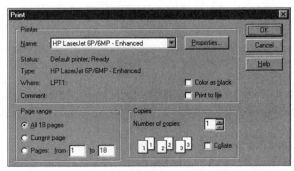

- **All:** Prints all pages in the drawing.

- **Current:** Prints the page that is currently displayed on the screen.

- **Pages:** Prints a range of pages; enter the first page number in the From box and the last page number in the To box.

5. **In the Copies box, enter the number of copies that you want.**

6. **Click OK.**

See? That wasn't so hard.

Some Windows applications also give you the option of printing a group of selected pages, such as 2, 4, and 7. Visio doesn't provide this option. To print a group of selected pages, you need to print each page individually by entering in the Pages option from 2 to 2, printing that page, entering from 4 to 4, printing again, and so on.

Adding Headers and Footers to a Drawing

A *header* refers to text that appears at the top of each page of a drawing; a *footer* is text that appears at the bottom of each page. Headers and footers are optional. If you decide to add them to a drawing, you can include text such as a title, file name, date, or automatic page numbers. You decide where you want them to appear in the header or footer area — left, center, or right.

To add a header or footer to a drawing, follow these steps:

1. **Choose File⇨Open to display your drawing.**

2. **Choose File⇨Page Setup; then click the Header/Footer tab.**

   Visio displays the Page Setup dialog box shown in Figure 2-8.

3. **In the appropriate header or footer box (Upper Left, Upper Center, Upper Right, and so on), type the information that you want to appear.**

4. **In the Margins area, enter a size for the header margin and footer margin.**

   You can type up to 128 characters in each header or footer box. I can't imagine why you would want that much information, but if you do, be sure to estimate the space that you need when entering a margin size.

5. **To format the header and footer text, click the Choose Font button, which displays the Font dialog box shown in Figure 2-9.**

   (Note that formatting applies to all header and footer text; you can't format each one individually.)

6. **In the Font dialog box, choose a Font, Size, Font style, Effects, and Color for the header and footer text.**

7. **Click OK to close the Font dialog box.**

8. **Click OK to close the Page Setup dialog box.**

Click the Print Preview Tool button or choose File⇨Print Preview to see how your header and footer text will look when you print your drawing. (Header and footer text is only visible in Print Preview or on the printed drawing.)

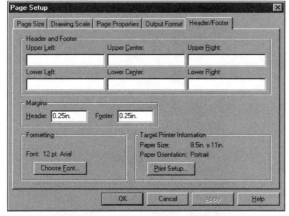

Figure 2-8:
Type the text for headers and footers in this dialog box.

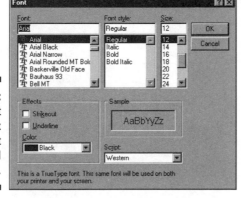

Figure 2-9:
Use the Font dialog box to format header and footer text.

In a tiled drawing, Visio prints headers and footers on each tile, as shown in Figure 2-10. When you have to tile a drawing to print it, you may want to put header and footer information on a background page (a separate page that works as an "underlay") instead. See Chapter 8 for details about creating background pages.

To add common text — time, date, file name, and page number — to a header or footer, you can enter one of the formatting codes shown in Table 2-2 in the Page Setup dialog box in the Header/Footer tab. For example, to add the current date, enter &d. Be sure to include any spacing that you want to precede and follow the text.

Table 2-2	Formatting Codes for Headers and Footers
Item	*Code You Type*
File name	&f
Current date	&d
Current time	&t
Page number	&p
Total number of pages printed	&P
File extension	&e
File name and extension	&f&e
Page name	&n
Ampersand	&&

Header

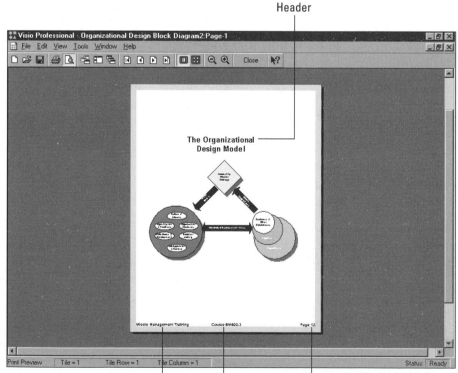

Figure 2-10:
Headers and footers contain information that you want repeated on each printed page.

Footer

Part II
Creating Basic Drawings

"Don't let Mort work on the office diagram next time."

In this part . . .

*I*f you don't have a whole lot of time to spend figuring out Visio, make sure that you check out this section. I show you the basic drawing stuff: How to get some shapes into a drawing, how to connect shapes, and how to throw some text in there, too, so that you can describe your drawings.

Chapter 3

Getting into Shape

• •

• •

Shapes are the single most important element of Visio; they're the building blocks that you use to create diagrams, drawings, charts, and graphs. Regardless of the type of drawing that you need to create — flowcharts, network diagrams, architectural drawings, project time lines — all are created, not by drawing (thank goodness!), but by using shapes. In this chapter I show you all the different types of shapes in Visio and how to work with them.

What's in a Shape?

If you think you may not have enough shapes to choose from when you're building your drawings, think again. Visio Standard includes more than 1,500 shapes; Visio Professional and Technical contain nearly twice and three times as many shapes, respectively. Shapes are stored on *stencils,* which are collections of related shapes that are displayed in their own window on your Visio screen. You create most of your drawings using stored Visio shapes, but you can also create and store your own shapes, which I tell you more about in Chapter 7.

A shape can be as simple as a single line or as complex and detailed as a network component for a computer system. A complex shape can also contain special programming that causes the shape to behave in a particular way.

For example, a bar chart shape from the Charting Shapes stencil automatically adjusts the length of its bars when you type in a percentage for one of the bars (see Figure 3-1). You can also control special aspects of other shapes, such as the vanishing point of a three-dimensional shape like a cube. You can store data with a shape as well, tracking capital equipment and generating inventory reports, for example. (For more information about storing data in shapes, see Chapter 13.) Now you know why Visio shapes are called *SmartShapes,* because many of them have built-in "brainy" behavior.

Open or closed shapes

Shapes can be classified as either open or closed, as shown in Figure 3-2. An open shape is one in which the end points aren't connected, such as a line, arc, or an abstract shape. A closed shape is a fully connected object like a polygon.

What difference does it make whether a shape is open or closed? You can fill a closed shape with a color or a pattern. You can't fill an open shape, but you can add end points such as arrows and other symbols.

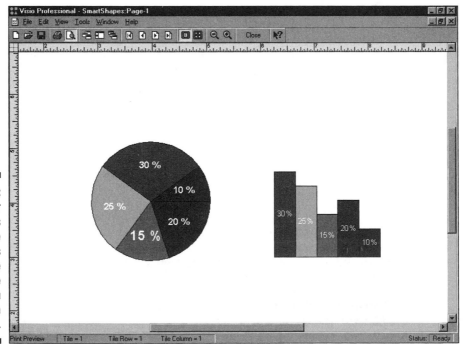

Figure 3-1:
The bar chart bars and pie chart slices adjust to the proper size when you type a percentage.

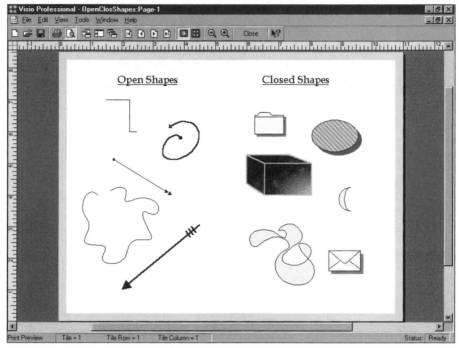

Figure 3-2: Check out these examples of open and closed shapes.

One- or two-dimensional shapes

All Visio shapes are either one-dimensional or two-dimensional. Two-dimensional shapes have length and height. When you select a two-dimensional shape, you can see its handles (see Figure 3-3). *Handles* — green squares that appear at each corner and on each side of a shape — let you change the length and height of a shape. Even a non-rectangular shape (like the pie chart) has a rectangular "frame" with handles at the corners and on each side when the shape is selected. The frame consists of a green dotted line that fully encloses the shape.

One-dimensional shapes are easy to spot on any Visio stencil; they have a yellow background. Other shapes have a gray background.

A line is an example of a one-dimensional shape. It has only two *end points* — small green boxes — that are visible when you select the line (see Figure 3-4). The beginning point — that is, the point from which you begin drawing — contains an *x*, and the end point contains a + symbol.

Handles   Frame

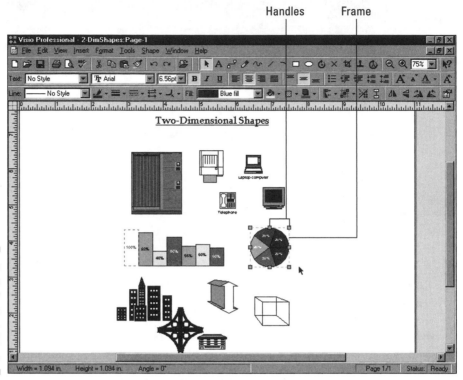

Figure 3-3:
You see
wide variety
in these
two-
dimensional
shapes.

You can resize the length of a one-dimensional shape, but not its height; a one-dimensional shape has no height. (Yes, a line has *thickness,* which you can alter using a formatting command, but thickness is not the same thing as height.)

An arc is considered a one-dimensional shape, even though it may seem to be a two-dimensional shape. Notice in Figure 3-4 that it has only two end points; it doesn't have a frame with handles at each corner and on each side. The handle at the top of the arc is called a *control* handle; it lets you adjust the bend of the arc. I show you more about working with control handles on other types of shapes later in this chapter.

The only time that you see a shape's handles is when the shape is selected, and the type of handles that you see depends on the tool you use to select the shape. You see more examples throughout this chapter.

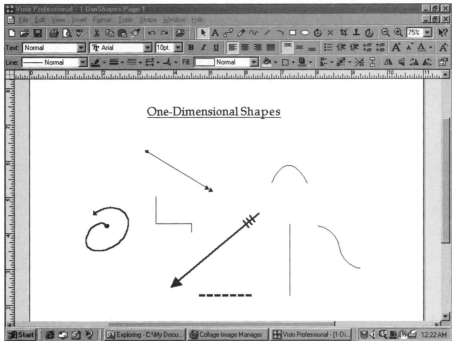

Figure 3-4:
Examples of
one-
dimensional
shapes.

Dragging Shapes into Your Drawing

So, how do you get shapes into a drawing? You drag 'em in. It's almost too simple. Position the mouse pointer over the shape on the stencil that you want in your drawing, click *and hold* the left mouse button down, and then drag the shape into the drawing area. Release the mouse button when the shape is where you want it. (As simple as it is, don't be embarrassed if you click a shape, then click the drawing area and wonder why your shape isn't there. This may happen a couple of times before you remember to hold the mouse button and *drag!*)

You can drag a shape into a drawing as many times as you want; the master shape stays on the stencil. As you drag a shape into your drawing area, you see an outline of the shape on the screen. When you release the mouse button, the actual shape is in your drawing. The shape may not be exactly the size that you want, but I show you how to change it soon enough (later in this chapter).

Remember that you can open as many stencils as you need while creating a drawing. Just choose File⇨Stencils.

Selecting Shapes

Believe it or not, selecting a shape in a drawing is even easier than dragging it onto a drawing — just click the shape. When you select a shape, its green handles become visible. You need to select a shape before you can move it, copy it, delete it, or change it in any other way.

Sometimes you may want to perform the same task (like moving or copying) on several shapes at the same time. To select more than one shape, hold down the Shift key as you click each shape that you want to select. The green handles are visible on the first shape that you select; the handles are blue on subsequent shapes that you select.

You can also select shapes by dragging a selection box around them (see Figure 3-5). Select the Pointer Tool button (the one that looks like an arrow) on the toolbar, and then drag the mouse around the shapes that you want to select. As you drag the mouse, you draw a *selection box* around the shapes. You must fully enclose all the shapes that you want to select; if you cut across a shape, it isn't selected.

Handles   Selection box

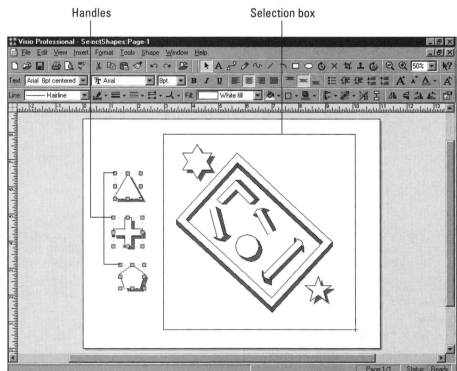

Figure 3-5:
You can
select
shapes
individually
or with a
selection
box.

If you select a bunch of shapes and then decide to exclude one of them, you can deselect it without deselecting them all. Just hold down the Shift key and click that particular shape again. When the selection handles disappear, you can tell that you successfully deselected the shape. To deselect all shapes, click in any blank area of the drawing.

Moving, Copying, Stamping, and Deleting Shapes

You can manipulate shapes in many ways after you drag them into your drawing. In this section I show you some of the most common ways that you can alter your shapes. You use several toolbar buttons that I picture in Table 3-1, so if you're not sure what a particular tool looks like, head for the table.

Table 3-1	Tools on the Standard Toolbar
Button	*Function*
📋	Copy
📋	Paste
✂	Cut
🔨	Stamp

When I tell you to drag a shape, you have to click the shape with the left mouse button and hold the button as you move the shape.

Moving shapes

After you have shapes in your drawing, you may want to move them around. Moving a shape is simple; just drag the shape wherever you want it. As you drag a shape, watch the vertical and horizontal rulers. The shape's position is highlighted on the rulers, so if you want to place a shape 3 inches from the top border and 2 inches from the left border of your drawing, it's easy to see where the shape's frame is aligned using the rulers.

You can *constrain* the movement of a shape by holding the Shift key as you drag. If you drag horizontally, the shape moves right and left only and stays at the same vertical position. If you drag vertically, the shape moves up and down and stays at the same horizontal position.

In Chapter 6 I show you how to snap shapes into alignment using rulers, a grid, and alignment commands, which can make the placement of your shapes more exact.

Copying and pasting shapes

To copy a shape, start by selecting the shape that you want to copy. You can then use one of these four methods to copy the shape:

- ✔ Press Ctrl+C.
- ✔ Click the Copy button on the Standard toolbar.
- ✔ Select Edit➪Copy.
- ✔ Hold the Ctrl key and drag. (You see a + symbol attached to the mouse pointer.)

I prefer keyboard shortcuts because they're so fast. All of these methods place a copy of the shape (or shapes) on the Windows Clipboard.

To paste the shape in a new location

- ✔ Press Ctrl+V.
- ✔ Click the Paste button on the Standard toolbar.
- ✔ Choose Edit➪Paste.
- ✔ Release the Ctrl key and mouse button.

Stamping shapes

If you need to use a shape over and over again, the stamp feature in Visio is a nifty tool that saves you dragging time. This tool works just like a rubber stamp; wherever you stamp it, the shape is pasted into your drawing. Follow these steps to use the Stamp tool:

1. **Click the Stamp Tool button (refer to Table 3-1) on the Standard toolbar.**

2. **In the stencil, click the shape that you want to stamp.**

3. **Drag the mouse into the drawing area.**

   Notice that your mouse pointer now looks like a stamp.

4. **Click the mouse where you want to stamp the shape.**

   Keep clicking until you've added all the stamped shapes that you want in your drawing.

5. **Click the Pointer Tool button to switch back to the regular mouse pointer.**

Deleting shapes

You can delete a shape in one of three ways. First select the shape, and then do one of the following:

✔ Press the Delete key.

✔ Click the Cut button on the Standard toolbar.

✔ Choose Edit⇨Cut.

✔ Press Ctrl-X.

Using the Delete key is the easiest way. If you think that you may want to bring the shape back, use Cut. This way the shape is stored on the Clipboard so that you can paste it in the drawing again (as long as you paste it before you cut anything else).

You use the same method to delete more than one shape at a time. Select all shapes that you want to delete (either click on them or draw a selection box around them), then delete them using one of these methods:

✔ Press the Delete key.

✔ Click the Cut button on the Standard toolbar.

✔ Choose Edit⇨Cut.

✔ Press Ctrl-X.

If you delete something by mistake, you can choose Edit⇨Undo (or press Ctrl+Z) to bring it back. By default, Visio has ten levels of Undo, so you can undo up to the last ten commands that you performed.

Handling Handles, Endpoints, and Other Stuff

Earlier in this chapter you saw that shapes display handles when you select them. Oddly enough, these are called *selection* handles! (In the case of one-dimensional shapes, the handles are called *end points*.) But many shapes have other types of handles, too, which are usually designed to control the shape in some way. In fact, the many types of handles and control points can be very confusing! Use this rundown of the important ones to help you sort them out.

The handles a shape displays depend on the tool that you use to select the shape. You can select shapes with any of the tools listed in Table 3-2. The tool that you choose depends on the task that you want to perform. For instance, if you want to alter the form of a shape, you use the Pencil tool. If you want to draw an abstract shape, you use the Freeform tool. Throughout this section, you use each of these tools for different functions. (I also included these tools on the Cheat Sheet for you as a handy reference.)

Table 3-2	More Tools on the Standard Toolbar
Button	**Tool**
▲	Pointer tool
A	Text tool
✏	Pencil tool
∿	Freeform tool
╱	Line tool
⌐	Arc tool
▢	Rectangle tool
◯	Ellipse tool
↻	Rotation tool

When you drag a shape into your drawing but you're not exactly sure how to use it, right-click on the shape, and then choose Shape Help from the short-cut menu that pops up. Visio displays a help pop-up box specific to the shape that you select. All the information that you need to know about controlling or manipulating the shape is provided.

Control handles

In addition to selection handles, some shapes have another handle (or two) called a *control* handle. Unless you look very closely, you may confuse selection handles with control handles. Both are green squares, but control handles are darkly shaded. They appear somewhere on or near the shape and let you control some aspect of the shape. In the cube that's selected in Figure 3-6, the control handle lets you adjust the *vanishing point* of the cube. In other words, you control the depth of the cube, the length of the cube, and the angle from which you view the cube. In a bar chart (a shape from the Charting Shapes stencil), the control handles let you change the number of bars and their relative height.

If you've ever worked in a Windows environment, you know that when you pass the mouse pointer over various tools on the toolbar, a helpful yellow box explaining the function of that tool pops up. Visio uses this method to describe a shape's control handles as well. And it's a good thing, because it's difficult to guess what some of the control handles are used for. The other way to find out is to right-click on a shape in your drawing, then choose Shape Help from the shortcut menu. Shape Help tells you how to work with the shape, including its control handles.

Figure 3-6:
Control handles let you control a special aspect of a shape.

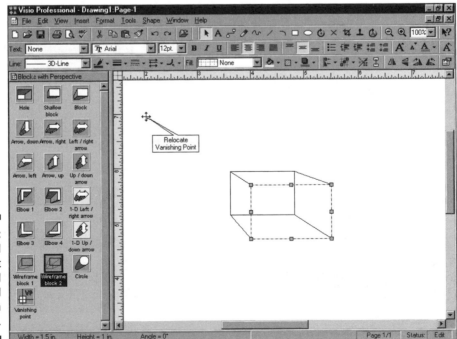

Control points

Control points are green circles that appear between vertices on certain shapes, lines, and arcs when you select them with the Pencil tool. Control points are different from control handles because they let you control the "shape of a shape." So, if you want to make a straight-sided rectangle look like a bulging rectangle, you drag the rectangle's control points. If you want to change a straight-sided pentagon to a curved one, you drag the shape's control points. Figure 3-7 shows how a pentagon shape looks before and after its control points are moved.

Vertices

Just as control points let you change the sides of a shape, *vertices* let you change the corners of a shape. (Technically, vertices are the point at which two lines intersect, but think of them as corners if that seems clearer.) You can display vertices, green diamond-shaped points, by selecting a shape with the Line, Arc, or Pencil tool (refer to Table 3-2).

Pencil tool⌐   ⌐Control point

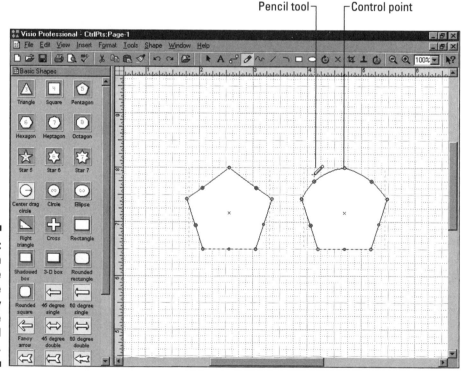

Figure 3-7:
You can curve the top of the pentagon by dragging the control points.

When you select a vertex, it turns magenta. You can drag the vertex in any direction, which changes the length and angle of the lines that form the vertex. In Figure 3-8, the slope of the roof is altered by dragging the top vertex.

For information on adding and deleting vertices, see Chapter 7.

You can seldom display vertices on shapes that you drag into a drawing, particularly complex shapes; however, you can always display vertices on shapes that you draw. (After all, if a Visio shape isn't quite right, you may want to draw your own.) Some Visio shapes are complex enough that moving a vertex may destroy the shape. See Chapter 7 for information about drawing your own shapes.

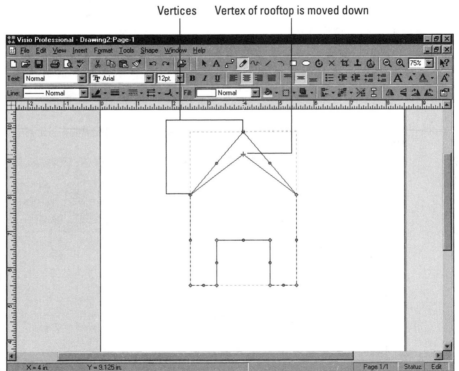

Figure 3-8:
Drag a
vertex to
change a
shape.

Rotation handles

You can rotate many Visio shapes so that you can place them at the angle you prefer. To display a shape's rotation handles, click the Rotation Tool button (refer to Table 3-2) on the Standard toolbar; then select the shape. Rotation handles appear as round green handles at the corners of a shape's frame. When a rotation handle appears in each corner, you can rotate the shape from any corner you choose. When you choose the Rotation tool, the mouse pointer changes to a right angle with a curved arrow. When you move the pointer over a rotation handle on the shape, the mouse pointer changes to two curved arrows in the shape of a circle (see Figure 3-9).

The *center of rotation,* which marks the point around which the object moves, is a green circle with a plus symbol. In Figure 3-9, the hourglass shape on the left is shown at its original angle. The shape on the right is rotated to the right using the rotation handle in the upper-right corner of its frame.

To rotate a shape, drag a rotation handle using a circular motion. The mouse pointer changes to a rotation pointer and you see an outline of the frame as you rotate it around the center of rotation. (Check out Chapter 7 for more details on rotating shapes.)

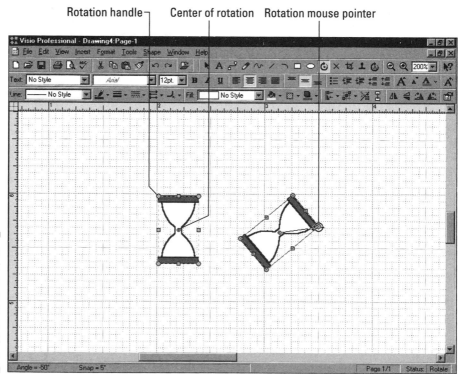

Rotation handle ⌐   Center of rotation   Rotation mouse pointer

Figure 3-9:
The center of rotation marks the point around which the object rotates.

Eccentricity handles

In simple, non-techie terms, an elliptical shape is an oval. In Visio, an elliptical shape can also be *part* of an oval, as in an oval-shaped arc. (Circles and circular-shaped arcs are *not* elliptical shapes.) Eccentricity handles are designed to let you adjust two aspects of an elliptical shape: its angle and its *off-centeredness,* or *eccentricity.* So, for example, if you draw an arc, you can use the eccentricity handles to change the angle at which the arc sits relative to its endpoints, and the eccentricity of the arc relative to its endpoints.

Eccentricity handles are visible only when you select a shape with the Pencil tool. Eccentricity handles are always a set of two green circles, each with a plus symbol. A third green circle (also with a plus symbol) sits between the two eccentricity handles. This is actually a control point used for changing the *height* of a curve. All three circles are connected by a dotted green line. The line represents the angle at which the curve sits relative to the curve's endpoints (see Figure 3-10).

Control point

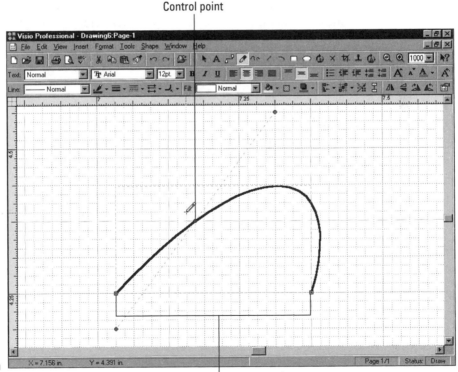

Figure 3-10:
Eccentricity handles let you change the angle and eccentricity of an elliptical shape like an arc.

Eccentricity handles

To change the height of an arc, click on the control point at the top of the arc and drag it in any direction. To change the angle of an arc, drag either of the eccentricity handles up or down. To change an arc's eccentricity, drag either eccentricity handle closer to the control point or farther away from the control point. (The closer to the control point the eccentricity handles are, the more circular the arc becomes.) The best way to figure out how to work with eccentricity handles is to play around with them!

Connection points

Connection points are the locations on a shape where you can connect the endpoints of other, one-dimensional shapes. For example, you use connection points in an organization chart because each box is connected to another by a one-dimensional connector line. The locations where the endpoints of connectors are glued to the boxes are called connection points.

Connection points are visible by choosing View⇨Connection Points. They appear as small blue *x*s and can be located almost anywhere on a shape — usually at corners, midpoints of lines, or centers of shapes (see Figure 3-11). Displaying connection points can make your screen look very cluttered. I recommend displaying them only when you need them — to connect shapes to one another using lines or connector shapes. When you don't need them, turn them off by choosing View⇨Connection Points again.

Padlocks

Sometimes Visio locks shapes so that you can't change a particular aspect of the shape, such as rotating, flipping, moving, deleting, selecting, or resizing it. When a Visio shape is locked against sizing or rotating, it displays padlocks at the corners of its frame instead of selection handles (see Figure 3-12). (When it's locked against changes other than those named above, padlocks don't appear, but you still can't make the change.) You can also lock any shape against change. You may want to do this when you know some inexperienced Visio users are going to be snooping around in your drawings!

You can lock an unlocked shape at any time by using the Format⇨Protection command. See Chapter 13 for specific instructions on protecting shapes.

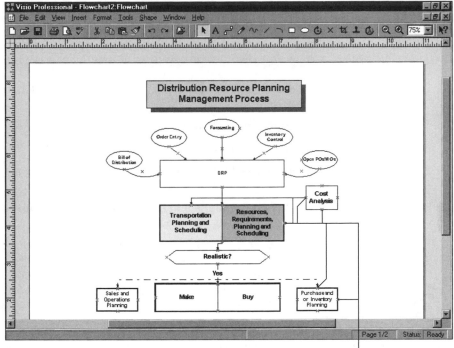

Figure 3-11:
Connection points tell you where you can glue connectors or lines to a shape.

Connection points

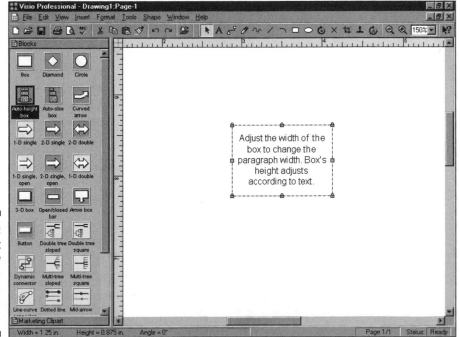

Figure 3-12:
Padlocks let you know that you can't rotate or resize a shape.

Sizing Up Your Shapes

It's pretty likely that you may want to resize some of the shapes that you use in your drawings. Use the following steps to adjust the size of your shapes.

1. **Select the shape with the Pointer Tool (refer to Table 3-2) and do one of the following.**

   • **To change a shape's width,** drag a side handle.

   • **To change its height,** drag a top or bottom handle.

   • **To change height and width at the same time,** drag a corner handle.

   • **To maintain the shape's height-to-width proportions,** press and hold the Ctrl key as you drag a corner handle.

2. **Release the mouse button when the shape is the size that you want.**

The previous steps may seem to imply that all shapes are parallelograms. They're not; but remember that every shape has a rectangular *frame*, which is a parallelogram, so that the shape can be resized in width, height, or both proportionally.

If you want a shape to be a specific size, for instance 2 x 1.5 inches, remember to watch the status bar at the bottom of the screen as you resize the shape. The status bar displays the shape's height and width as you move the mouse.

Finding the Shapes That You Want

Because Visio offers so many shapes (a minimum of 1,500 depending on the Visio product that you have), you need a way to search for a shape. After all, when you open and close dozens of stencils, it's easy to forget exactly where you saw a shape that you like.

Shape Explorer lets you search for a shape by its name, a stencil name, a template name, a keyword, a phrase that describes the shape that you want, or the type of drawing that you want to create.

To use Shape Explorer, follow these steps:

1. **Choose File⇨Stencils⇨Shape Explorer.**

   Visio displays the dialog box shown in Figure 3-13.

2. **In the Search For box, type a word or phrase that describes the shape that you're looking for.**

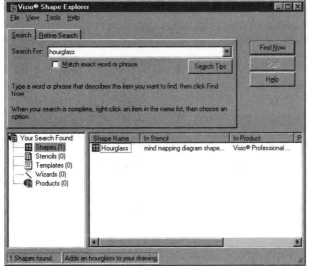

Figure 3-13:
The Visio
Shape
Explorer
dialog box
helps you
quickly find
shapes that
you're look-
ing for.

3. **Click the Find Now button.**

   Visio searches shapes, stencils, templates, wizards, and Visio Products (Standard, Professional, Technical, Enterprise, and add-on shapes) and displays the results in the lower-right section of the dialog box. (If the shape's icon is displayed in full color, you can add it to your drawing. If the icon is grayed, the shape belongs to a stencil that isn't installed on your system, and you can't add it to your drawing.)

4. **To add the shape to your drawing, right-click the shape's icon and then choose Add to Drawing.**

   If you prefer to open the entire stencil that the shape is on so that you can use other shapes as well, right-click the shape's icon, then choose Open Containing Stencil.

5. **Close the Visio Shape Explorer dialog box by clicking the Close button in the upper-right corner.**

If you're having trouble finding the shape that you want, be sure to click the Search Tips button in the Shape Explorer dialog box. It offers detailed, useful information about how to type the word or phrase so that Shape Explorer can easily find the shape that you're looking for.

If you want to narrow your search, click the Refine Search tab in the Shape Explorer dialog box and then remove check marks from the categories that you *don't* want Visio to search. For example, if you only want to search shapes and stencils, remove the check marks from the Templates, Wizards, and Products check boxes to speed up your search. To further refine your search, click the Details button to specify whether you want to search for names, descriptions, or keywords, and then click OK.

Chapter 4

Say What?: Incorporating Text

● ●

In This Chapter

▶ Adding text to a drawing

▶ Working with text: Editing, copying, pasting, moving, and deleting

▶ Changing alignment, margins, and tabs

▶ Creating bulleted and numbered lists

▶ Changing the look of text: Color, font, size, and style

▶ Rotating text

● ●

*R*egardless of the type of drawing that you're creating, you probably want to add text to it somewhere. I just know that you want a title, label, caption, page number, description, or explanation on this drawing! You're in luck, because Visio allows you to build *text blocks* into each Visio shape. A text block is a special frame for holding text. Whether you use 'em or not is up to you, but if you need to work with a text block, I show you everything you need to know in this chapter.

Adding Text to a Drawing

In this section I show you how to add text to existing shapes and how to add freestanding text to a drawing. Throughout this chapter as you work with text, you use the tools shown in Table 4-1.

To add text to a shape in your drawing:

1. **Click a shape to select it.**

2. **Begin typing your text.**

   When you begin typing, you see the shape's text block — a frame defined by a green dotted line — because Visio zooms in on the text block. You're not seeing things — keep typing. For those of you who aren't able to read 4-point type (and I contend that's most of you), Visio zooms in so that you can actually read what you're typing!

And don't worry — Visio keeps up with you even if you enter a 400-line caption (well, that may be a bit much . . .). If you enter a lot of text, Visio thoughtfully wraps the text to the next line for you automatically. If you enter more text than the text block can hold, Visio enlarges the text block as you continue to type.

3. **When you finish typing your text, click anywhere outside the text block.**

Voila! You can see the original shape again, along with your text. The drawing in Figure 4-1 is an excellent example of how extensively you can use text in a drawing.

Table 4-1	Tools on the Standard Toolbar
Button	**Tool or Function**
	Copy
	Paste
	Pointer tool
A	Text tool
	Text Block tool
	Format Painter tool

You can't tell where a shape's text block is going to show up until you type something in it. If you're curious about its location before you enter text, you can quickly pop it up by double-clicking the shape or selecting the shape, and then pressing F2.

The formatting of the text in a text block is different depending on the shape. Some shapes may display left-aligned text while others may right-align the text or orient the text vertically. I show you how to change text characteristics in "Changing the Way Your Text Looks" later in this chapter.

Some of you adventurous types may want to include text in a drawing that's not part of a shape. That's cool — Visio is prepared for your kind! You can include such *freestanding text* in a drawing quite easily by following these steps.

1. **Click the Text Tool button (refer to Table 4-1) on the Standard toolbar.**

   Your mouse pointer changes to look like a sheet of paper with text.

2. **Drag the pointer to draw a text box as large (or as small) as you want.**

   Your text block is outlined in the familiar green dotted line and an insertion point appears in the center.

3. **Type your text.**

4. **After you enter all the text that you want, click anywhere outside of the text block.**

Note that in Step 2 above, the insertion point appears in the center of the text block because the text is set for center alignment. I show you how to change this setting in "Changing the lineup" later in this chapter.

You can also use a text block when you create your own shapes by drawing with the Pencil, Line, Freeform, Rectangle, or Ellipse tools. You create and add text to the text block in the same way I just described. For more information about creating your own shapes, see Chapter 7.

Okay, let's clear up one thing. Technically speaking, freestanding text isn't really freestanding, it's a shape in and of itself. Does that matter? Not really — you just need to know that text is always enclosed within a text block; it never just floats around aimlessly!

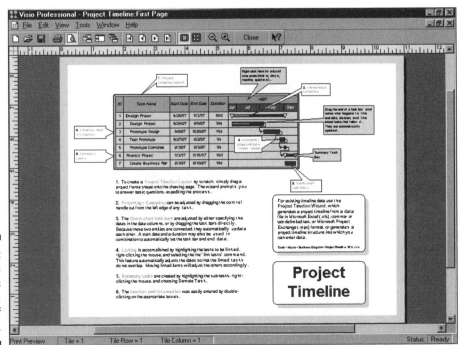

Figure 4-1:
Some drawings contain a great deal of text.

Editing Text

Of course, the minute that you click outside a shape to "set your text in stone," you may decide it's time to change some aspect of your text. Maybe you want to add to it, delete from it, or just start all over again.

Changing text in Visio is easy enough. Just follow these steps.

1. **Click the Text Tool button (refer to Table 4-1), and then click a shape to display its text block (see Figure 4-2).**

2. **Place the insertion point where you want to change the text by clicking the mouse button.**

3. **Begin typing, selecting, deleting, or backspacing to make your changes.**

   • **To delete characters to the right of the insertion point:** Press the Delete key.

   • **To delete characters to the left of the insertion point:** Press the Backspace key.

   • **To select the text and type over it:** Highlight the text with the mouse or hold down the Shift key while you highlight the text with the arrow keys. After you highlight the text that you want to delete, begin typing your new text. Whatever you type wipes out the text that you selected.

4. **After you make changes to your text, click anywhere outside of the text block.**

   Your shape or freestanding text is visible again.

Speaking of word processors, if you've used a word processing program before, you find that nearly everything about the way text works in Visio is the same as a word processing program. (It doesn't matter which one; they're all pretty much the same when it comes to basic typing and editing.) If you're very familiar with word processors, you can probably just skim the sections of this chapter that discuss copying, pasting, moving, deleting, and so on.

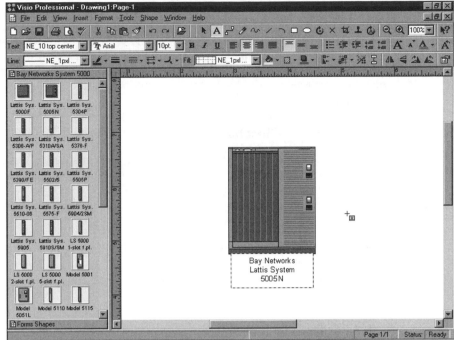

Figure 4-2:
When you
use the Text
tool to click
a shape,
Visio
displays its
text block.

You can also open a text block by clicking the Pointer Tool button (which looks like an arrow) on the Standard toolbar and then double-clicking the shape or freestanding text, but watch out! Using this method, Visio automatically selects all the text in the shape. If you don't want to replace all the text, *be sure to click somewhere in the text block to position the insertion point before you begin typing.* If you begin typing without doing so, Visio replaces your text with what you type. If you replace text accidentally, use Edit⇨Undo or press Ctrl+Z to bring back your old text.

Text Manipulations

In any drawing, you invariably end up manipulating text in *some* way, whether it's copying, pasting, moving, resizing, changing the alignment, margins, tabs, and so on. This section guides you through the maze of making all these changes after you enter the text.

Copying and pasting without the glue

Sometimes you may want to copy text from one place to another — anything to avoid retyping! Actually, copying text is a good idea for another reason: consistency. If you want a chunk of text to be exactly the same somewhere else in your drawing, the best way to ensure this is to copy the text.

Don't worry about whether the text you're copying is part of a shape or is freestanding text; the steps that you follow are the same. You can paste text into a shape's text block by selecting the text block first. If you don't select a text block, but rather paste the text by clicking somewhere in the drawing, Visio pastes the text into its own text block somewhere near the middle of the drawing page. You can then move the text block where you want it.

You can copy and paste text using the following steps:

1. **Click the Text Tool button (refer to Table 4-1) on the Standard toolbar and click a shape.**

   Visio displays the shape's text block.

2. **Select the text that you want to copy.**

3. **Click the Copy button (refer to Table 4-1) on the Standard toolbar, or choose Edit⇨Copy, or press Ctrl+C.**

4. **Choose where you want to paste the text:**

   • **To paste into a shape's text block,** double-click the shape.

   • **To paste freestanding text,** click any blank area of the drawing.

5. **Click the Paste button on the Standard toolbar, choose Edit⇨Paste, or press Ctrl+V.**

Remember, the text that you copy remains on the Windows Clipboard until you copy something else. If you need to paste again and again, feel free!

You can quickly choose the Copy and Paste commands from a pop-up short-cut menu by right-clicking your mouse when a text block is selected.

Moving a text block

Keep in mind that you don't know where a shape's text block is placed until you enter some text in it. You may find that you don't like the position of the text block and want to move it. In Figure 4-3, the text block for the star on the left covers up part of the shape. You can move the text block below the star (like the star on the right) to make the text readable and the shape more visible.

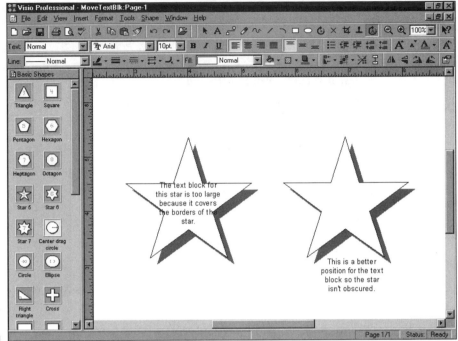

Figure 4-3:
Sometimes
moving a
text block is
the best
solution.

Even if you move the text block halfway across the drawing page, *it's still attached to its shape.* If you move the shape, the text moves with it; if you copy the shape, the text is copied with it; if you paste the shape, the text is pasted with it; if you rotate . . . well, you get the idea.

To move a text block independently of its shape, use these steps:

1. **Click the Text Block Tool button (refer to Table 4-1) on the Standard toolbar.**

   Your mouse pointer changes to look like a sheet of paper with lines of text.

2. **Click the shape that has text that you want to move.**

   The green text block frame and handles are visible.

3. **Move the mouse over the text block frame until it changes to a pointer that looks like a double rectangle.**

4. **Drag the text block to reposition it.**

5. **Click the Pointer tool again to bring back your normal mouse pointer.**

Moving a freestanding text block is easy because a freestanding text block is nothing more than a shape. You move it just like you move any other shape. Use these steps:

1. **Click the Pointer Tool button (refer to Table 4-1) on the Standard toolbar if it isn't already selected.**

2. **Click the freestanding text block that you want to move.**

   The green selection handles and frame appear.

3. **Make sure the mouse is pointing somewhere inside of the text block.**

   (The mouse pointer changes from black to white.)

4. **Drag the text block to a new location.**

Resizing a text block

Sometimes you may need to resize a text block to fit a shape a little better. In Figure 4-4 the text block for the star on the left is too large because it covers up part of the star's borders. On the right, the text block is resized.

Use these steps to resize a text block:

1. **Click the Text Block Tool button (refer to Table 4-1) on the Standard toolbar.**

   When you move the mouse pointer over the text in the text block, the pointer changes to a double rectangle.

2. **Click the shape, and the green text block frame and handles appear.**

3. **Move the mouse pointer over a side handle to resize the shape's width or a top or bottom handle to resize the shape's height.**

   The mouse pointer changes to a double-headed arrow.

4. **Drag the handle to resize the text block.**

5. **Click the Pointer Tool button again to bring back your normal mouse pointer.**

Changing the lineup

Whenever you create text in a drawing, you need to pay attention to alignment. *Horizontal alignment* refers to the way characters line up left to right in a text block. In most text documents, text is left aligned; however, when you're working with a drawing, center, right, and justified alignments all work well in particular drawings. An example of each style is shown in Figure 4-5.

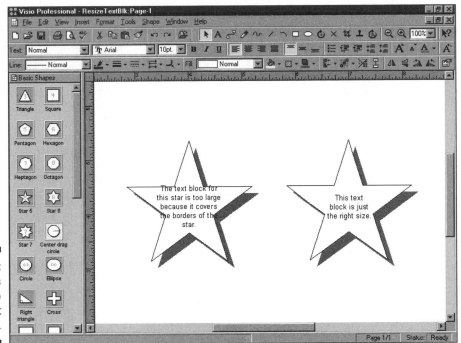

Figure 4-4:
Sometimes you need to resize a text block.

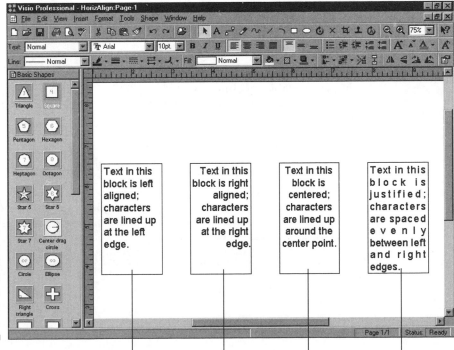

Figure 4-5:
Use any of four horizontal alignment styles where appropriate.

Left alignment   Right alignment   Center alignment   Justified

For horizontal alignment, Visio's Text toolbar contains the following tools shown in Table 4-2.

Table 4-2	Text Alignment Tools on the Text Toolbar
Button	*Tool*
	Align Left
	Center
	Align Right
	Justify

To change horizontal text alignment, follow these steps:

1. **Click the Text Tool button (refer to Table 4-1) on the Standard toolbar.**
2. **Click the shape that contains the text that you want to change.**

    Visio displays the text block.
3. **Select the paragraph that you want to align.**
4. **Click the Align Left, Center, Align Right, or Justify Tool button.**

    Visio reformats the selected text.

I highly recommend that you use these tools, because they are faster than choosing menu commands. If you prefer to use menu commands, alignment settings are available by choosing Format⇨Text, clicking the Paragraph tab in the Text dialog box, and selecting the check box of the alignment option that you want.

Note that because horizontal alignment applies to a paragraph, you can align separate paragraphs differently in the same text block.

Vertical alignment refers to the alignment from top to bottom in a text block. When working with a text document, vertical alignment is not something you typically think about, because your text appears on a page with margins. However, when your text is contained in a text block — which is really nothing more than a box — you have the choice of aligning the text with the top of the box, with the bottom of the box, or centering the text in the box (see Figure 4-6).

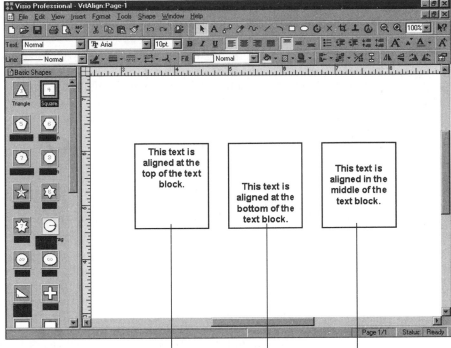

Figure 4-6:
Vertical
alignment
places text
at the top,
center, or
bottom of a
text block.

Top alignment   Bottom alignment   Middle alignment

You can use the following tools on the Text toolbar (shown in Table 4-3) to vertically align your text.

Table 4-3	Vertical Alignment Tools on the Text Toolbar
Button	**Tool**
	Align Top
	Middle
	Align Bottom

To set vertical alignment for a text block, follow these steps:

1. **Click the Text Tool button (refer to Table 4-1) on the Text toolbar.**

2. **Click the shape that contains the text that you want to change.**

   Visio displays the text block.

3. **Click the Align Top, Middle, or Align Bottom button.**

   Visio adjusts your text.

Again, to set alignment, I recommend that you use one of the alignment tools provided on the Text toolbar to the time it takes to select menu commands. If you prefer to use menu commands, alignment settings are available by choosing Format⇨Text, clicking the Text Block tab in the Text dialog box, and selecting an option from the Vertical Alignment drop-down list.

Note that unlike horizontal alignment, vertical alignment applies to *all* the text in a text block.

Margins: Finding some breathing room

Text block margins define the white space that surrounds text in a text block. Visio sets text block margins very narrowly — about ⅛ of an inch. In most cases, these narrow margins are fine, because the outline of the text block usually isn't visible. But if you decide to outline a text block with a frame, these margins can be so narrow that the text doesn't look right. Figure 4-7 shows two text blocks. The text block on the left uses standard margins; the margins for the text block on the right are increased to ½ inch. Not only does the text block on the right look better, the words are more readable. And you don't get that claustrophobic feeling looking at it!

Visio uses *points* as the default unit of measurement for text and margins. 72 points is roughly equivalent to 1 inch, so 4 points is about ⅛ of an inch. (I say roughly because points were originally based on the size of common typewriter fonts. Today, system fonts vary in relative size.)

If you prefer to have Visio measure text and margins in inches (or any of 19 other units of measure!), you can change the default setting. Just choose Tools⇨Options, click the Default Units tab, and change the Text setting. The drop-down box lists all the choices for units.

To change a text block's margins, use these steps:

1. **Click the Text Block Tool button (refer to Table 4-1) on the Standard toolbar.**

   When you move the mouse pointer over the text in the text block, the pointer changes to a double rectangle.

2. **Click the shape that has the text block you want to change. The green text block frame and handles appear.**

3. **Choose Format⇨Text.**

   Visio displays the Text dialog box.

4. **Click the Text Block tab (see Figure 4-8).**

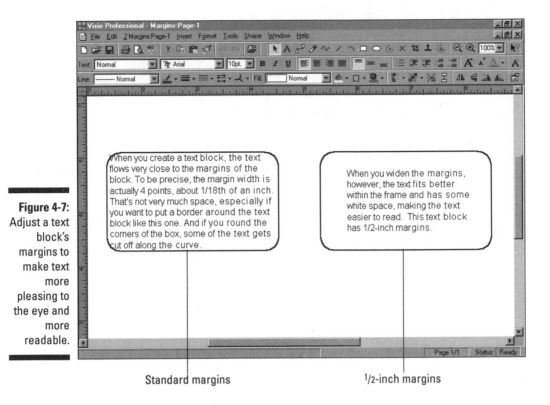

Figure 4-7:
Adjust a text block's margins to make text more pleasing to the eye and more readable.

Standard margins   ¹/₂-inch margins

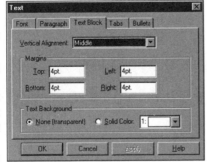

Figure 4-8:
The Text Block tab in the Text dialog box lets you set margins.

5. **In the Top, Bottom, Right, and Left boxes, type a number.**

   Visio measures margins in points (72 points = 1 inch). If you prefer to use inches, enter them as decimal numbers and type **in** after the number (such as .5 in).

6. **Click Apply if you want to make more changes in the Text dialog box.**

7. **To return to your drawing, click OK.**

TIP

You can pop up the Text dialog box quickly by right-clicking on your shape and choosing Format⇨Text.

Picking up the tab

Some types of text call for a tabular format, even in a drawing. You may want to include a simple table in a drawing, with items aligned in rows and columns. To create this type of layout, you need to set *tab stops* (or just *tabs*), the points where you want your cursor to jump when you press the Tab key.

You can set tabs to be left aligned, right aligned, centered, or decimal aligned. Examples of each of these are shown in Figure 4-9. When you use a decimal-aligned tab, be sure to type the decimal point in your entry. If you don't enter a decimal point, the entry is left aligned.

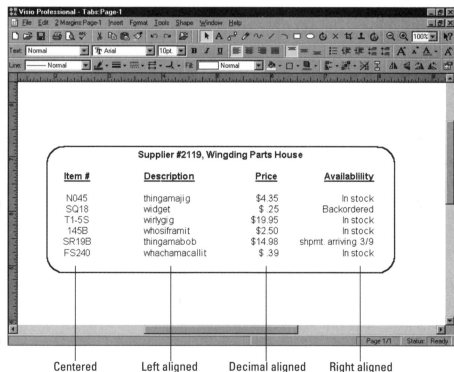

Figure 4-9:
Tabs can be left aligned, right aligned, centered, or decimal aligned.

Use these steps to set tabs for a text block:

1. **Click the Text Block Tool button (refer to Table 4-1) on the Standard toolbar.**

   When you move the mouse pointer over the text in the text block, the pointer changes to a double rectangle.

2. **Click the shape with the text that you want to alter, and the green text block frame and handles appear.**

3. **Choose Format⇨Text.**

   Visio displays the Text dialog box.

4. **Click the Tabs tab (see Figure 4-10).**

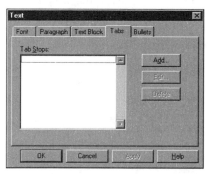

Figure 4-10:
Use the
Tabs tab in
the Text
dialog box
to set tab
positions.

5. **To add tabs, click the Add button.**

   Visio displays the Tab Properties dialog box (see Figure 4-11).

6. **Type a number (in inches or decimal inches) for the tab stop in the Position box.**

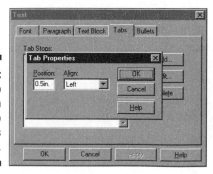

Figure 4-11:
Set tab
stops in
the Tab
Properties
dialog box.

   7. **In the Align box, choose an alignment style from the drop-down menu (Left, Center, Right, or Decimal), and then click OK.**

      Visio returns to the Tabs dialog box.

   8. **Click OK.**

When you return to your text block you can use the tabs by pressing the Tab key.

Creating bulleted lists

Bulleted lists are very common in drawings and diagrams — probably because they help summarize and separate material. Fortunately, creating bulleted lists in Visio is easy because Visio does it for you automatically.

You can set up a bulleted format for text that you already typed, or in a blank text block. If you set up a bulleted list in a blank text block, Visio inserts and formats the bullets as you type the text.

Use these steps to created a bulleted list:

   1. **In the text block, select the text that you want to format with bullets. If the text block is empty, just select the text block itself.**

   2. **Choose Format⇨Text.**

      The Text dialog box appears.

   3. **Click the Bullets tab to display the bullet options shown in Figure 4-12.**

   4. **Click a bullet style; then click OK.**

      Visio returns to your drawing. If you selected text in Step 1, it is formatted instantly. If the text block was empty, the bullets appear automatically when you begin typing.

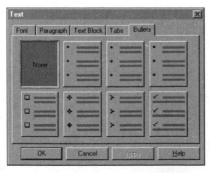

Figure 4-12:
The Bullets
tab offers
several
styles and
formats.

Creating numbered lists

The process for creating numbered lists is a bit more complicated than the process for creating bulleted lists, and it isn't automatic. I recommend that you format the text block for a numbered list *before* you enter the text. Because the process isn't automatic, it's easier to type the numbers and the text all at once. (It isn't required, however.) In the following steps I show you how to manually indent a numbered list; keep in mind that you may want to alter the steps slightly for your particular text.

You can add a numbered list to a text block using these steps.

1. **In the text block, select the text that you want to format as a numbered list. If the text block is empty, just select the text block itself.**

2. **Choose Format⇨Text.**

   The Text dialog box appears.

3. **Click the Paragraph tab to display the options on the Paragraph tab (shown in Figure 4-13).**

Figure 4-13:
Use the Paragraph tab in the Text dialog box to set up a numbered list.

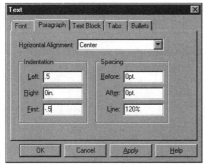

4. **In the Horizontal Alignment box, choose Left.**

5. **In the Indentation section, type .5 in the Left box, which marks the left indentation of the paragraph.**

6. **In the Indentation section, type –.5 in the First box, which marks the indentation for the first line of the paragraph.**

7. **Click OK.**

   Visio returns to your drawing.

In case you're wondering what you just did in these steps, you created what is known as a *hanging indent* (the first line hangs out to the left of the rest of the paragraph). You set the *wrap* point (the point where text wraps on the second, third, and following lines) to .5 inches.

If you haven't typed your text yet, type the number for the first item (such as 1. or I.), press Tab, and then type the text. Press Enter when you finish the first item. Repeat the process for all items in the list.

If you already typed your text, move your insertion point to the beginning of the line for each item, type the correct number, and then press Tab. Visio reformats the existing text.

In the steps above, you use .5 (½ inch) for indentation because it is an accepted standard. You aren't required to use this increment; you can just as easily use .2 inches or 1.2 inches. In either case, make sure you use the same number for the Left and First (Left being positive and First being negative).

Setting the indentation and spacing of text

To set indentation for a paragraph, you use the Paragraph tab in the Text dialog box. Indenting is like widening the margins on the left and/or right sides of a paragraph(without *really* widening the margins). For example, you may want to indent a special paragraph a ½ inch on the right and the left sides to give it emphasis. You can also make the first line of a paragraph stand out by indenting only that line.

The Paragraph tab in the Text dialog box also lets you adjust line spacing. For example, you can automatically add extra space before or after paragraphs. Like margins, line spacing is measured in points unless you change the unit of measurement using the Tools⇨Options command (described earlier in the chapter in "Margins: Finding some breathing room"). For extra space before or after a paragraph, type a number in the Before or After box (refer to Figure 4-13).

To set indentation and line spacing for a paragraph, use these steps:

1. **Click the Text Tool button (refer to Table 4-1) on the Standard toolbar.**

   The mouse pointer changes to look like a sheet of paper with text.

2. **In the text block or freestanding text box, select all or part of the paragraph that you want to indent.**

3. **Choose Format⇨Text.**

   Visio displays the Text dialog box.

4. **Click the Paragraph tab.**

5. **To set indentation for the paragraph you selected, type a number (measured in inches or decimal inches) in the Left, Right, and First boxes.**

6. **To set line spacing for the selected paragraph, type a number (measured in points) in the Before, After, and Line boxes.**

   Before and After set the number of spaces preceding and following the paragraph; Line sets the spacing within the lines of the paragraph.

7. **Click OK to return to your drawing.**

Changing the Way Your Text Looks

When you draw a text block and enter text, Visio automatically uses Arial, 12 point, black characters on a transparent background. Simple. Sedate. Readable. Nothing dramatic. Are existing Visio shapes set up to display anything more dramatic? Not really. You may find some variation — maybe 8 point Arial instead of 12 point — but nothing to get excited about.

If you want more pizzazz in your text, it's up to you to create it. You have the option of changing the font, size, color, and style of text. You can also designate a case, position, and language (no, Visio won't translate English into Portuguese for you!).

Use these steps to make changes to the text itself:

1. **Select the text that you want to change.**

2. **Choose Format⇨Text or right-click your mouse and choose Text from the shortcut menu.**

   The Text dialog box appears, as shown in Figure 4-14.

Figure 4-14:
The Font tab in the Text dialog box gives you options for changing your text.

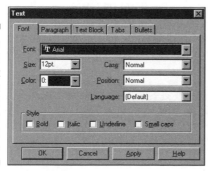

- **To change the font:** Click the Font drop-down list and choose a font style.

- **To change the text size:** Click the Size drop-down list and choose a point size for the selected text.

- **To change the text color:** Click the Color drop-down list and choose a color for the selected text.

- **To change the case:** Click the Case drop-down list and choose Normal (the default setting), All Caps, or Initial Caps.

- **To change text position:** Click the Position drop-down list and choose Subscript or Superscript.

- **To change the language of the Spell Checker:** Click the Language drop-down list and choose a language other than English.

- **To change the style:** Click the check boxes for Bold, Italic, Underline, or Small Caps.

3. **Click Apply.**

4. **Repeat Steps 3 and 4 if you want to try other options.**

5. **Click OK.**

    Visio returns to your drawing and reformats the selected text.

 Unfortunately the Font tab of the Text dialog box doesn't show you a preview of the fonts, so you can't see how the font looks before you choose it. The next best thing is to move the dialog box out of the way so that you can see your selected text. This way, when you click the Apply button you can see how the text looks without closing the dialog box and starting all over again.

Adding a colorful background

If you aren't satisfied with colorful characters alone, you can change the background color of a text block as well. Just think of all the wonderful color combinations you can come up with! Remember, though, your text needs to be *readable*. The more contrast between the text and background colors, the better.

An important thing to realize about text blocks is that they are transparent, which means that if your text block falls over the outline of a shape, the shape will show through, obscuring the text (see Figure 4-15). To solve this problem, you can change the text block background to solid white (or whatever color matches the shape underneath).

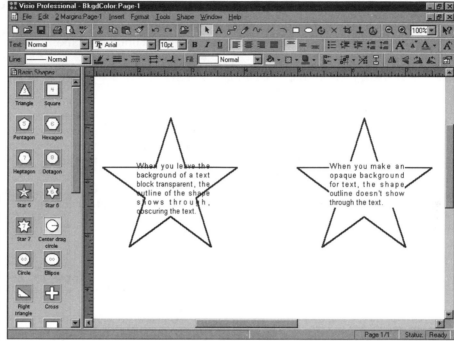

To change the background color of a text block, follow these steps:

1. **Click the Text Tool button (refer to Table 4-1) on the Standard toolbar.**

2. **Select the text block that you want to change.**

3. **Choose Format⇨Text, or right-click the text block and choose Text from the shortcut menu.**

   Visio displays the Text dialog box.

4. **Click the Text Block tab, shown in Figure 4-16.**

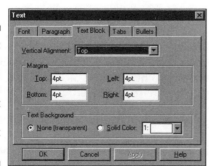

 5. In the Text Background area, choose a color from the Solid Color drop-down list.

 To make an opaque background on an unfilled shape, choose white.

 6. Click OK.

Copying formatting to other text

When you use your precious time and energy to set up a text block with a magenta background, chartreuse text, Elephant font, 38 point font size, underline, bold, italic, and small caps, you don't want to have to do it all over again manually to make a matching text block! This task is much simpler if you just *copy* the format, and you can. Use these steps:

 1. Click the Text Tool button (refer to Table 4-1) on the Standard toolbar.

 2. Click the text block with the formatting that you want to copy.

 3. Click the Format Painter Tool button (refer to Table 4-1) on the Standard toolbar.

 Your mouse pointer now includes a paintbrush.

 4. Click the text block that you want to copy the format to.

 Visio applies the format instantly.

The previous steps copy all aspects of the actual text formatting. Vertical and horizontal alignment, margin settings, indentation, and tabs are considered formatting that belongs to the *text block*. If you want to copy these as well as the text formatting, use the same steps but click the Pointer Tool button on the Standard toolbar in Step 1 instead of the Text Tool button. Using this method, Visio copies all text block and text attributes to the target text block. Copying formatting not only saves you time — it ensures consistency when consistency is important to you.

Rotating text

One of Visio's most versatile features is the ability to rotate text. For most Visio shapes the text is oriented horizontally, but sometimes you may need to rotate the text at an angle. Figure 4-17 shows a triangle on the left with a horizontal text block. In the triangle on the right, the text block is rotated and moved so that the text runs parallel to the triangle's side.

To change the rotation of a shape's text block, follow these steps:

 1. Click the Text Block Tool button (refer to Table 4-1) on the Standard toolbar.

When you move the mouse pointer over the text in the text block, the pointer changes to a double rectangle.

2. **Click the text block.**

The green selection handles appear, along with round rotation handles at each corner of the frame.

3. **Move the mouse pointer over one of the rotation handles.**

The mouse pointer changes to two curved arrows in the shape of a circle.

4. **Drag the text in the direction that you want to rotate the text.**

If you want to rotate the text to a specific angle, such as 45 degrees, or 125 degrees, watch the status bar as you rotate the text. Moving in a counter-clockwise direction produces a positive angle up to 180 degrees; moving clockwise displays negative angles up to –180 degrees.

If you want the text to align with a particular part of the shape (such as a border or outline), it may be necessary to move the text block after you rotate it.

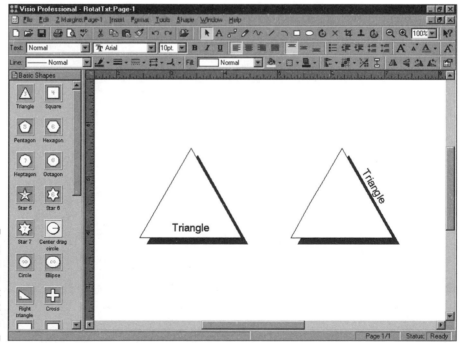

Figure 4-17:
Rotate
text to
complement
the shape it
labels.

Chapter 5

Connecting Shapes

● ●

In This Chapter

▶ What the heck are connectors, anyway?

▶ Looking at (and adding) connection points to shapes

▶ Unraveling a sticky mystery: Glue

▶ Creating connectors — in many ways

▶ Jumping across connectors

● ●

I urge you up front to read straight through this chapter, not because it's a *New York Times* best-seller pageturner, but because skipping around can lead to a lot of frustration and confusion! Of course, you don't have to read this chapter all the way through, but the relationship between glue, shapes, and connectors is intertwined. Don't let this scare you off — reading through this chapter can help you in your basic understanding of Visio.

Figuring Out Connectors

Connector is a term that is unique to Visio. The simple, non-techie explanation is that connectors are lines between boxes. The proper definition is that connectors are special one-dimensional (1-D) shapes that you use to connect two-dimensional (2-D) shapes to one another. This technical definition allows for the fact that connectors are not always lines; they can also be 1-D shapes like arrows, arcs, hubs, and other specialized shapes (like an Ethernet cable) that connect 2-D shapes.

So, where and why do you use connectors? You use connectors to show:

✔ The relationship between two shapes

✔ A hierarchy

✔ A path in a process

✔ That two shapes are connected (This one seems rather obvious!)

Let's face it, some drawings don't make any sense without connectors. Imagine an organization chart without connectors — you may have the president reporting to the copy room clerk! (Which doesn't always sound like a bad idea, does it?) You find connectors in all sorts of drawings, from network diagrams, to process flowcharts, to Web page diagrams. In Figure 5-1, the 2-D executive shape in the organization chart is connected to the 2-D manager shapes; manager shapes are then connected to 2-D position shapes. All connectors are 1-D shapes.

You can use any 1-D shape as a connector for a 2-D shape. You may not have noticed it before, but 1-D shapes always have a yellow background on a Visio stencil; 2-D shapes are displayed with a gray background. The different background colors tell you instantly how you can use a shape.

Connectors are more than just lines or shapes — they have built-in intelligence. Some connectors are *smart,* meaning that they can reconnect to a different point on a shape, if necessary, when you move the shape. Other connectors are *dynamic,* meaning that they can change form or their paths around shapes depending on the shapes they're connected to. You see examples of both throughout this chapter.

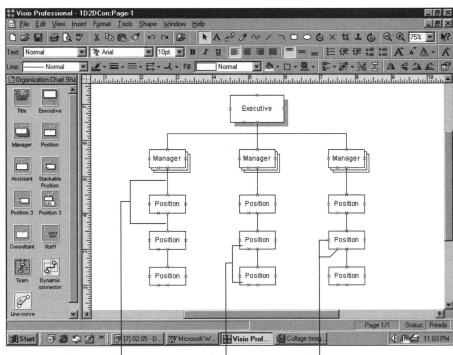

Figure 5-1:
Connectors
are 1-D
shapes that
you use to
bridge 2-D
shapes.

1-D connector shapes   2-D shapes   Connection points

In this chapter, you work with various tools on the Standard and Shape toolbars. These tools are listed in Table 5-1.

Button	Tool Name	Toolbar
Table 5-1	**Toolbar Tools for Working with Connection Points**	
	Pointer tool	Standard
	Connector tool	Standard
	Connection Point tool	Standard
	Connect Shapes tool	Shape

Working with Connection Points

Did you notice the blue Xs that appear on the sides of each shape? (Refer to Figure 5-1.) They're called *connection points* and are the places on a shape where you can hook up a connector.

If you don't see connection points on your screen, choose View⇨ Connection Points. You can toggle them on and off using this menu command. Or, if you display the View toolbar on your screen (choose View⇨ Toolbars⇨View), it contains a tool called Connections that lets you toggle connection points on and off. (The Connections Tool button looks like a square with an X in the middle of each side.)

Every shape has at least one connection point. If you look again at Figure 5-1, you can see that at least one side of each of the organization chart shapes has *two* connection points. Unfortunately, there isn't any formula for how many connection points a shape has or where they are located. One shape may have 2 while another has 12. Connection points can appear inside a shape, outside a shape, or on the line or border of a shape.

Connection points are for your eyes only; they don't print when you print your drawing.

If a shape doesn't have a connection point where you need it, add one! Use these steps:

1. **Select the shape.**

2. **Click the Connection Point Tool button on the Standard toolbar.**

The mouse pointer changes to an arrow with an X.

3. **Press and hold the Ctrl key, and click the location on the shape where you want to add a connection point.**

You can add as many connection points as you like (although I can't recommend getting carried away). You can place them on a shape, inside a shape, or outside a shape.

If you're having trouble placing connection points where you want them, you may have better luck if you turn the Snap function off. Choose Tools⇨ Snap & Glue. In the Snap & Glue dialog box, click the Snap check box to remove the check mark, and then click OK. (See Chapter 6 for more information about the Snap function and how it works.)

To delete a connection point:

1. **Click the connection point that you want to remove with the Connection Point tool.**

The connection point turns magenta.

2. **Press the Delete key.**

Voilà! The connection point is gone.

Gluing Connectors to Shapes

Put your Elmer's away — you don't need it when you're using Visio! *Glue* is a feature built into Visio connectors. Glue lets you stick connectors to shapes and keep them there. This may not seem like an important function to you now, but it will be when you start moving connected shapes all over the place.

Creating a glueless drawing is a monotonous task. Without glue, you have to move a connector each time you move a shape. If the distance between shapes changes, you have to adjust the length of the connector. Then you have to reattach the connector to the shape after you move it. If the path between two shapes changes, you have to reroute the connector. Now, multiply those changes by about 15 times because you probably move shapes *at least* that many times in a drawing before it's done. See? Glue isn't sounding so bad now, is it? Without glue, creating drawings is a lot more work than you ever imagined.

Figuring out if glue is dynamic or static

The concept of glue is pretty simple, but now I'm going to make it more complicated. Glue is such a great idea that Visio has two kinds: dynamic and static. I describe static glue first, although using dynamic glue is more adventurous.

Static glue

Static glue forms a *point-to-point* connection (take that literally, as in exact location to exact location) between shapes. This means that if you use static glue to connect two boxes from points on the top of each box, no matter where you move the boxes, those connectors don't budge! They stay connected to the top of each box, even if the drawing doesn't seem to make sense or looks goofy.

In Figure 5-2, the organization chart was originally arranged like the one at the top of the figure — with connectors attached to the tops of the boxes. Each connector uses static glue. At the bottom of the figure, the organization chart is rearranged, and the connectors are *still* attached to the top of each box. And yes, it looks goofy. This is how static glue behaves. Think of static glue as stubborn and unyielding. Yet, static glue has its purpose — you may create drawings where you want connectors to stay exactly where you put them.

When it's really important to you *how* shapes are connected and that connectors stay exactly where you put them, use static glue. Static glue is also good for drawings that you create quickly and that you're not likely to change a great deal.

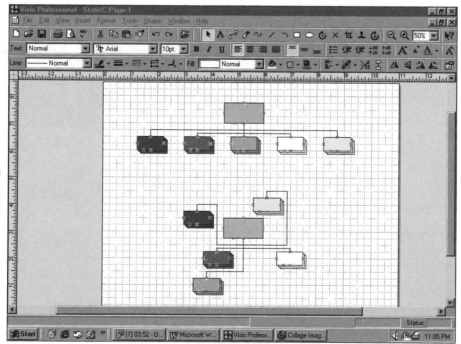

Figure 5-2:
Static glue keeps connectors attached to the same point, even when you move shapes.

Dynamic glue

Unlike static glue, dynamic glue is looking for adventure; it loves to travel and find new places to rest! Yet, it's a *sensible* traveler. When you move a shape that has a connector attached with dynamic glue, the connector attaches itself to a different connection point if necessary — one that makes sense in the drawing!

Because dynamic glue doesn't care where it attaches, it forms what are called *shape-to-shape* connections (as opposed to *point-to-point* connections). Figure 5-3 shows the same boxes pictured in Figure 5-2, but in Figure 5-3 the connectors use dynamic glue. If you move shapes with dynamic connectors, the connectors move to more logical connection points (usually the nearest point) on each box instead of sticking to a specific connection point.

You want to use dynamic glue when you anticipate moving shapes around a lot, and when it's not important to you that shapes connect at specific points.

Sometimes the similar terminology in Visio can be confusing. For instance, the term *dynamic* is used to describe *glue* as well as *connectors*. It's easy to confuse the two, even though they're entirely different animals! *Dynamic* simply means *changeable*. *Dynamic glue* is able to attach a connector to a different point on a shape whereas a *dynamic connector* is able to change its shape and path, if necessary. These concepts may still be confusing now, but they become clear the more you work with glue and connectors.

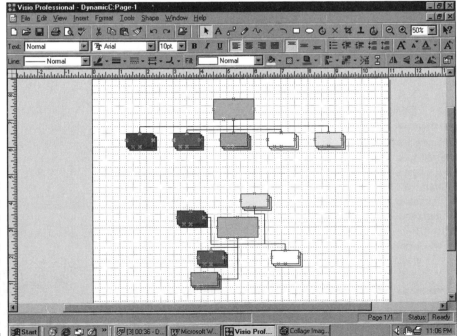

Figure 5-3:
Dynamic
glue lets
connectors
move to
different
points when
you move
shapes.

Determining your glue type

You need to know how to tell whether a connector uses dynamic glue or static glue. The answer is visible in the connector's endpoints when you select the connector. You see one of two things:

✔ **When a connector uses static glue,** the connector's endpoints are dark red and are the size of other endpoints and selection handles. The beginning point has a + in it; the ending point has an X in it.

✔ **When a connector uses dynamic glue,** the endpoints are a lighter shade of red and are slightly larger than other endpoints and selection handles.

Determining which type of glue your connectors use is as simple as that. (I considered including a figure for you, but red endpoints don't show up very well in shades of gray.)

Switching from one glue to another

Before I leave this whole gluey topic, I want to show you how to *switch* a connection from one type of glue to another. Why? Because knowing how to switch from one to the other is important depending on the type of drawing you're creating, how much you want to control connections, and how much you're going to change the drawing as you work on it. You may create a connection with dynamic glue, and then decide that you want the connector to *always* stay attached to a shape's lower-left corner no matter where you move the shape.

You can't glue some connectors using dynamic glue — it just isn't available to all connectors. In order to glue dynamically, a connector must be able to bend around other shapes when necessary. If the connector isn't programmed to bend, you can only use static glue. Unfortunately, you have no way to know whether dynamic glue is available or not until you try it with a specific connector. If you keep trying over and over, and it's not working, the problem isn't you! Save yourself the frustration and use a different connector (see "Adding Connectors to Shapes," later in this chapter).

To change a static connection to a dynamic one, follow these steps:

1. **Click the Pointer Tool button (refer to Table 5-1) on the Standard toolbar.**

2. **Select the connector that you want to change.**

3. **Press and hold the Ctrl key as you drag either endpoint away from the shape, and then drag it back toward a different connection point.**

   When you release the mouse button, the endpoint is attached to the shape and is light red and slightly larger than other endpoints. This tells you the glue is dynamic.

When you switch a connector to dynamic glue, don't be surprised if the end-point jumps to a different point than the one you choose. Remember that dynamic glue is smart; it chooses the *nearest* logical point to connect to. If you move the shape the connector is attached to, the connector may choose yet another point to attach to.

To change a dynamic connection to a static one, use these steps:

1. **Click the Pointer Tool button (refer to Table 5-1) on the Standard toolbar.**

2. **Select the connector that you want to change.**

3. **Drag either endpoint away from the shape; then drag it to the point where you want to attach the connector.**

   When you release the mouse button, the endpoint is dark red, which tells you that the connector is now using static glue.

Setting glue options

If you read any other parts of this chapter, you may have gotten the idea that connection points are the only spot on a shape where you can attach a con-nector. Wrong! You can attach connectors to connection points, guides, shape handles, and shape vertices, depending on which of these options you choose. The Snap & Glue dialog box in Figure 5-4 shows these four options listed in the Glue To box. Guides and Connection Points are selected for you automatically. If you want to glue connectors to handles and vertices, you need to click these check boxes as well. Or, you can deselect any of the four options. (Guides are lines that you can add to a drawing to help you position and place shapes accurately. See Chapter 6 for more on guides.)

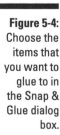

Figure 5-4:
Choose the items that you want to glue to in the Snap & Glue dialog box.

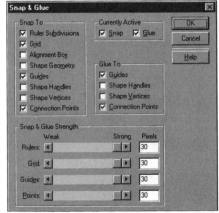

Use these steps to set glue options:

1. **Choose Tools⇨Snap & Glue.**

   Visio displays the Snap & Glue dialog box (refer to Figure 5-4).

2. **In the Glue To box, click the check boxes of the points that you want to glue connectors to.**

3. **Click OK.**

Adding Connectors to Shapes

The first half of this chapter makes you a glue expert; in this half I show you how to put some connectors in a drawing. Visio gives you *many* options.

The following three methods automatically use dynamic glue to connect shapes (see "Dynamic glue" earlier in this chapter):

- ✔ Connecting shapes as you drag shapes into your drawing
- ✔ Drawing connectors with the Connector tool and the Ctrl key
- ✔ Connecting shapes using the Connect Shapes tool

These three methods automatically use static glue to connect shapes (see "Static glue," earlier in this chapter):

- ✔ Dragging connector shapes into your drawing
- ✔ Drawing connectors with the Connector tool
- ✔ Pulling connectors from control handles on shapes

You don't need to memorize every method to add connectors right away. I divide the list of methods into two categories for a reason. You know what type of drawing you need to create. If it's important to connect to specific points, and you aren't moving shapes around a lot, you should use a method that uses static glue. If you are adding or deleting shapes a lot, or moving shapes around a lot, and you don't particularly care where connectors attach, use a method that uses dynamic glue.

As you're connecting shapes, it's important to remember to use Shape Help. Just right-click the shape that you want help with. When the shortcut menu appears, click the Shape Help option. A pop-up Help message tells you how to work with the shape. An example is shown in Figure 5-5.

Dynamic Connector

Use to connect shapes point-to-point or shape-to-shape with adjustable, bent lines.
To connect other shapes point-to-point, glue an endpoint on this shape to a
connection point × on the other shapes.
To connect other shapes shape-to-shape, drop this shape on the page, then
Ctrl+drag each endpoint on this shape to the other shapes. If you move 2-D shapes
connected shape-to-shape, the ends of the connector move to connect the shapes'
closest points.
If this shape crosses any existing lines on the drawing page, it creates a line jump.
This shape routes around 2-D placeable shapes.
To add text, select the shape, then type.

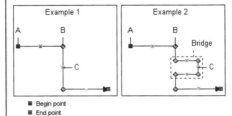

■ Begin point
⊞ End point
× Midpoint
◇ Vertex

A   Drag a begin point or an endpoint to glue point to point, or Ctrl+drag to glue
shape to shape.
B   Drag a vertex to reposition it while maintaining the angles of the line segment.
Ctrl+drag a vertex to reposition it without maintaining the angles of the line segment.
C   Drag a midpoint to move a connector line segment while maintaining the angles
between it and the segments on each side of it.
Ctrl+drag a midpoint to create a new vertex. Shift+drag a midpoint to create a
"bridge" in a line segment, as shown in Example 2.

Figure 5-5:
Shape Help
gives
detailed
explanations
for working
with a
shape.

The following sections discuss each of the methods for adding shapes to a drawing.

Connect shapes as you drag shapes

I prefer connecting shapes as I drag them into my drawing because this method lets me combine two steps into one. This method is particularly useful for process drawings, like flowcharts.

To use this method, you use the Connector tool on the Standard toolbar (refer to Table 5-1). This method uses dynamic glue (shape-to-shape connections), so if you move shapes around later, the connectors reconnect to the closest logical points.

1. **Choose File➪Stencils to open the stencils that you want to use.**

2. **Click the Connector Tool button (refer to Table 5-1).**

   The mouse pointer switches to Connector tool, a sort of elbow-shaped arrow.

3. **Drag a shape that you want to use onto the drawing page.**

4. **Drag another shape into the drawing.**

   Visio connects the two shapes automatically, using dynamic glue.

5. **Repeat Step 4 until all the shapes that you want are in the drawing.**

6. **Click the Pointer Tool button to switch back to the regular mouse pointer.**

If you want to turn off this feature so that shapes *aren't* automatically connected when you drag them into your drawing, just click the Pointer tool again. (The Pointer tool looks like an arrow.)

Figure 5-6 shows two boxes that were connected as they were dragged into the drawing. You can see that the Connector tool is highlighted, the mouse pointer is the Connector tool (a sort of elbow-shaped arrow), and the connector is glued dynamically.

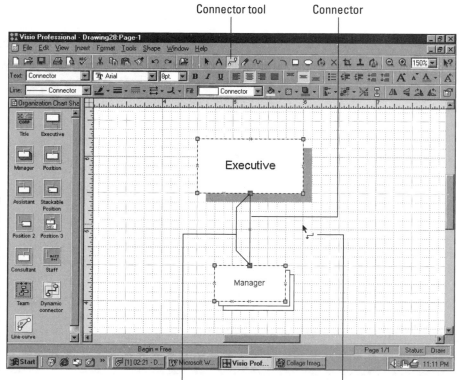

Figure 5-6: These two boxes were connected automatically as they were dragged onto the drawing.

If this method isn't working for you, you may be trying to connect 1-D shapes to one another. This method automatically connects 2-D shapes only. It's not typical to connect 1-D shapes to each other. If you need to do this, however, you can draw connectors, which I show you in the next section.

Using the Connector tool to draw connectors

If your drawing already contains 2-D shapes, you can use the Connector tool to go back and make connections later using either static (point-to-point) or dynamic (shape-to-shape) glue. This tool creates *dynamic* connectors: the incredible, bendable, shapeable, flexible, elbow-jointed connectors I tell you about in "Figuring Out Connectors" earlier in this chapter. If it needs to, the connector bends to form an elbow-joint connector like the one shown in Figure 5-7.

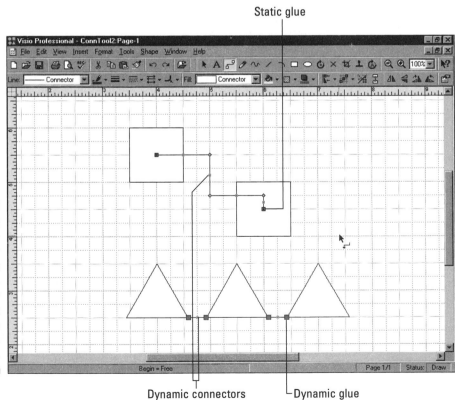

Figure 5-7: The Connector tool creates a dynamic connector that can bend to make connections.

To use the Connector tool to connect existing shapes with static glue, follow these steps.

1. **Click the Connector Tool button (refer to Table 5-1) on the Standard toolbar.**

   The mouse pointer changes to an elbow-shaped arrow.

2. **Move the mouse pointer over a connection point on a shape.**

   You see a bold, black border around the connection point.

3. **Click the connection point and then drag the mouse to a connection point on another shape.**

   The connector attaches between the points using static glue (point-to-point connection).

Using the Connector tool and the Ctrl key

If you want to use dynamic glue when you connect two existing shapes in a drawing, follow these steps:

1. **Click the Connector Tool button (refer to Table 5-1) on the Standard toolbar.**

   The mouse pointer changes to an elbow-shaped arrow.

2. **Move the mouse pointer over a connection point on a shape.**

   You see a bold, black border around the connection point.

3. **Hold the Ctrl key as you click the connection point and then drag the mouse to a connection point on another shape.**

   The connector attaches between the shapes using dynamic glue (shape-to-shape connection).

Using the Connect Shapes tool

The Connect Shapes tool is powerful, and it's a timesaver, too. This tool automatically connects two or more existing 2-D shapes in the order that you want them connected. This is a quick way to connect a series of shapes that you already placed in a drawing (see Figure 5-8).

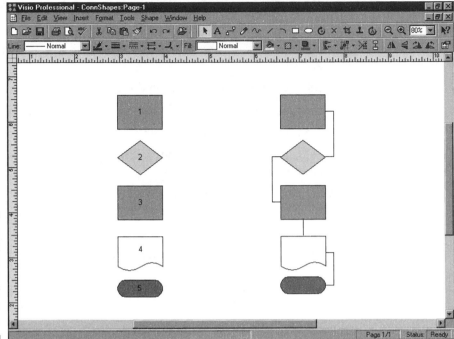

Figure 5-8:
The Connect
Shapes tool
connects a
series of
shapes
automatically.

To use this method, follow these steps:

1. **Click the Pointer Tool button (refer to Table 5-1) on the Standard toolbar.**

2. **Hold down the Shift key and click all the shapes in the order that you want to connect them.**

3. **Click the Connect Shapes Tool button (refer to Table 5-1) on the Shape toolbar.**

   Visio automatically connects all the shapes using dynamic glue.

A really cool variation to this method lets you connect the shapes with the type of connector you choose (something other than a line). For example, suppose you want to connect four boxes with block-style arrows or arrow-tipped lines. These are examples of 1-D shapes that you can find on the Connectors stencil. The Blocks, Basic Shapes, and Blocks with Perspective stencils also contain some nifty 1-D shapes to use as connectors. In Figure 5-9, I selected the Flow Director 1 shape from the Connectors stencil to use as the connector between flowchart shapes.

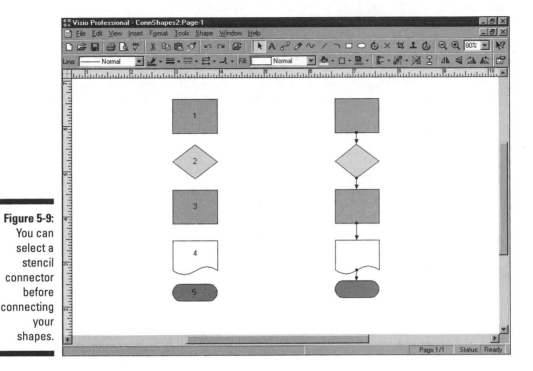

Figure 5-9:
You can
select a
stencil
connector
before
connecting
your
shapes.

To connect existing shapes with the connector that you choose, follow these steps:

1. **Click the Pointer Tool button (refer to Table 5-1) on the Standard toolbar.**

2. **Choose File⇨Stencils.**

   Open the stencil that contains the 1-D connector that you want to use.

3. **On the stencil that you opened, click the shape that you want to use for a connector.**

4. **In the drawing, hold down the Shift key and click all the shapes in the order that you want to connect them.**

5. **Click the Connect Shapes Tool button (refer to Table 5-1) on the Shape toolbar.**

   Visio automatically creates shape-to-shape (dynamic glue) connections between all the shapes that you selected using the connector you chose.

Dragging connector shapes into your drawing

Another way to connect shapes is to drag 1-D shapes into your drawing from stencils. Some of the best stencils for 1-D connector shapes are:

- ✔ Basic Shapes
- ✔ Blocks
- ✔ Blocks with Perspective
- ✔ Connectors

Most stencils usually contain at least one connector shape. If the stencil you're using for 2-D shapes doesn't contain the connector that you want to use, open the stencil that does using the File➪Stencils command.

1-D shapes that you can use as connectors appear with a yellow background on stencils.

Pulling connectors from shapes

Control handles are those shaded, green, square handles on shapes that let you control different aspects and behavior of a shape. (For all the details on control handles, see Chapter 3.) On some shapes, the control handles let you create connectors by "pulling" them out of the control handle.

To find out how you can use a shape's control handle, select the shape, move the mouse pointer over the control handle, and pause for a few seconds. If the control handle is for adjusting the connector (like the one shown in Figure 5-10), a tip pops up that says Reposition Connector. Some shapes have more than one control handle, and the one you choose may not be the right one. If not, try a different control handle. If you don't find one for adjusting connectors, you have to use a different method for creating connectors.

To pull a connector from a control handle, use these steps:

1. **Click the Pointer Tool button (refer to Table 5-1) on the Standard toolbar.**

2. **Click the shape that you want to pull a connector from.**

3. **Pause the mouse pointer over the control handle to make sure it says** Reposition Connector; **then drag the mouse to a connection point on the shape where you want to attach the connector.**

4. **Release the mouse button on the connection point.**

   Visio attaches the connector using static glue.

Control handle   Control handle tip

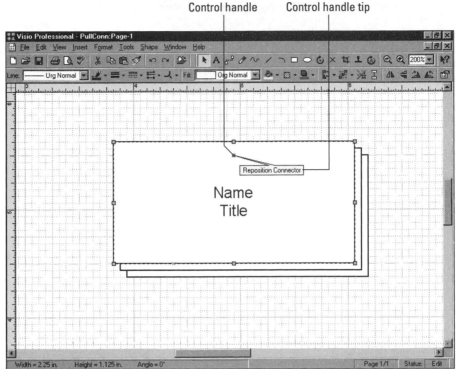

Figure 5-10:
The control
handle tip
indicates
this control
handle is for
a connector.

If you select the first shape again, you can see that, unlike other connectors, this connector is part of the shape. If you move the shape, the connector remains connected to the shape that you attached it to. Keep in mind that with most connectors that are part of a shape, you can't switch the glue from static to dynamic.

Handling Connectors That Cross Paths

In some drawings, such as flowcharts or network diagrams, you may run into problems when connectors cross each other. In a simple drawing, this may not be an issue. But when a drawing is complex, connectors that cross paths can make a drawing difficult to follow.

To solve this problem, Visio lets you add a *jump* to a connector — a sort of "wrinkle" in a line. The jump clarifies which two shapes are connected and which ones are not (see Figure 5-11).

Jump on horizontal connector

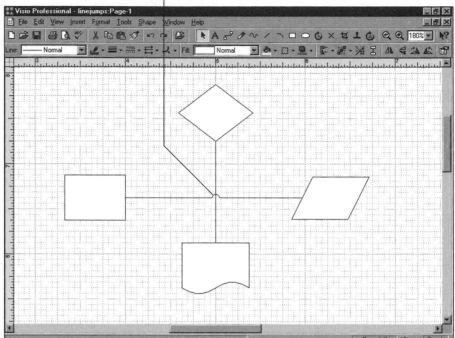

Figure 5-11:
In this drawing, jumps are set for horizontal connectors.

To define line jumps, use these steps:

1. **Choose File➪Page Setup.**

   Visio displays the Page Setup dialog box.

2. **Click the Page Properties tab, shown in Figure 5-12.**

3. **In the Add Line Jumps To box, click one of the options shown in the drop-down list.**

   - None

   - Horizontal Lines

   - Vertical Lines

   - Last Routed Line (the last of the two connectors that you drew)

4. **Click OK.**

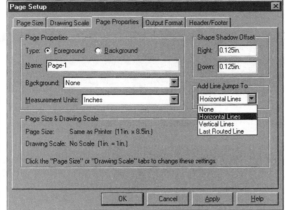

Figure 5-12:
The Page
Properties
tab in the
Page Setup
dialog box.

Using Routable Connectors and Placeable Shapes

This section covers a difficult topic, so I try to make it as simple as possible for you. A *routable connector* is one that can change its path so that it doesn't cut across another shape to get to the one it's connected to. The connector that connects the two octagons in Figure 5-13 is routable because it refuses to cut across the upper triangle. The connector that connects the two triangles *isn't* routable because it plows right through the three-dimensional box that's in its path. (Granted, this is a pretty goofy-looking diagram, but it illustrates the point!)

So, a routable connector is one that is capable of changing its path to get out of the way of other shapes. Is *every* connector routable? No way. To be routable, a connector must be *dynamic.* You can determine if a connector is dynamic immediately, because when you select it, it has an elbow joint, control points, and vertices, all of which can be manipulated. If you refer to Figure 5-13, you can see that the connector between the two octagons is dynamic because it has all of these features.

And for the other half of the story: the placeable shape. Here's the catch: A routable connector works only with a *placeable shape,* any shape that you specify as one that will work with a routable connector. Look again at Figure 5-13. The 3-D box is *not* a placeable shape, so the connector that connects the triangles isn't routable; it runs right through the 3-D box.

Routable connector   Non-routable connector

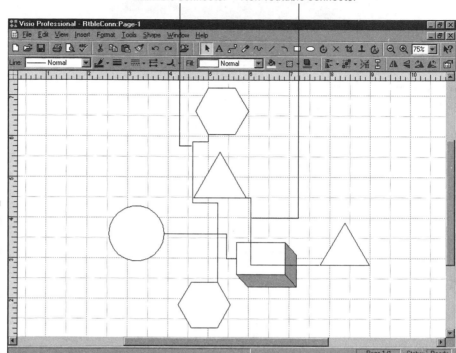

Figure 5-13:
Routable
connectors
are "polite"
to placeable
shapes;
nonroutable
connectors
are not.

In a nutshell: Routable connectors and placeable shapes — you must have one to have the other. So how do you get both? Fortunately, Visio does half of the work for you automatically; it sets all shapes to be placeable *if Visio decides they need to be.* That's cool. That way, you don't have to worry about it!

You have the option of changing this setting by choosing Format➪Behavior. In the Layout Behavior box, choose Layout And Route Around to make a shape placeable, or choose Do Not Layout And Route Around to make a shape non-placeable.

You can get a routable connector in one of three ways:

 ✔ **When you connect shapes using the Connect Shapes command,** you automatically get a routable connector.

 ✔ **Use the Dynamic Connector,** a shape that appears on many stencils and is *always* available on the Connectors stencil. (It looks like an elbow-jointed connector with a box at each end.)

 ✔ **Before you begin a drawing, click the Connector Tool button on the Standard toolbar; then drag shapes into the drawing area.** Using the Connector Tool, the shapes are automatically connected using a dynamic connector.

When you use routable connectors, you can tweak the path of the connector by moving control points and vertices that make up the "elbow joint" of the connector. For detailed steps on working with a shape's control points and vertices, see Chapter 7.

Using Auto Layout for Connected Drawings

Visio has an automatic layout feature for drawings that typically include connected shapes, like organization charts, network diagrams, and flowcharts. This feature saves you the trouble of rearranging shapes manually when you revise (add or delete) shapes in a large drawing. If you're in a hurry, the auto layout feature also lets you draw sloppy drawings quickly and have Visio arrange the shapes for you. An example of a messy, hastily drawn organization chart is shown in Figure 5-14.

If you click the Connector tool before you start dragging shapes into your drawing, Visio automatically connects one shape to the next using dynamic connectors. (If you choose not to use the Connector tool, be sure to add dynamic connectors between shapes.) After all the shapes are in the drawing, you're ready to use the auto layout feature.

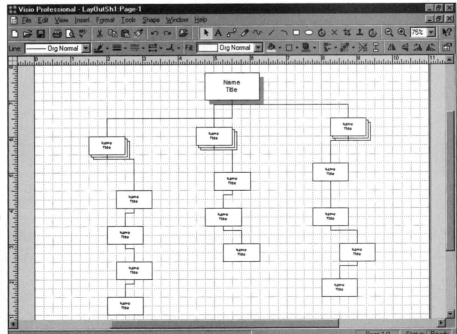

Figure 5-14:
Use auto layout to arrange and position these shapes.

To use Visio's auto layout feature in a drawing where the shapes are connected, follow these steps.

1. **Drag all the shapes and connectors into the drawing.**

2. **Select all the shapes and connectors.**

3. **Choose Tools⇨Lay Out Shapes.**

   The Lay Out Shapes dialog box, shown in Figure 5-15, appears.

Figure 5-15:
Choose auto layout features under the General tab of the Lay Out Shapes dialog box.

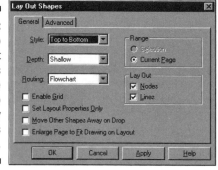

4. **In the Style drop-down list, choose Top to Bottom, Left to Right, or Radial.**

   Choose Top to Bottom or Left to Right for linear drawings like organization charts. Choose Radial for non-linear drawings like some network diagrams.

5. **In the Depth drop-down list, choose Shallow, Medium, or Deep.**

   In an organization chart, for example, you choose Deep if the chart contains more shapes up and down than across — that is, more positions, fewer managers. If the chart contains more shapes running across the chart than up and down (more managers than positions) you probably choose Shallow. If the drawing is pretty evenly weighted, use Medium.

6. **In the Routing drop-down list, choose Flowchart or Right Angle.**

   Choose Flowchart if the drawing uses both straight and right-angle connectors. Choose Right Angle if the chart uses *only* right-angle connectors.

7. **In the Range box, click the Selection or Current Page radio button.**

   Choose Selection to have Visio lay out all the shapes that you selected in Step 1.

   You can choose Current Page and lay out all the shapes on the current page.

8. **In the Lay Out box, click the <u>N</u>odes or <u>L</u>ines check box.**

   Choose Nodes to automatically lay out 2-D shapes, or choose Lines to automatically lay out connectors. (You can also choose both.)

9. **Click OK.**

Visio automatically arranges the shapes so that your drawing looks like the one shown in Figure 5-16.

Don't worry about using the Advanced tab in the Lay Out Shapes dialog box unless you're running out of room in a drawing. This tab lets you specify minimums for spacing and sizing. You can set spacing in decimal inches between connectors and 2-D shapes, and between connectors and other parallel connectors. You can set a minimum box (2-D shape) size and *avenue* size (the space between 2-D shapes) (see Figure 5-17).

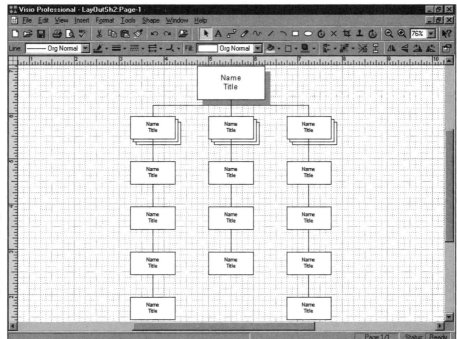

Figure 5-16:
Use Auto
Layout to
automat-
ically
arrange the
shapes.

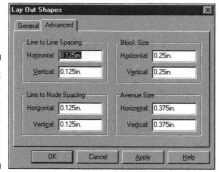

Figure 5-17:
The
Advanced
tab lets you
set spacing
and sizes.

Don't forget: If you don't like the way the auto layout feature arranges your drawing, choose Edit⇨Undo or press Ctrl-Z.

Part III
Customizing Your Work

The 5th Wave   By Rich Tennant

"I used Visio to create this 3-D wallpaper and now half the staff is complaining of headaches. Must be these dang VDT screens!"

In this part . . .

In this part you start to get into the nitty-gritty of Visio. I show you more about positioning shapes precisely, drawing your own shapes and manipulating them, and making more sophisticated drawings using pages and layers. You also get a brief summary of Visio's wizards and an inkling of what they can do for you.

Chapter 6

Making Your Drawings Precisely Right

● ●

● ●

*T*his chapter is all about how to measure, place, and line up elements in a drawing using the tools Visio provides. The tools I show you make these tasks easy and save you time. You don't have to use all of these ideas; just pick and choose the ones that make the most sense for your drawings.

Checking Out Your Options

The list below gives you a preview of the terms I use in this chapter so that you aren't scratching your head wondering what the heck I'm talking about.

✔ **Alignment and distribution:** Alignment refers to shapes lining up evenly; distribution refers to objects being spaced evenly.

When shapes aren't aligned and distributed evenly in a drawing, your eye senses that something is wrong. Visio helps you align and distribute shapes automatically.

✔ **Grid lines:** These prominent vertical and horizontal lines make the drawing area look like graph paper.

In many of the figures in this book, I often turn off the grid so that you can focus just on the topic at hand. However, the grid is a useful tool for measuring and placing shapes.

✔ **Guides:** You can add guide lines to a drawing to help you position and place shapes accurately.

If you draw a person on paper, you may lightly sketch in horizontal lines at the shoulder, waist, and knees as guides for helping you proportion the figure. You place guides in a Visio drawing for the same purpose.

✔ **Rulers:** These are the objects on the top and left side of the drawing area that look curiously like — well, like *rulers!* Rulers, as you may expect, act as measuring devices.

✔ **Scale:** Scale is the ratio of real-life objects to the shapes in your drawing. Remember the last time you looked at a map? The scale was probably 10 miles per 1 inch or something close to that. Unless you're able to print on life-size paper, you have to scale a drawing when it includes objects that are larger than the paper!

✔ **Snap:** This feature pulls or attracts shapes to any object that you specify: another shape, a grid line, a guide, a connection point. This function helps you place shapes accurately.

If you plan on using some of the sections in this chapter to help you with Visio, check now to make sure that Rulers, Grid, Guides, and Connection Points are checkmarked on your View menu (just click them). If not, they won't show up on your screen, and you'll think I'm just making 'em up (or seeing things)!

You may also find it useful to display the View toolbar if you use any sections in this chapter. To display the View toolbar, choose View➪Toolbars➪View. The View toolbar contains the tools listed in Table 6-1. The Grid tool toggles the grid on and off; the Guides tool toggles guides on and off; and the Connections tool toggles connection points on and off.

Table 6-1	Tools on the View Toolbar
Button	*Tool*
⊞	Grid
┼	Guides
⌐⌐	Connections

Using the Drawing Grid

Whenever you create a new drawing, Visio automatically displays a drawing grid — horizontal and vertical lines that make the drawing area look like graph paper. The grid helps you place shapes where you want them in a drawing.

Just as you can buy graph paper in different grid sizes, you can set the grid density (fine, normal, or coarse) for your drawing. Why would you care about density? If you create a drawing with very small shapes, you probably want a finer density, say, lines every ⅛ inch or so. On the other hand, if you use very large shapes in your drawing, a ½-inch grid is more than adequate (see Figure 6-1); ⅛-inch increments are just wasted.

Keep in mind that the actual density that you see on your screen depends on your monitor and the resolution that you use. To figure out what fine, normal, and coarse mean on your monitor, experiment with them! Use the steps that appear later in this section to change grid density.

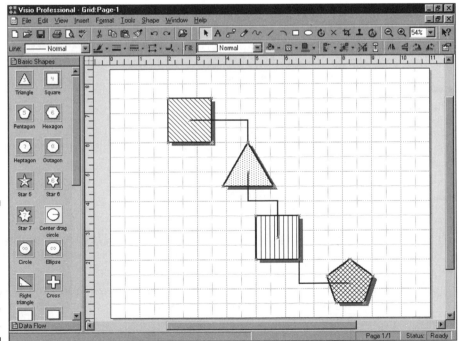

Figure 6-1:
In this drawing, a ½-inch grid is adequate for these large shapes.

The grid in Visio is automatically *variable*. That is, when you zoom in on a drawing, grid lines are closer together; if you zoom out, the grid lines are farther apart. This is a great feature when you want to place shapes right on the money. It doesn't help much to zoom in really close on a shape if the grid doesn't change, because it would be like trying to place shapes on paper every ⅛ inch using a ruler that was only marked in ¼-inch intervals. You can only place a shape really precisely if the grid gets denser. Of course, like most settings in Visio, you can turn off the variable grid and use a fixed grid instead if you want (see the steps that follow). If you use a fixed grid, the density stays the same, regardless of the zoom percentage you use. Typically, a grid is evenly spaced horizontally and vertically; that is, when horizontal lines occur every ½ inch, vertical lines do, too. However, you can set an uneven grid if you like, with ½-inch horizontal grid lines and ¼-inch vertical grid lines, for example.

To change grid settings or set a fixed grid, use these steps.

1. **Choose Tools⇨Ruler & Grid.**

   Visio displays the Ruler & Grid dialog box, as shown in Figure 6-2. Notice that the Ruler & Grid dialog box includes identical areas for horizontal and vertical grid lines so that you can set variables independently.

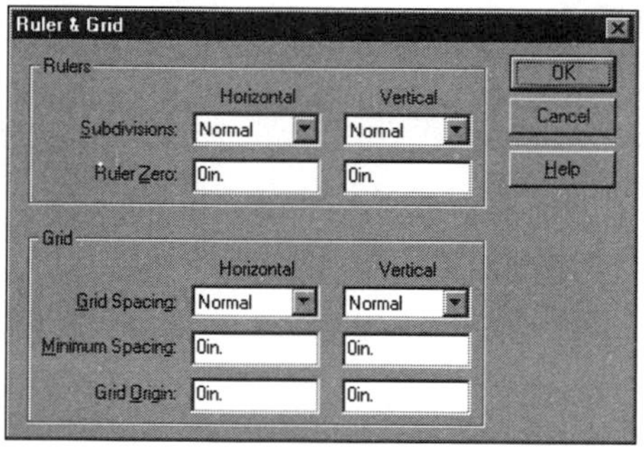

Figure 6-2:
The Ruler & Grid dialog box lets you set grid variables.

2. **Click the drop-down lists for Grid Spacing Horizontal and Grid Spacing Vertical; then click Fine, Normal, or Coarse. To set a fixed grid, click Fixed.**

3. **If you want to get picky about the *minimum* spacing to use (for Fine, Normal, or Coarse), type a number (in inches) in the Minimum Spacing boxes.**

4. **Click OK.**

Note: The grid doesn't print when you print your drawing; it's a visual aid only.

If you ever want to turn off the drawing grid, choose View➪Grid. This command toggles the grid display on and off. Turning off the grid helps you see how the drawing will look when you print it.

Setting Your Scale

When you create a drawing that doesn't represent real life objects — like, say, a flowchart — you don't need to worry about scale. Who cares if your *decision* shape is 1⅛ inch wide and your *process* shape is 1¾ inch wide? When you use a template to create a flowchart (or any other type of drawing with abstract shapes) Visio automatically sets the drawing scale to 1:1 (drawing size:actual size).

However, when you create a drawing with shapes that represent real-life objects (anything larger than a page), the drawing must be *scaled* so that all objects fit on the page in proper relation to one another. For example, suppose that you want to create an office layout. If you use the Office Layout template, Visio automatically sets the drawing scale to ¼ inch:1 foot. That is, every ¼ inch shown on the printed page represents 1 foot of office space. Terrific — all the work is done for you! An example of a ¼ inch:1 foot office layout is shown in Figure 6-3.

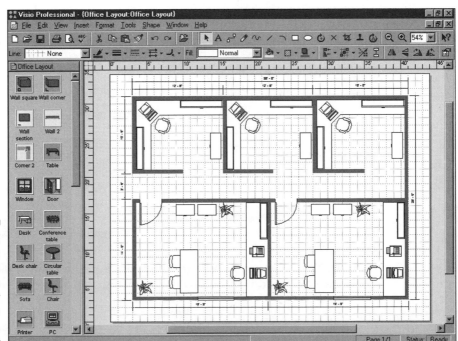

Figure 6-3:
The ¼ inch:
1 foot scale
works
perfectly for
this office
layout.

If you're not using a template (or if you want to adjust the scale set by a template), you can set a drawing scale yourself, but you're going to have to work for it! Well, at the very least, you need to understand the three elements involved:

- **Page units** represent the measurements on the printed page (like a 6-foot couch that's only ½ inch on the printed page).
- **Drawing units** represent real-life measurements (like 320 feet for a building landscape plan).
- **Drawing scale** is the ratio between these two.

To get an accurate scale in your drawing, *you must set all three of these elements*. If you set only the drawing scale, you may end up with inches:inches when you want feet:yards. That's because the default setting for page units and drawing units is typically *inches*. (I say *typically,* because many templates define inches as the unit of measure.)

To set page units, follow these steps:

1. **Choose Tool⇨Options.**
2. **In the Options dialog box, click the Default Units tab.**
3. **In the Page box, choose the unit of measure that you want from the drop-down list.**
4. **Click OK.**

To set drawing units, use these steps:

1. **Choose File⇨Page Setup.**
2. **In the Page Setup dialog box, click the Page Properties tab.**
3. **In the Measurement Units box, choose the unit of measure that you want from the drop-down list.**
4. **Click OK.**

Use these steps to specify a drawing scale:

1. **Choose File⇨Page Setup.**
2. **In the Page Setup dialog box, click the Drawing Scale tab, shown in Figure 6-4.**
3. **In the Drawing Scale area, click the radio button of one of the scale categories (Architectural, Civil Engineering, and so on).**

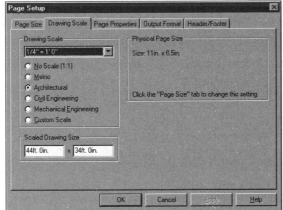

Figure 6-4:
The
Drawing
Scale tab in
the Page
Setup dialog
box.

4. **Click the drop-down list of measurements to display the preset scales; then click on the scale that you want to use.**

   If you don't want to use any of the preset scales listed, go back to Step 3 and choose Custom Scale; then enter a scale in the box provided.

5. **Check the Scaled Drawing Size area of the dialog box.**

   It tells you how much "real estate" you can cover on the drawing page with the current settings. If it's too large or too small, go back to Step 4 and choose a different scale that fits the page size better. For example, if you need to draw an office plan that's 50 feet by 50 feet and the Scaled Drawing Size shows only 40 feet by 30 feet, you need to adjust the drawing scale.

6. **Click OK.**

Check the Page Size tab in the Page Setup dialog box to make sure that your page matches your paper size. If it doesn't, set the correct page size and orientation. For more information on these settings, see Chapter 2.

When you change the scale of a drawing, it applies only to the current page of the drawing. If the drawing has multiple pages, including background pages, you must change the scale separately for each page. For more information about working with multi-page drawings and background pages, see Chapter 9.

Snapping Shapes into Place

Snap is a terrific timesaving feature of Visio. You can't imagine how much time you waste trying to place shapes precisely *without* using snap. The snap feature in Visio works like a magnet. You can *attract* a shape to one or more elements that you choose so as to position or align the shape correctly. When snap is turned on, you see a shape jump to certain points as you drag the shape around the drawing area. The jump you see is snap in action.

You can snap shapes to any of the following eight elements. The first four work with two-dimensional (2-D) shapes; the last four are for snapping one-dimensional (1-D) shapes to 2-D shapes.

- **Alignment box:** A shape's frame (displayed only when a shape is selected)

- **Connection points:** Blue Xs that appear on shapes when View⇨Connection Points is checked

- **Grid lines:** Horizontal and vertical graph paper lines in the drawing area

- **Guide lines or guide points:** Special lines or points that you add to a drawing to help you align shapes

- **Ruler markings:** Any mark that appears on the ruler (1 inch, ½ inch, and so on)

- **Shape geometry:** The outline of a shape

- **Shape handles:** The square green points on a selected shape that you use to resize shapes

- **Shape vertices:** The green diamond-shaped points that you use to change the angle of a line or add a new point

When you start Visio, snap is automatically turned on for rulers, grid lines, connection points, and guides. This means that whenever you drag a shape around the drawing area, it jumps to align itself to ruler subdivisions, grid lines, guides, or connection points on other shapes. For example, suppose you want to place three rectangles 1 inch apart. As you drag the shapes, they jump to the nearest grid line or ruler subdivision, letting you place the rectangles exactly 1 inch apart (see Figure 6-5). Without snap, you can spend a great deal of time shooting in the dark trying to space and line up these suckers! Even with all your effort, they *still* may not line up correctly.

You can choose any combination of the elements from the list above or choose none. Turning on all snap options at the same time is a little distracting because your shape jumps every time it gets near *anything*. I recommend that you turn on only those snap options that you really want to use. For instance, you may not want to choose grid and ruler at the same time. Since grid lines rarely correspond to ruler markings, it's not clear where your shape is jumping when both of these options are selected at the same time.

Along with choosing snap elements, you get to set the *strength* of snap. It's sort of like choosing between a tiny refrigerator magnet or a 10-pound horseshoe magnet. The bigger the magnet, the harder snap pulls shapes from farther away. (I doubt that you need to set strength; in all my years of working with Visio I've never noticed snap not pulling hard enough!)

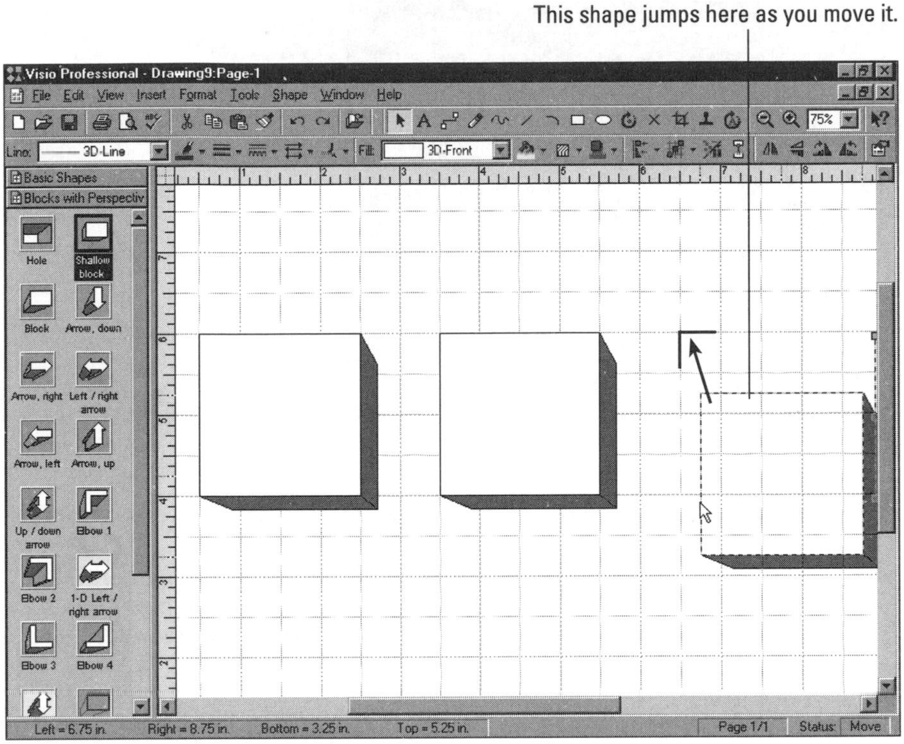

This shape jumps here as you move it.

Figure 6-5:
With snap, shapes jump into position automatically.

To change snap settings or turn snap off altogether, use these steps:

1. **Choose Tools⇨Snap & Glue.**

   The Snap & Glue dialog box, shown in Figure 6-6, appears.

2. **In the Snap To section, click the check boxes of elements that you want shapes to snap to when you move them.**

3. **In the Snap & Glue Strength area, adjust the pull by moving the slides along the slide bar.**

4. **Click OK.**

If you want to turn snap off altogether, choose Tools⇨Snap & Glue. In the Currently Active section of the dialog box, click the Snap check box to remove the check mark, and then click OK. When you turn snap off, shapes move freely (no more Mexican jumping beans!) when you drag them around the drawing area.

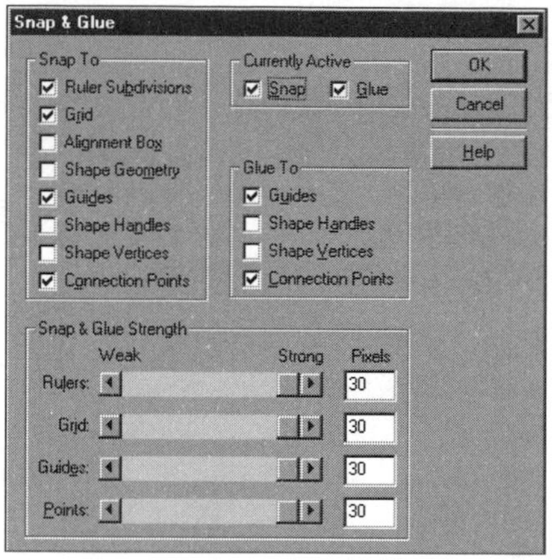

Figure 6-6:
Choose
Snap
elements
and strength
in the Snap
& Glue
dialog box.

Measuring Up with Rulers

I don't know about you, but I always feel more comfortable when I know how much space I have to move around in and what my boundaries are. The rulers tell you just that. Using vertical and horizontal rulers on the drawing page, you can tell exactly how much space you have in a drawing and how big or small elements are.

The rulers in a Visio drawing typically display inch measurements, unless you choose a different unit of measure. You have many other choices. For example, you may want to use yards or miles for drawings that represent real-life objects, such as landscape plans. If you use the metric system, you may want to switch ruler units to centimeters or millimeters. To switch default measurement units for the rulers, follow these steps:

1. **Choose File⇨Page Setup.**

   Visio displays the Page Setup dialog box.

2. **Click the Page Properties tab, shown in Figure 6-7.**

3. **Click the drop-down arrow for Measurement Units; then click the units that you want to use.**

4. **Click OK.**

The zero point for the rulers is generally in the lower-left corner of the drawing page, although you can change this if you want. Why would you want to? Well, suppose you're drawing an office layout. You may find the drawing easier to work with if you move the zero points to align with the left and upper walls (see Figure 6-8).

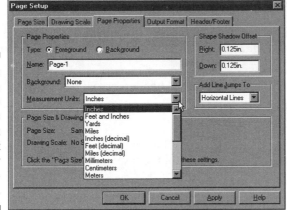

Figure 6-7:
Use the
Page
Properties
dialog box
to set
default ruler
measure-
ment units.

Figure 6-8:
The zero
point for
rulers is
moved to
align with
the left and
upper walls
of the floor
plan.

New zero points

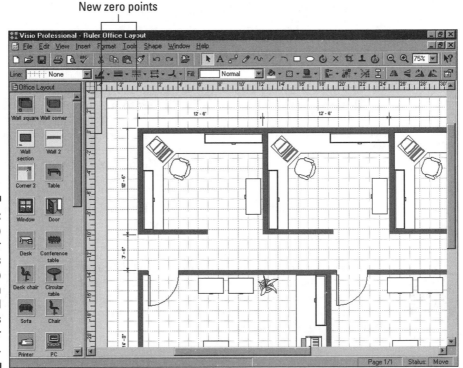

To change the zero point of both rulers, follow these steps.

1. **Move the mouse pointer to the gray square where the vertical ruler and horizontal ruler intersect (in the upper-left corner of the drawing area).**

   The mouse pointer changes to a 4-headed arrow.

2. **Hold down the Ctrl key; then drag the mouse where you want the zero point of both rulers to be.**

   As you move your mouse, watch the faint dotted line that appears on each ruler, marking the position of the mouse.

3. **Release the mouse button when the zero point is positioned where you want it.**

If you want to change the zero point of just one ruler, use the same type of procedure but drag from one ruler only. For example, if you want to place the zero point on the horizontal ruler 2 inches in from the left edge of the paper, follow these steps:

1. **Point to the *vertical* ruler until you see the double-headed arrow mouse pointer.**

2. **Hold the Ctrl key and drag the mouse until the vertical line is positioned where you want the zero point to be on the horizontal ruler.**

If you prefer not to do all this dragging, you can choose <u>T</u>ools⇨Ruler & <u>G</u>rid. When the Ruler & Grid dialog box is displayed (refer to Figure 6-2), enter zero points (measured in inches) in the Ruler Zero boxes for horizontal, vertical, or both rulers.

To reset the zero points of both rulers back to their default position, just double-click on the intersection of the rulers in the upper-left corner of the drawing area.

This is a handy time to use the snap feature I discuss earlier in the chapter. Before you adjust the zero point for your rulers, turn on snap for rulers if it isn't on already. (I show you how in "Snapping Shapes into Place.") With ruler snap turned on, your mouse jumps to ruler subdivisions so that you can place the zero point easily.

Using Guides to Guide You

As if you don't already have enough ways to position shapes in a drawing, Visio gives you two more! They're called *guide lines* and *guide points,* and they work in combination with snap. Use guide lines when you want a bunch of shapes to stand in a row like soldiers (see Figure 6-9). Use guide points when you want to pinpoint a shape in an exact location.

To make guide lines and guide points work, you gotta turn on snap for guides. Otherwise your guides aren't doing anything except cluttering up your drawing. (See "Snapping Shapes into Place" earlier in this chapter to set snap elements.) In Figure 6-9, all the shapes are snapped to the guide line because snap is set to work on guides and shape handles. To snap shapes to a guide, just drag the shape near the guide. The shape snaps automatically to the guide. When you select the shape, the shape's red selection handles clearly indicate that the shape is glued to the guide. (Visio uses dynamic glue to glue shapes to guides. See Chapter 5 for more information about dynamic glue.)

Guide line

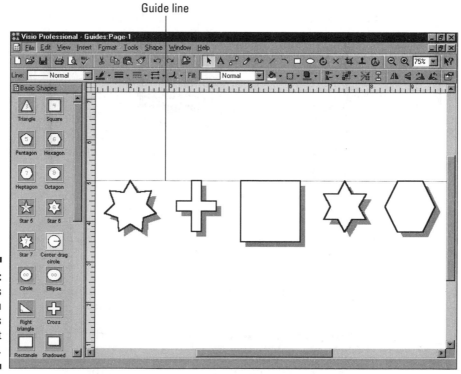

Figure 6-9:
Guide lines help you keep shapes in a straight line.

The really useful thing about guide lines and guide points — after you create them — is that you can move them. When you do, all the shapes attached to the guides move right along with them.

Creating guide lines

To create a guide line, use these steps:

1. **Move your mouse pointer over the vertical ruler (to create a vertical guide) or over the horizontal ruler (to create a horizontal guide) until the mouse pointer changes to a double-headed arrow.**

2. **Drag the mouse.**

   As you drag, the guide appears as a blue line that runs across (or up and down) the drawing page.

3. **Stop dragging the guide when it's positioned where you want it.**

   The line turns green because it's selected.

What? Now you want a diagonal guide line? Okay. Just create a horizontal or vertical guide, and then rotate it. You can use these steps:

1. **Select the guide line that you want to rotate.**

2. **Choose <u>S</u>hape⇨Si<u>z</u>e & Position.**

   The Size & Position dialog box appears.

3. **Click the Rotated radio button.**

4. **In the Angle box, type the degree angle of rotation (such as 45).**

5. **Click OK.**

   Visio rotates the selected guide to the angle that you specify.

Creating guide points

You can also create *guide points* when you want to pinpoint the corner of a shape in an exact location. On the screen, a guide point looks like a plus symbol (+). To create a guide point, use these steps:

1. **Move your mouse pointer over the intersection of the vertical and horizontal rulers.**

   The mouse pointer changes to a 4-headed arrow.

2. **Drag the mouse.**

   One vertical and one horizontal blue line follows the movement of your mouse on the drawing page.

3. **Stop dragging the mouse when the intersection of the guides is positioned where you want it.**

   The blue lines disappear and the guide point (a green cross) is displayed on the screen.

In Figure 6-10 on the left, it's clear that the lower-right corner of the square is connected to the guide point, but it's not so clear that the star is connected. That's because each one is connected at a selection handle on the shape's *frame.* If the star wasn't selected (so that you can see its frame), you'd probably guess that it *isn't* connected. If you want the tip of the star to touch the guide point, like the star on the right, turn on snap for connection points, because the star has a connection point at each tip. (See "Snapping Shapes into Place" earlier in this chapter to set snap elements.)

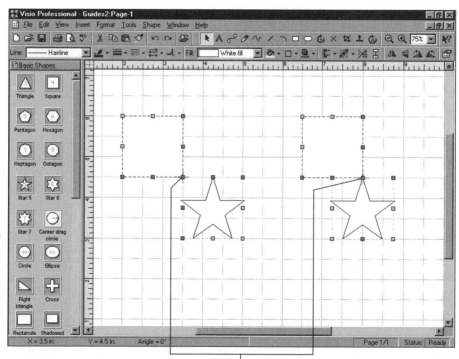

Figure 6-10:
Guide points
let you
place a
shape at an
exact point.

Guide points

If you want to use multiple guides spaced evenly across your drawing, this is a great tip for creating them. Create the first guide and then hold down the Ctrl key as you drag a copy of the guide to the next increment that you want — say 1 inch. Now press F4. It automatically creates another guide 1 inch from the last guide. Press F4 as many times as you want to keep creating evenly spaced guides at the same increment you originally chose.

Aligning and Distributing Shapes

Besides using guides, Visio gives you another way to align shapes automatically. Suppose that you create a flow chart like the one on the left in Figure 6-11. The boxes aren't lined up, the connectors look goofy, and the whole thing looks like you threw it together in a few seconds! The one on the right was aligned using Visio's automatic alignment feature.

With the click of a toolbar button, you can horizontally align the tops, bottoms, or middles of selected shapes, or vertically align the left edges, right edges, or middles of selected shapes.

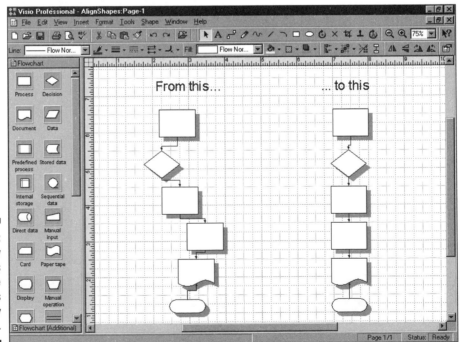

Figure 6-11:
The left flow chart is messy; the right one is perfectly aligned.

To align several shapes either horizontally or vertically, use these steps:

1. **Select the shape to which you want the other shapes to align.**

2. **Hold the Shift key as you select all other shapes that you want to align to the first shape.**

3. **Choose Tools⇨Align Shapes, or you can click the Align Shapes Tool button on the Shapes toolbar (it looks like a box and a triangle left-aligned).**

   The Align Shapes dialog box, shown in Figure 6-12, appears.

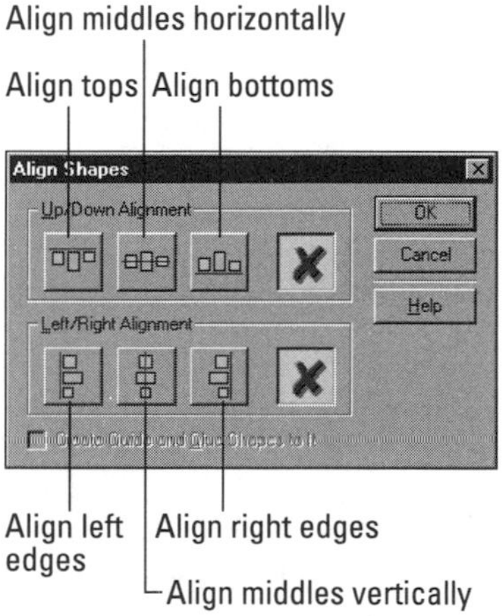

Align middles horizontally

Align tops | Align bottoms

Figure 6-12:
The Align
Shapes
dialog box.

Align left | Align right edges
edges
└─Align middles vertically

4. **Click the alignment style that you want.**

   If you think that you may add more shapes to your drawing that you'll want to align with these, consider clicking the Create Guide and Glue Shapes to It option at the bottom of the dialog box.

5. **Click OK.**

   Visio aligns all shapes to the first shape that you selected.

The first shape that you choose is like the baseline shape; all other shapes that you choose align to this first shape.

Notice the Align Shapes tool has a down-arrow next to the tool icon. If you click the arrow instead of the tool itself, Visio displays a mini-version of the dialog box. Just click the alignment style that you want.

Ever try to space several shapes evenly — say, ½ inch apart — across an area? It can be very frustrating when you have to do it manually! Visio calls this *distributing* shapes and makes it easy for you by providing a toolbar tool (or a menu command, if you prefer) similar to the Align Shapes command. Use these steps to distribute shapes:

1. **Select all shapes that you want to distribute.**

2. **Choose Tools⇨Distribute Shapes, or click the Distribute Shapes Tool button (it looks like three boxes aligned diagonally) on the Shape toolbar.**

   The Distribute Shapes dialog box, shown in Figure 6-13, appears.

Figure 6-13: The Distribute Shapes dialog box shows eight styles.

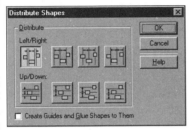

3. **Click the distribution style that you want to use.**

   If you think that you may add more shapes to your drawing that you'll want to distribute with these, consider clicking the Create Guides and Glue Shapes to Them option at the bottom of the dialog box.

4. **Click OK.**

   Visio distributes the shapes automatically.

Just like with the Align Shapes toolbar button, the Distribute Shapes tool has a down-arrow next to the tool icon. You can click the down-arrow to reveal a mini-version of the dialog box.

Chapter 7

Shape Up!

*B*ecause Visio provides so many shapes in its stencils, you can use Visio quite successfully without ever needing to customize shapes. But if you're really the adventurous type, you'll have Visio making shapes *your* way. In this chapter you discover how to get creative with Visio by drawing your own shapes or changing existing shapes.

Drawing Your Own Shapes

As if there aren't enough shapes for you to choose from in Visio, you can make your own, too. Actually, you may find yourself making your own shapes frequently, particularly if you work in a specialized field, like architectural design for zoos, or something equally zany. Visio gives you many tools for drawing shapes, and I show them to you in Table 7-1.

Using the Line tool

As the name implies, you can use the Line tool on the Standard toolbar to draw lines or shapes that are made up of straight lines. In Visio, lines are considered one-dimensional (1-D) shapes. The point where you start drawing a line displays an *endpoint,* a box with an X in it that's green when you select it.

The point where the line ends has an endpoint with a + symbol. Visio calls both of these endpoints *vertices* (see Figure 7-1), even though your high school geometry book said a *vertex* is a point at which two lines intersect. Go figure! Between the two vertices is a *control point,* which you use to control the shape of a shape, as I show you later in this chapter.

Table 7-1	Tools for Drawing Shapes
Button	*Tool*
	Arc tool
	Ellipse tool
	Format Painter tool
	Freeform tool
	Line tool
	Pencil tool
	Pointer tool
	Rectangle tool
	Rotation tool

To draw a simple line, follow these steps:

1. **Click the Line Tool button (refer to Table 7-1) on the Standard toolbar.**

   The mouse pointer changes to a line and a + symbol.

2. **Place the mouse pointer where you want the line to begin; then drag the mouse to where you want the line to end.**

   To draw a line at a 45-degree angle from your starting point, hold the Shift key as you drag the mouse.

3. **Release the mouse button.**

   The line is selected and the endpoints are displayed. (The control point is displayed if you switch to the Pencil tool on the Standard toolbar, which looks like a pencil.)

4. **Click any blank area of the drawing to deselect the line.**

Using the Line tool, you can also draw a shape by connecting a series of line segments. To connect segments as you draw, use these steps:

1. **Click the Line Tool button (refer to Table 7-1) on the Standard toolbar.**

   The mouse pointer changes to a line and a + symbol.

2. **Draw your first segment by dragging the mouse.**

3. **Point to the endpoint of the first segment; then drag the mouse to draw the second segment of your shape.**

   Repeat Step 3 as many times as you want.

4. **To close the shape, draw another segment from the endpoint of the last segment that you drew to the beginning point of the first segment that you drew, and then release the mouse button.**

   The shape becomes a *closed* shape. You see it fill with white (see Figure 7-2) because the default fill color is white (not transparent).

If your background color is white, and your grid is turned off, you can't see the white fill.

Vertices

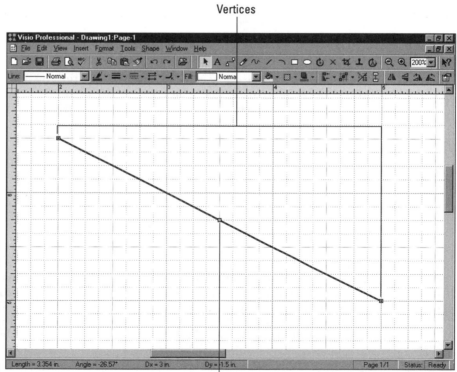

Figure 7-1:
Every line
has a
control point
between
two
vertices.

Control point

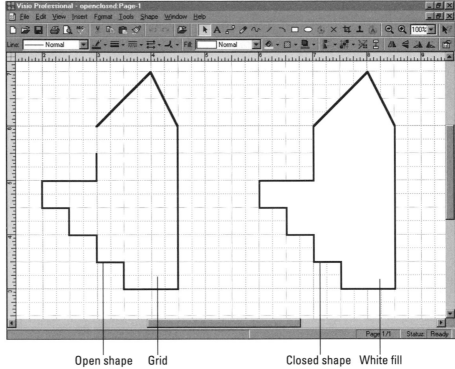

Figure 7-2:
You can tell that the shape on the right is closed because you can't see the grid through it.

Open shape   Grid   Closed shape   White fill

Whenever you draw shapes by connecting segments, turn on Snap (Tools⇨Snap & Glue), particularly for connection points, grid lines, or vertices. Snap helps you connect segments automatically. To review how Snap works, see Chapter 6.

If you don't draw all the line segments for a shape consecutively, you won't get a closed shape. You can tell right away because the shape isn't filled, even though the segments appear to be connected.

Using the Pencil and Arc tools

The Pencil tool works almost exactly like the Line tool. If you move the Pencil tool in a straight line, it draws a straight line. But, if you move the mouse in a curved direction, the Pencil tool draws a portion of a circle. The size and circumference of the circle depend on how far you move the mouse. Because you can draw curves and straight lines with the Pencil tool, use it when your shape includes both curves and lines (see Figure 7-3).

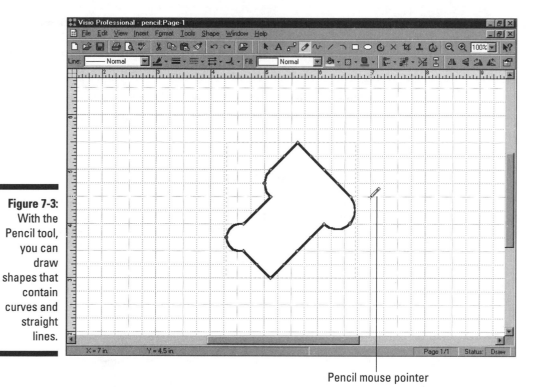

Figure 7-3:
With the Pencil tool, you can draw shapes that contain curves and straight lines.

Pencil mouse pointer

To draw a closed shape using the Pencil tool, follow these steps:

1. **Click the Pencil Tool button (refer to Table 7-1) on the Standard toolbar.**

2. **Draw the first segment by dragging the mouse; then release the mouse button.**

   Drag in a straight line for a line; drag in a circular direction for a curve.

3. **Draw the second segment by pointing to the endpoint of the previous segment, dragging the mouse, and then releasing the mouse button.**

   Repeat Step 3 as many times as you like.

4. **Finish the shape by connecting the endpoint of the last segment to the beginning point of the first segment.**

Well, it may seem obvious that the Arc tool lets you draw arcs! So how is it different from the Pencil tool, which also lets you draw arcs? The Arc tool always draws one-quarter of an ellipse whereas the Pencil tool always draws a portion of a circle (not an ellipse and not one-quarter). Use the Arc tool when you want a less-than-circular curve. Use the Pencil tool when you want to draw true circular curves. (I show you later in "Using the Ellipse and Rectangle tools" how to use the Ellipse tool to draw complete circles and ellipses.)

To draw an arc (one-quarter ellipse) using the Arc tool, follow these steps:

1. **Click the Arc Tool button (refer to Table 7-1) on the Standard toolbar.**

2. **Place the mouse where you want the arc to begin.**

3. **Drag the mouse in the direction you want the arc to go.**

4. **Release the mouse button where you want the arc to end.**

Using the Freeform tool

I call the Freeform tool the "doodling" tool. It works the same way a pencil works in your hand when you aren't drawing anything in particular. The Freeform tool (it looks like a squiggly line) obediently follows every curve and scribble you make. Just drag the Freeform tool to create, well — freeform shapes, like the one shown in Figure 7-4.

If you have a drawing tablet on your computer system, the Freeform tool is great because it's easier to draw with a pen than with a mouse. The Freeform tool also duplicates handwriting quite well when you use a pen.

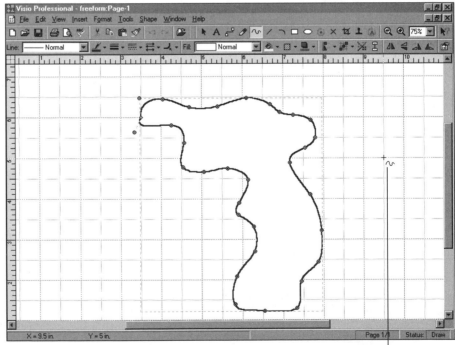

Figure 7-4:
Use the Freeform tool to create curved, irregular shapes.

Freeform mouse pointer

Using the Ellipse and Rectangle tools

You can see earlier in this chapter how to use the Arc and Pencil tools to draw curves (elliptical or circular). You can use either of these tools to draw four connected segments that form a complete circle or ellipse, but why do it the hard way? Visio cuts four steps down to one step by providing an Ellipse tool. The following steps tell you how to use it:

1. **Click the Ellipse Tool button (refer to Table 7-1) on the Standard toolbar.**

2. **Put the mouse pointer where you want the ellipse to be placed.**

3. **Drag the mouse in any direction.**

    To draw a perfect circle, hold the Shift key as you drag the mouse.

4. **Release the mouse button when the ellipse is the size and shape that you want.**

If you want the ellipse to be a particular size, watch the status bar as you drag the mouse. It tells you the exact width and height of your ellipse as you draw. (If you hold the Shift key to draw a circle, the height and width display the same number.) You can also choose Shape⇨Size and Position after you draw the shape; then enter exact dimensions in the Height and Width boxes.

The Rectangle tool works exactly the same way as the Ellipse tool. You can use the Line tool to create a rectangle by drawing and connecting four segments, but the Rectangle tool draws a rectangle for you in one easy step.

1. **Click the Rectangle Tool button (refer to Table 7-1) on the Standard toolbar.**

2. **Put the mouse pointer where you want the rectangle to be placed.**

3. **Drag the mouse in any direction. To draw a perfect rectangle, hold the Shift key as you drag the mouse.**

    To create a rectangle of a specific size, watch the status bar for height and width measurements as you draw.

4. **Release the mouse button when the rectangle is the size and shape that you want.**

Reshaping Shapes

Suppose that you find a shape in Visio that's almost what you want but not quite. You can modify it in many ways by tweaking a shape a little or a lot until it's just what you want it to be.

Moving and adding vertices

You can change the shape of any shape in Visio by dragging part of it to a new position. It's easy. In Figure 7-5, I changed a simple isosceles triangle by dragging the upper-right *vertex* to a new place. Remember, a vertex appears at the end of every line and the point at which lines intersect, which means that you see a vertex at each point of the triangle. Vertices are marked by green diamond shapes and are visible on a selected shape when you use any of the following tools on the Standard toolbar:

- ✔ Arc tool
- ✔ Freeform tool
- ✔ Line tool
- ✔ Pencil tool

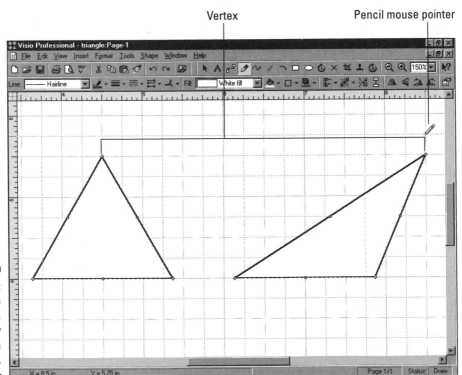

Figure 7-5:
It's easy to reshape a shape by dragging a vertex.

To move a vertex, use these steps:

1. **Select the shape using the Pointer Tool button (refer to Table 7-1) on the Standard toolbar.**

2. **Using the Pencil tool, Freeform tool, Line tool, or Arc tool, point to the vertex that you want to move.**

   (All of these tools are available on the Standard toolbar and are shown in Table 7-1.)

   When you're within *selection range* of the vertex, the mouse pointer changes to a four-headed arrow.

3. **Click the vertex.**

   When selected, the color switches from green to magenta.

4. **Drag the vertex wherever you want it; then release the mouse button.**

You can also add a vertex to any shape by using these steps:

1. **Using the Pointer Tool button (refer to Table 7-1) on the Standard toolbar, select the shape.**

   You see the shape's selection handles.

2. **Switch to the Pencil tool.**

   You see the shape's vertices and control points.

3. **Hold down the Ctrl key; then click a point where you want to add a vertex.**

   Visio adds the vertex (diamond shape) and a control point (round shape) between the new vertex and the previous one.

4. **Repeat Step 3 for as many vertices as you want to add.**

To be exact, when you add a vertex to a shape, you're actually adding a *segment*. That's because Visio automatically adds a control point between the new vertex and the previous one. Voilà! A new segment. You can use the control point to change the shape of the segment, as I show you in the next section of this chapter.

Why would you want to add a vertex to a shape? For an example, check out the five-pointed star in Figure 7-6. It's not bad, but perhaps you want it to look a little snazzier — maybe with five smaller points between the five existing points. To accomplish this task, you need to add some vertices and move others. Currently, vertices appear at the tip of each point on the star and at each inverted angle of the star.

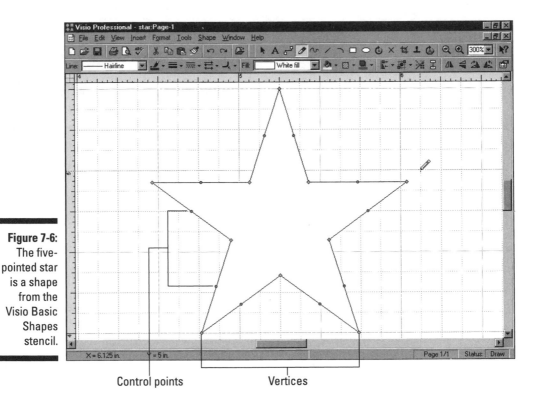

Figure 7-6:
The five-
pointed star
is a shape
from the
Visio Basic
Shapes
stencil.

Control points   Vertices

To create the ten-pointed star shown in Figure 7-7, you pull the inverted angle
vertex — call it A — out to a point. Before you can do that, though, you need
to add a new vertex on either side of A — call them B and C. If you pull A
without adding B and C, you just make a fatter star with shallower inverted
angles. Adding the vertices B and C gives the new tip two new points from
which to begin.

Moving control points

Suppose, instead of adding five new points to the star in Figure 7-6, you just
want to round out the lines of the star and make it look like one of the stars in
Figure 7-8? You use the *control points,* the round shapes that appear between
two vertices.

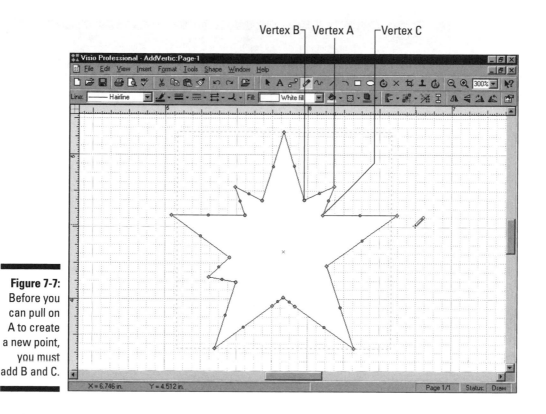

Figure 7-7:
Before you can pull on A to create a new point, you must add B and C.

To move a control point, use these steps.

1. **Select the shape using the Pointer Tool button (refer to Table 7-1) on the Standard toolbar.**

   You see the shape's selection handles.

2. **Switch to the Pencil tool.**

   You see the shape's vertices and control points.

3. **Point to the control point that you want to move.**

   The mouse pointer changes to a four-headed arrow.

4. **Click the control point.**

   The selected control point switches from green to magenta.

5. **Drag the control point; then release the mouse button.**

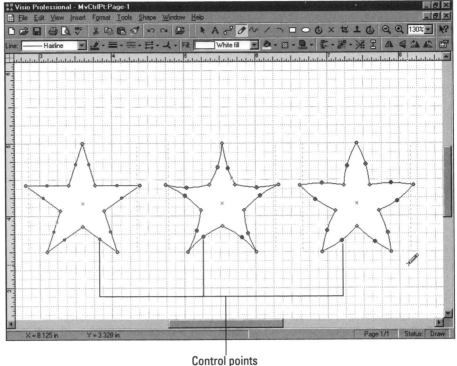

Figure 7-8:
The control points on the legs of each star can be moved to create a different form.

Control points

> You can make your changes more precise by zooming in on your shape and using the rulers to track the movement of a control point.

Rotating Shapes

Rotating shapes is something you may need to do frequently. A shape may not be facing the correct angle when you drag it into the drawing. Or it may be easier to draw a shape at one angle and rotate it later.

You can rotate nearly all Visio shapes. You can see easily whether a shape can be rotated or not by selecting it with the Rotation tool. If the shape has large, round handles that appear at the corners of the shape's frame, it can be rotated. You also see a *rotation pin* (a round handle with a + symbol) at the center of the shape. This is the point around which the shape is rotated. (If a Visio shape can't be rotated, it's with good reason — probably because it doesn't make any sense, or because it's inaccurate to rotate the shape.)

Visio provides three ways to rotate a shape:

- ✔ **Rotation handles** on a shape let you drag the shape to rotate it. Use this method when you want to change a shape's angle quickly but not necessarily precisely.

- ✔ **Rotate Right and Rotate Left tools** on the Shape toolbar let you rotate a shape 90 degrees at a time (clockwise or counterclockwise). Use this method when you know that you want to rotate a shape in 90-degree increments. These tool buttons show two triangles with an arrow to show the direction of rotation.

- ✔ **A menu command** (Shape⇨Size & Position) lets you rotate a shape at a precise angle that you specify. This is the best method to use when the precise angle of rotation is a priority.

To rotate a shape using the Rotation tool, use these steps:

1. **Click the Rotation Tool button (refer to Table 7-1) on the Standard toolbar.**

2. **Click the shape that you want to rotate.**

   The rotation handles are visible at the corners of the shape's frame, and the rotation pin appears at the center of the shape.

3. **Move the mouse pointer over one of the rotation handles.**

   The pointer changes to the rotation pointer, which looks like a right angle with a curved arrow.

4. **Drag the mouse pointer clockwise or counterclockwise, depending on the direction that you want to rotate the shape.**

   Watch the status bar to see how far (in degrees) the shape is rotating.

5. **Release the mouse button when the shape is positioned where you want it.**

The closer you place the mouse to the rotation pin as you're rotating a shape, the more the rotation angle jumps, sometimes skipping degrees. The farther away you place the mouse pointer from the rotation pin, the more precise the angle of rotation.

Figure 7-9 shows how shapes are rotated using the Rotation tool. You can see the rotation symbol in the figure.

When you know you want to rotate a shape 90 degrees at a time, the quickest way is to use these steps:

1. **Click the shape that you want to rotate.**

2. **Click the Rotate Right or Rotate Left Tool button on the Shape toolbar.**

You can click the Rotate Right or Rotate Left tool buttons (which look like two triangles with an arrow pointing right or left) repeatedly to continue rotating the same shape in 90-degree increments. This method saves you the trouble of dragging a shape to rotate it or using a menu command.

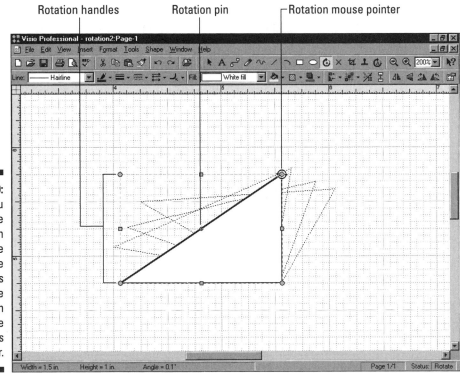

Figure 7-9:
When you use the Rotation tool, the shape rotates around the rotation pin at the shape's center.

When precision is really important to you, use the menu command to rotate shapes. You can rotate a shape at a precise angle, as small as .01 degree. Use these steps:

1. **Select the shape that you want to rotate.**

2. **Choose Shape⇨Size & Position.**

   The Size and Position dialog box, shown in Figure 7-10, appears.

3. **In the Angle box, type a positive number for a counterclockwise angle of rotation. Type a negative number for a clockwise angle of rotation.**

4. **Click OK.**

   The dialog box closes, and Visio displays your shape on the screen. Notice that the angle you entered in the dialog box is shown on the status bar.

Figure 7-10:
The Size &
Position
dialog box
lets you
enter an
angle of
rotation.

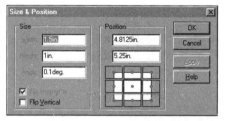

For most Visio shapes, the rotation pin is right in the center of the shape. If you want a shape to rotate around a different point, you can move the rotation pin. You may need to do this if you want to keep a particular point on the shape anchored. For example, in Figure 7-11, the center of rotation for the triangle is moved from the center to the left — outside of the triangle. Now the shape rotates around this point.

Use these steps to move a shape's rotation pin:

1. **Click the Rotation Tool button (refer to Table 7-1) on the Standard toolbar.**

2. **Select the shape.**

   The shape's rotation handles and rotation pin appear.

3. **Drag the rotation pin to a new position.**

4. **Release the mouse button.**

New rotation pin ─── ┌─Original rotation pin

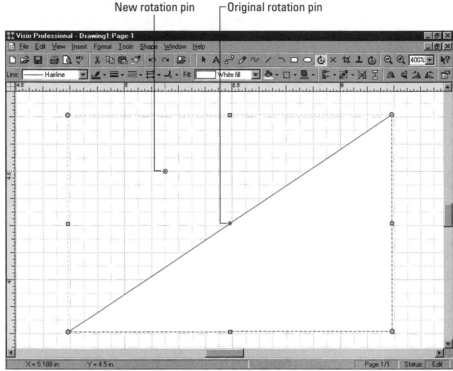

Figure 7-11:
Move the
rotation pin
to reposition
the center
of rotation
on a shape.

When moving the rotation pin, it helps to zoom in on the shape. This lets you place the pin more precisely and also displays a finer grid. If you don't want the rotation pin to snap into place, turn snap off by choosing Tools⇨ Snap & Glue; then click the Snap check box to remove the check mark.

Flipping Shapes

Sometimes you may need to *flip* a shape. Flipping is nothing more than taking a shape and turning it over so that it faces the opposite direction. You can flip a shape horizontally or vertically, as shown in Figure 7-12, using the Flip Horizontal or Flip Vertical tools on the Shape toolbar. Select the shape first; then click one of the flip tools.

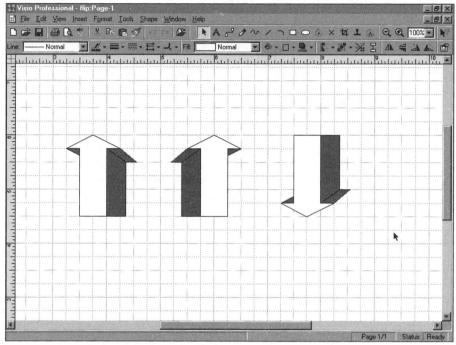

Figure 7-12:
The shape
on the left is
flipped
horizontally
and then
vertically.

Creating Shapes the Fun Way

Near the bottom of the Visio Shape menu is a command called Operations.
Huh? Sounds pretty serious! Well, it's not serious at all. In fact, this command
should be called Fun Stuff. When you select this command, you see a submenu with a long list of choices. Actually, they're tools — tools you may have
never imagined — for creating shapes in new ways.

The following list gives a brief explanation of each to get you interested.

- ✔ **Combine:** Creates a new shape from overlapping shapes by cutting out
  the areas that overlap.
- ✔ **Fragment:** Breaks shapes into separate shapes along the lines where
  they overlap.
- ✔ **Intersect:** Creates a new shape from *only* the area where two or more
  shapes overlap. All other areas are deleted.
- ✔ **Subtract:** When shapes overlap, subtract cuts away the areas that overlap the first shape that you select.
- ✔ **Union:** Creates a new shape from overlapping shapes by using the
  perimeter of all the shapes as the new outline.

It may take a while before you remember exactly what each command does. That's okay, just fool around with them! If you don't like the results that you get, just choose Edit➪Undo and try another one. I illustrate each of these commands because they're easier to see than describe.

Uniting shapes

The first fun stuff command is called *Union*. As the name implies, union *unites* two or more overlapping shapes. How does it do that? By making a new shape from only the outside edges of the overlapping shapes. The inside edges are erased, and the new shape takes on the shape of the perimeter of all the shapes. Figure 7-13 shows an example.

To use the union feature, follow these steps:

1. **Drag the shapes that you want to unite into the drawing area.**

   If you want to draw shapes, draw them now.

2. **Move the shapes where you want them, making sure each one over-laps at least one other shape.**

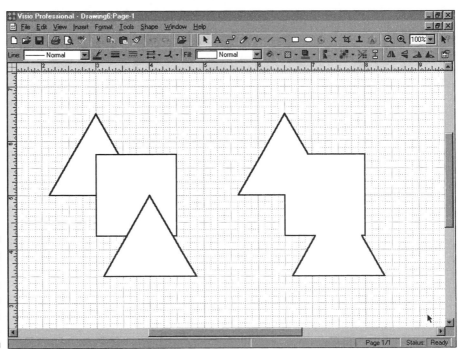

Figure 7-13: Individual shapes on the left are united into a new shape.

3. **Click the Pointer Tool button (refer to Table 7-1) on the Standard toolbar; then draw a selection box around all the shapes.**

4. **Choose Shape➪Operations➪Union.**

   Visio unites all the shapes into one shape.

If some of your shapes aren't overlapped, the Union command doesn't unite them. Though they're treated as one shape, they still appear to be separate.

Combining shapes

The *Combine* command is a bit misleading. It may be more accurate to call it the "Cutout command," because that's what it does. Check out the shapes in Figure 7-14. On the left side of the figure, the two shapes are placed on top of each other. On the right, the Combine command uses the outline of the star to cut out the center of the other shape. (You know this is a cutout because you can see the grid through the star.) After this example, you may think of Combine as the "doughnut command."

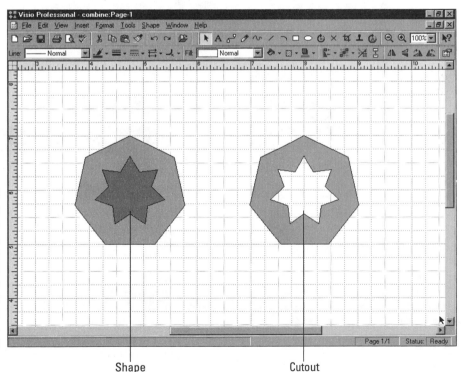

Figure 7-14:
The shapes on the left are combined to create the cutout shape on the right.

Shape   Cutout

Follow these steps to combine shapes:

1. **Draw all the shapes that you want to combine.**

2. **Arrange the shapes so that they overlap one another.**

3. **Using the Pointer Tool button (refer to Table 7-1) on the Standard toolbar, draw a selection box around all shapes that you want to combine.**

4. **Choose Shape⇨Operations⇨Combine.**

   Visio creates cutouts where the smaller, fully-enclosed shapes overlap the larger ones.

Figure 7-15 shows a more complex example of combined shapes. On the left, each shape is a different shade of gray. Notice that after the shapes are combined, the shape becomes one shape and takes on the shade of the small triangle, the shape at the top of the heap.

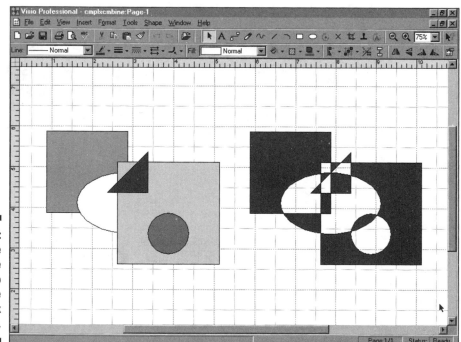

Figure 7-15: You can use the Combine command to create complex shapes.

Fragmenting shapes

Fragmenting sounds rather dangerous, but it's actually harmless and quite fun. It's a great way to create new shapes from overlapped shapes. Figure 7-16 shows several overlapped shapes on the left. On the right, the same shapes are fragmented and spread apart so that you can see exactly what fragmenting does. It's sort of like cutting apart all the pieces where they overlap and making jigsaw puzzle pieces out of them.

To fragment shapes, follow these steps:

1. **Drag all the shapes that you want into the drawing area, or draw them.**

2. **Move the shapes so that they overlap each other.**

3. **Use the Pointer Tool button (refer to Table 7-1) on the Standard toolbar to draw a selection box around the shapes.**

4. **Choose Shape⇨Operations⇨Fragment.**

   Visio breaks all the shapes into separate shapes along their overlapping lines. You can't control the distance Visio uses to separate the shapes, but you can move the shapes individually after they're fragmented.

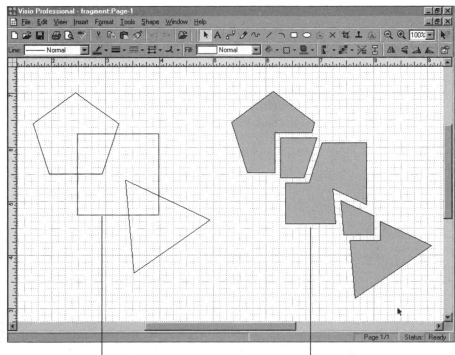

Figure 7-16:
Fragmenting is a great way to create new shapes.

Overlapping shapes   Fragmented shapes

Intersecting shapes

Intersecting shapes is a severe move. Visio cuts away all parts of a shape that don't overlap *all* other shapes. In Figure 7-17, you can see that this drawing began with three overlapping circles. Notice that each circle overlaps both of the others (not just one). (I emphasize the inner triangle in the shapes in the figure to make the triangle more visible.) After intersecting these shapes, the only thing that's left is the small three-sided shape from the center where all circles overlap one another.

To fragment shapes, use these steps:

1. **Drag all the shapes that you want into the drawing area or draw them.**

2. **Move the shapes so that they *all* overlap every other shape at some point.**

3. **Use the Pointer Tool button (refer to Table 7-1) on the Standard toolbar to draw a selection box around the shapes.**

4. **Choose Shape⇨Operations⇨Intersect.**

   Visio removes all extraneous parts of the shapes and leaves only that portion where *all* shapes overlap one another.

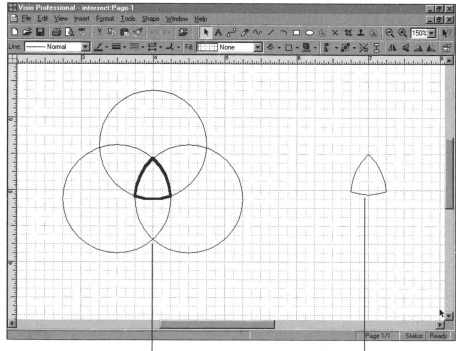

Figure 7-17: Intersecting shapes cuts away all but the parts of a shape that overlap all other shapes.

Overlapped shapes   Intersected shape

Subtracting shapes

Subtract is a feature that works just like it sounds: When two shapes overlap each other, the overlapping part is subtracted — removed — from the first shape that you select. *The first shape you select* is an important point to remember; you need to know which shape you want left behind when you finish subtracting. If you select the wrong shape, you're left with the part you *don't* want. In Figure 7-18, the circle and star on the left are the original shapes. The partial star in the center is what's left if you select the star first — before selecting the circle and the subtract command. The partial circle on the right is what's left if you select the circle first.

Follow these steps to use the subtract command:

1. **Drag the shapes that you want to work with into the drawing area, or draw them.**

2. **Position the shapes so that they overlap one another.**

3. **Use the Pointer Tool button (refer to Table 7-1) on the Standard tool-bar to select the shape that you want to keep after using the subtract command.**

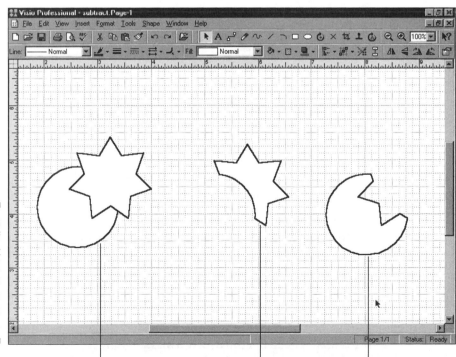

Figure 7-18:
The result of the subtract command depends on which shape you select first.

Original shapes   Star selected first   Circle selected first

4. **Now, select the shape that you want to subtract.**

5. **Choose Shapes⇨Operations⇨Subtract.**

   Visio removes the shape that you selected in Step 4 and leaves what remains of the shape that you selected in Step 3.

Give Your Shapes a Makeover

Although many of the Visio shapes are pretty cool, some of them are pretty basic — just an outline of something with no color, weight, pattern, or shadow. Pretty boring, huh? Well, you can jazz up the more basic shapes by adding things like line color and weight, fill color and pattern, and shadowing. These features are typically referred to as *formatting* (a boring word itself).

You usually select a shape first and then apply some special type of formatting to it. Well, if you're doing it to one shape, why not do it to more than one at the same time? You can! This saves you a lot of time when you decide that all 382 whatchamacallits in your drawing should be blue and green checkerboards with a purple outline and a magenta shadow. Select all your shapes (no, don't click each one individually, use the Pointer tool to draw a selection box around them); then apply the formatting that you choose.

If you can't select all the shapes that you want with a selection box, remember that you can hold down the Shift key and click the rest of your stray shapes to add them to the selection.

Changing line style

Every shape has an outline, usually drawn in a thin, black line. Not only can you change the color of the line, you can change the *weight* (thickness) of it as well as the *pattern*. You can make it fat and green and dash-dash-dashed, or dainty and pink and dot-dot-dotted. You can also decide if you want squared or rounded corners on your shape.

When you work with a one-dimensional (1-D) shape like a simple line, you can also add endpoints to the beginning or end of the shape, and determine the size of the endpoints.

Use these steps to make all these changes to a shape's line:

1. **Select the shape that you want to change.**

2. **Choose Format⇨Line, or right-click the mouse, and then choose Format⇨Line from the drop-down menu that appears.**

   Visio displays the Line dialog box, as shown in Figure 7-19.

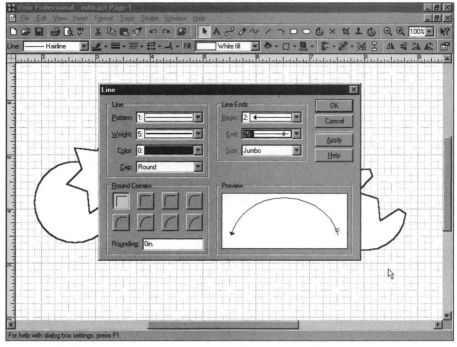

Figure 7-19:
Choose line
pattern,
color,
weight, and
style in the
Line dialog
box.

3. **Click the down-arrow in the Pattern box to choose a line pattern.**

4. **Click the down-arrow in the Weight box to choose a line thickness.**

5. **Click the down-arrow in the Color box to choose a line color.**

6. **Click the down-arrow in the Cap box to choose blunt lines (square) or soft lines (round).**

7. **To round the corners of your shape, click one of the rounding styles in the Round Corners box.**

   If you want the rounding to be a specific size (like beginning ⅛ inch from the corner), enter a decimal number in the Rounding box.

8. **If your shape is one-dimensional (1-D), choose endpoints and size in the Begin, End, and Size boxes.**

9. **View all your choices in the Preview area.**

10. **Click OK.**

Visio provides the following five tools that let you apply line style changes without opening a menu. Each one of these tools has a tiny drop-down arrow next to it that opens a list of choices when you click the arrow. These tools appear on the Shape and toolbar and are shown in Table 7-2.

Table 7-2		Line Style Tools
Button	**Tool**	**Function**
	Line Color tool	Lets you choose a line color
	Line Weight tool	Lets you choose a line thickness
	Line Pattern tool	Lets you choose a line pattern
	Line Ends tool	Lets you choose endpoints for a line
	Corner Rounding tool	Lets you choose a line corner style for a shape

To use any of these tools, select the shape first; then click one of the tools and select a style.

Adding fill color, pattern, and shadow

White, white, white can become very monotonous after a while. Why not add some excitement to your shapes? Make them colorful! Make them patterned! Make the pattern in striking colors! Give them some depth by adding shadows! (Am I too excited about all this?)

Well, maybe you don't want to add *all* of these features. There is such a thing as overkill. . . .

If you want to fill a shape with a solid color, that's cool. Just pick the color and that's that. When you fill a shape with a pattern, however, you have two colors to choose: *foreground* and *background*. The color that defines the pattern itself — dots, hash marks, stripes, criss-crosses — is the foreground color. The background is the color that shows through the pattern. Quite often, patterns are done in black and white, so you don't even think about the possibility of choosing colors for the foreground and background. You can use black and white in Visio as well, but it's good to know what foreground and background colors are so that you get the results that you expect.

Speaking of overkill, if you decide to add a shadow to your shape, it doesn't have to be a solid color, either. You can choose a pattern, foreground, and background color for it as well. (Now *that* is overkill.)

Follow these steps to accomplish any of these nifty tasks:

1. **Select the shape that you want to change.**

2. **Choose Format⇨Fill, or right-click the mouse and then choose Format⇨Fill from the shortcut menu that appears.**

   Visio displays the Fill dialog box, as shown in Figure 7-20.

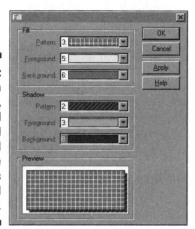

Figure 7-20:
Choose a
pattern,
foreground
color, and
background
color for the
shape's
fill and
shadow.

3. **In the Fill box, choose a Pattern, Foreground, and Background by clicking the down-arrow for each box.**

4. **In the Shadow box, choose a Pattern, Foreground, and Background by clicking the down-arrow for each box.**

   The Preview area shows a sample of the choices that you select.

5. **Click OK.**

   Visio returns to your drawing and reformats the selected shape.

Visio also provides timesaving toolbar buttons for these tools, as shown in Table 7-3. Select a shape that you want to change; then click the down-arrow next to the tool to display a drop-down list of choices.

Table 7-3	Fill Tools on the Shape Toolbar
Button	*Tool*
Fill: [White fill ▼]	Fill Style tool
🪣	Fill Color tool
▨	Fill Pattern tool
🖥	Shadow Color tool

The following list shows you how to use these tools.

- **The Fill Style Tool button** on the Shape toolbar lets you choose a fill color.

- **The Fill Color Tool button** on the Shape toolbar *also* lets you choose a fill color! Hmm. Why does Visio provide two buttons that do the same thing? Beats me. Choose from the color chips displayed, or click More Fill Colors to display the Fill dialog box (refer to Figure 7-20).

- **The Fill Pattern Tool button** on the Shape toolbar lets you choose a pattern style from the list. Or click More Fill Patterns to display the Fill dialog box (refer to Figure 7-20).

- **The Shadow Color Tool button** on the Shape toolbar lets you choose a shadow color. To choose a pattern, foreground color, and background color for a shadow, click More Shadow Colors to display the Shadow dialog box.

Do it again, please

Suppose you painstakingly format a shape with a purple- and red-patterned fill, a burgundy and chartreuse shadow, and a 4-point canary-dotted outline (no one ever accused you of having an eye for color). Now you want to apply those lovely colors and styles to another shape. Do you have to set all these features by hand again? Nope. Visio makes it easy for you. Ever notice that paint brush tool on your Standard toolbar? It's called the *Format Painter* tool, and it lets you *paint* a format from one shape to another. Use these steps:

1. **Click the shape with the lovely format that you want to copy.**

2. **Click the Format Painter Tool button (refer to Table 7-1) on the Standard toolbar.**

   Your mouse pointer changes to a paint brush.

3. **Click the shape that you want to apply that lovely format to.**

   Presto! All that beautiful color and style is instantly copied to your shape.

How do I get rid of all this formatting?

So, you decide that you don't like violet polka dots on an orange background with a green frame and a green and purple criss-cross shadow pattern? How do you get rid of it? Unfortunately, you can't click a tool that magically removes all the formatting that you add to a shape. You have to reset line, fill, pattern, and shadow features the same way that you add them. But you can reformat one shape and then use the Format Painter tool again to paint a plain style onto other shapes. This is the quickest way to undo what you did.

Arranging Shapes

Now that you have a bunch of fantastic shapes in your drawing, can you use some smart ways to arrange them? You bet. Some shapes are complex — shapes within shapes. It makes sense to tie them together somehow so that you don't rip them apart accidentally when you try to move them. It helps if you know how to stack shapes in the order that you want them. I show you both of these arranging tips in this section.

To group or not to group . . .

Nothing is more frustrating than spending a good deal of time creating a single shape out of many shapes, getting everything perfectly aligned, and then messing it all up when you try to move it or resize it. One way to avoid this is to group shapes so that they behave as a single shape.

In Figure 7-21, you see a knight shape from the Kids stencil. The knight on the left is the grouped shape. In the center, the knight shape is ungrouped, and all the individual shapes that make up the overall shape are selected. On the right, the individual shapes are separated so that you can see exactly how complex this knight shape is. This is an excellent example of how important grouping is. Ungrouped, it's easy to accidentally drag the knight off without his shield and horse. Grouping also lets you size, rotate, and flip the complete shape as a unit.

To group shapes, use these steps:

1. **Select all the shapes that you want to group.**

2. **Choose Shape⇨Grouping⇨Group or click the Group Tool button on the Shape toolbar.**

   Visio reframes the shapes with a single frame and handles.

To ungroup a shape, use these steps:

1. **Select all the shapes that you want to group.**

2. **Choose Shape⇨Grouping⇨Ungroup or click the Ungroup Tool button on the Shape toolbar.**

   Visio separates the grouped shape into its original shapes and displays all the shape frames with handles.

If you prefer to use shortcut keys, you can press Ctrl+G for Group and Ctrl+U for Ungroup.

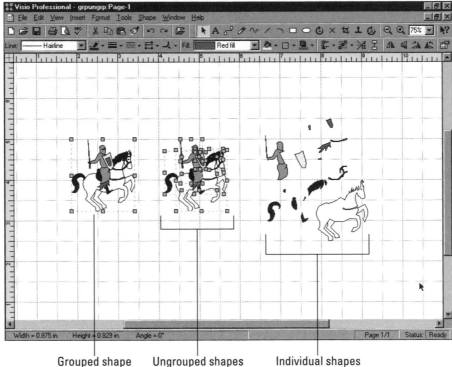

Grouped shape   Ungrouped shapes   Individual shapes

Figure 7-21: Grouped shapes are often far more complex than they appear.

Rearranging your stacks

Each time you draw or drag a new shape into the drawing area, Visio places it on top of other existing shapes. If you don't overlap the shapes, you never notice, but if you overlap shapes, you notice the overlap immediately. Particularly when you want the *first* shape you drew to be on top of the other fifty you drew afterward, and it keeps getting covered up — this can be very frustrating if you don't know what's going on! Think of each shape as being drawn on a separate piece of scratch paper. Each time you draw a shape, you drop the paper on your desk. Those that fall on top of others clearly overlap one another. Those that don't *still fall in a stacking order,* whether you're aware of it or not.

Visio provides two toolbar tools to help you rearrange the stacking order of shapes. On the Shape toolbar are the Bring to Front and Send to Back Tool buttons. These commands are also available on the Shape menu, along with two others: Bring Forward and Send Backward. What's the difference? Bring to Front brings a shape to the top of the stack whereas Bring Forward brings a shape up only one level in the stack. Likewise, Send to Back sends a shape to the bottom of the stack whereas Send Backward sends a shape down just one level in the stack. (Bring Forward and Send Backward are found only on the Shape menu; they don't have toolbar buttons.)

In Figure 7-22, the triangle was drawn first, so it's on the bottom of the stack. Say that you want to move it just above the rectangle but below the ellipse. If you try to move it without changing its order in the stack, it's almost completely hidden behind the rectangle. You need to use Bring Forward several times to raise its position in the stack.

To rearrange the stacking order of shapes, follow these steps:

1. **Select the shape that you want to rearrange.**

2. **Determine which command or tool that you need to use: Bring Forward, Bring to Front, Send Backward, or Send to Back.**

3. **Click the Bring to Front Tool button or the Send to Back Tool button on the Shape toolbar, or choose Shape⇨Bring Forward or Shape⇨ Send Backward.**

4. **Repeat Step 3 if necessary.**

If you prefer to use shortcut keys, you can press Ctrl+F for Bring to Front or Ctrl+B for Send to Back.

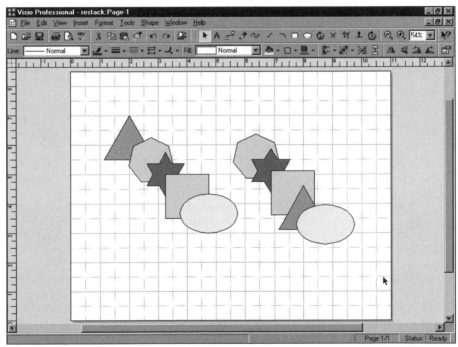

Figure 7-22:
You can rearrange the way that these shapes overlap one another.

Chapter 8

Working with Pages

*J*ust about now you may be thinking "A page is a page; what's to know? Pretty boring stuff." But there's a lot to know about pages in Visio! Visio files aren't like documents where text runs smoothly from one page to the next with a few interesting figures thrown in here and there. Some drawings have only one page; others may have multiple pages. And in Visio, pages are pretty independent animals! You can set a different page size, orientation, drawing scale, background, shadow, even a different header and footer, for each page in a single Visio file. You can also rotate a page to make drawing angled lines and shapes easier — then rotate it back again when you're finished drawing. This makes Visio very flexible; it also makes it a little more complex than your average text editor.

Remember that *drawing page* refers to the drawing area that you see on the screen, *printed page* refers to the paper you print on, and *printed drawing* refers to the actual drawing as printed on paper. (See Chapter 2 for more details on these printing terms.)

The Role of the Template

Remember that a template is designed to make creating a drawing easier because it sets up a drawing scale (like a typical architectural scale of ¼ inch = 1 foot), and it automatically opens the stencils that you may need to create a particular type of drawing (like the Office Layout stencil for creating an office floor plan). See Chapter 1 if you need a refresher on how to start a new Visio file using a template.

The other important things a template sets up is the size of the drawing page and the printed page (both usually 8½ x 11 inches) and the orientation of the page (portrait or landscape). These are settings that you need to be aware of when you work with pages in a drawing. Using a template is a definite advantage because it automatically matches the size and orientation of the drawing page to the size and orientation of the printed page, which ensures that your drawing prints correctly.

Reorienting a Page

Suppose that you're creating a network diagram in portrait orientation, and then realize that the drawing is too wide to fit on 8½-inch-wide paper. You can change the paper orientation to landscape rather than adjust the layout of your drawing. Switching to landscape orientation turns your drawing page 90 degrees so that it's wider than it is long.

When you change the orientation of your drawing page, however, you need to change the printer settings as well so that your printer expects to print in landscape mode. To change both of these settings, follow these steps:

1. **Choose File⇨Page Setup.**

   The Page Setup dialog box appears with the Page Size tab selected (see Figure 8-1).

2. **In the Page Orientation area, click Landscape or Portrait.**

3. **Click the Print Setup button to display the Print Setup dialog box (see Figure 8-2).**

   Note: Your printer may display a dialog box that is similar to this one, but not identical.

4. **In the Orientation area, click the Landscape or Portrait radio button.**

5. **Click OK.**

6. **Click OK in the Page Setup dialog box.**

Page Orientation area

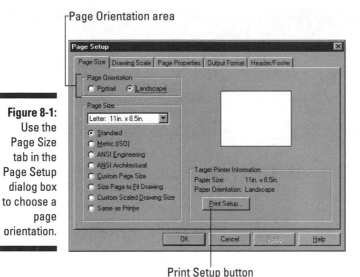

Figure 8-1:
Use the
Page Size
tab in the
Page Setup
dialog box
to choose a
page
orientation.

Print Setup button

When you switch page orientation, the shapes in your drawing don't mysteri-
ously disappear or get erased, but it's likely that some of them are straddling
the borders of the page, or may be completely off the page (see Figure 8-3).
Remember, you just moved the boundaries of the page, but the shapes are
still placed where they always were (within the old page boundaries). Now
that you have new boundaries, you need to move your shapes to get them
back onto the drawing page.

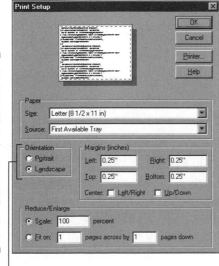

Figure 8-2:
Use the
Print Setup
dialog box
to match
your printer
orientation
to the
orientation
of your
drawing
page.

Orientation

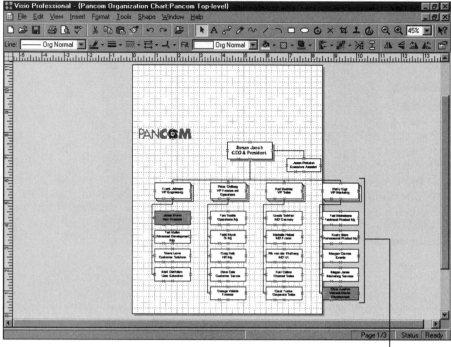

Figure 8-3:
When you
change the
drawing
page orien-
tation, some
of the
shapes are
no longer on
the page.

Shapes off the page

Choosing a Standard Page Size

Most of us print on standard-sized paper: 8½ x 11 inches. However, you may want to use a different paper size, and Visio lets you change your page size settings accordingly. Other common sizes are:

- ✓ **Metric:**148mm x 210mm
- ✓ **ANSI Architectural:** 9 x 12 inches

Visio gives you the following page size options as well:

- ✓ **Using a custom-scaled drawing size:** A nice option when you want to print a drawing half-size or in another scaled size.
- ✓ **Setting your page size to match the printer:** Sets your drawing page size to match the size your printer is currently set for.
- ✓ **Setting a custom page size:** Lets you define specific dimensions for the drawing page. (Believe it or not, legal — 8½ x 14 inches — isn't a standard size in Visio; it's a custom size.)
- ✓ **Sizing your page to fit your drawing:** Cuts out unused space on the drawing page.

The following steps show you how to change the page size as well as your printer setup. (Remember that you must change your printer setup to match, otherwise your drawings don't print correctly.)

1. **Display the page for which you want to change the size.**

2. **Choose File⇨Page Setup.**

   Visio displays the Page Setup dialog box (refer to Figure 8-1).

3. **Choose an option in the Page Size area.**

   (For Custom Page Size, see the following section, "Setting a Custom Page Size.")

4. **Click the Print Setup button to display the Print Setup dialog box (refer to Figure 8-2).**

   In the Paper area, choose the same size paper that you chose in Step 3. If that size isn't available, choose the closest size.

   Some printers don't have settings for odd-sized or custom-sized paper. Choosing the closest size may work with some printers; then again, it may not with others. Be sure to click the Preview tool before printing to see exactly how your drawing will print.

5. **Click OK to return to the Page Setup dialog box.**

6. **Click OK.**

Setting a Custom Page Size

The custom page size settings let you define special page dimensions, like 3 x 5 inches, or 6½ x 4 inches. This option isn't just for users who are lucky enough to have a super-duper printer that can print on paper as small as a postage stamp! (Are there any?) It's also a very useful feature for *positioning* a drawing, or *isolating* a drawing to a specific area of the printed page. Let me explain.

Suppose that you want to print a 3 x 5-inch Visio drawing in the upper-left corner of an 8½ x 11-inch piece of paper and leave the remaining white space for reviewers to write comments (see Figure 8-4). Or, how about when you want to *over print* a Visio drawing onto a preprinted page, such as a pre-printed form.

You can try to position the drawing in the right space on the size of paper that you're printing on, or you can simply set a custom page size for the drawing. However, you need to keep a couple of things in mind when you set a custom page size. If the drawing already contains shapes, they don't move; they stay where they always were. If they're outside of the new page dimensions, you have to move them inside. Second, the drawing (as an example, one that's 4 x 5 inches), always begins printing in the upper-left corner of your paper. If you want your drawing to print in the lower-right corner (or anywhere else, for that matter), don't use the Custom Page Size option, because you don't get the results that you want.

To change drawing page and printed page settings using menu commands, follow these steps:

1. **Display the drawing page that you want to change.**

2. **Choose File⇨Page Setup.**

   Visio displays the Page Size tab in the Page Setup dialog box (refer to Figure 8-1).

3. **In the Page Size area, click Custom Page Size.**

4. **In the Page Size field, type the page dimensions that you want.**

5. **Click the Print Setup button to display the Print Setup dialog box (refer to Figure 8-2).**

6. **In the Paper area, choose the paper size that you're printing on from the drop-down list.**

   (In this case, the drawing page size and paper size *don't* match.)

Drawing page   Printed page

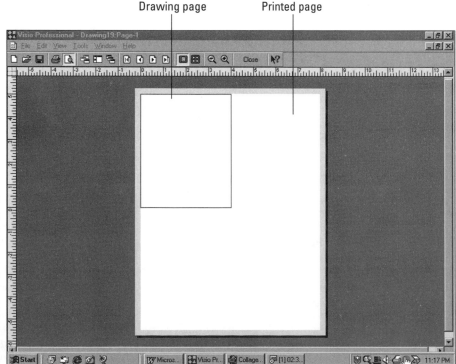

Figure 8-4:
Print
Preview
shows a
paper size
of 8½ x 11
inches, but
a drawing
page size of
4 x 5 inches.

7. **In the Orientation area, choose the orientation that best accommo-dates the custom drawing page size that you specified in Step 4.**

8. **Click OK to return to the Page Setup dialog box.**

9. **Click OK.**

You can also use these fun steps to change the size of the drawing page — by using the mouse.

1. **Display the drawing page that you want to change.**

2. **Click the Pointer Tool button (which looks like an arrow) on the Standard toolbar.**

3. **Press and hold the Ctrl key and then move the mouse pointer over the edge of the drawing page that you want to drag.**

   To resize the page in height and width at the same time, move the mouse pointer over one of the corners of the page. The mouse pointer changes to a double-headed arrow.

4. **Drag the mouse until the page is the size that you want, noting the page dimensions on the status bar.**

Another Page, Please . . .

When you create a new Visio drawing, it includes only one page. You can add pages to a drawing and, of course, you have many good reasons for doing so! Try some of these ideas:

- **Keep a set of related drawings,** such as a collection of maps with driving directions for your city, on separate pages in one Visio file.

- **Use pages to create overview drawings and detail drawings** — for example, your corporate, regional, and branch organization charts. You can even add *jumps,* similar to links between Web sites, from one page to another. (See Chapter 13 for more on adding jumps.)

- **Use pages to keep track of the history and revisions of a drawing,** which can work something like this: Page 1 is the original draft, Page 2 is the second draft, Page 3 is the review drawing, Page 4 is the revised drawing, Page 5 is the second review drawing, Page 6 is the final drawing.

- **Create a mini slide show** with a series of drawings on separate pages and present them in full screen view.

- **Include your company name and logo on background pages** so that the logo shows through on every page without being part of your drawing. The icing on the cake is that each page in your drawing can have its own background page, so that you can vary the content from page to page.

Adding and deleting pages

You can add as many pages to a drawing as you like. Pages are always added at the end of the drawing — in other words, you can't *insert* pages between other pages. (You can, however, reorder pages, as I show you later in the section "Reordering pages.") The new page that you add takes on all the attributes of the page that's currently displayed. If you want to change some of these attributes, you can do so at the time that you create the page, or later, using the File⇨Page Setup command.

Use these steps to add a page to a drawing:

1. **In your drawing, display the page with the attributes that you want the new page to have.**

   (Of course, that would be the *only* page in your drawing if you haven't added a page yet!)

2. **Choose Insert⇨Page.**

   Visio displays the Page Properties tab in the Page Setup dialog box, as shown in Figure 8-5. A name for the new page is suggested in the Name field.

Suggested name

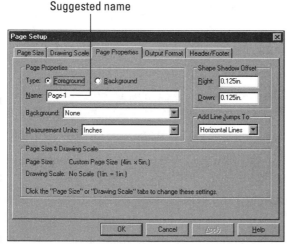

Figure 8-5:
Use the
Page
Properties
tab to set
attributes
for a new
page.

3. **Under Type, you can see that Foreground is already selected. To create a background page, click the Background button.**

4. **In the Name field, use the suggested name (Page-2, Page-3, and so on), or enter a new one.**

At this point, you're free to click on the Page Size or Drawing Scale tabs to change settings for the new page. This isn't necessary, however, if you want the new page to take on the attributes of the page that you displayed in Step 1.

5. Click OK.

The new page you add appears after all the other pages in the drawing (if you have five already, the new page is number six). If you decide later to change page size, refer to "Choosing a Standard Page Size" or "Setting a Custom Page Size" earlier in this chapter. To change drawing scale attributes, see Chapter 6.

To delete a page, use these steps:

1. Choose Edit⇨Drawing Page⇨Delete Pages.

The Delete Pages dialog box appears and lists all the pages in the drawing by name.

2. Click the page that you want to delete.

3. Click OK.

Visio removes the page from the drawing.

The Delete Pages dialog box doesn't let you select more than one page at a time, so if you want to delete other pages, you need to repeat the steps above.

Getting from one page to another

When you have multiple pages in a document, you need a quick way to bounce from one to the other. The quickest way to get there is with the Page toolbar, but it isn't displayed on your screen automatically. You can display the Page toolbar in one of two ways:

✔ Right-click your mouse in the toolbar area and then click Page

✔ Choose View⇨Toolbars⇨Page

Wherever Visio has room in the toolbar area, you see a very short toolbar pop up with the following tool buttons (shown in Figure 8-6):

✔ Glue

✔ Go To Page

✔ Next Page

✔ Previous Page

✔ Snap

Figure 8-6:
The Page
toolbar isn't
displayed
automat-
ically; you
have to ask
for it!

Previous Page

Snap   Go To Page

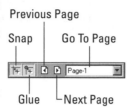

Glue   └Next Page

The Snap and Glue tools toggle these features on and off. You use the other three tools for page navigation. Click the Previous Page or Next Page buttons to move through pages one at a time. To go to a specific page, click the down-arrow on the Go To Page tool and select a page from the drop-down list that appears.

Show me all your pages!

When your drawing contains multiple pages, viewing more than one page at a time lets you compare one page to another quickly and easily. It also lets you edit each page without closing one and opening another over and over again. To display a new page, Visio opens the page in a separate window. Use these steps to open additional page windows:

1. **Choose Edit⇨Go To.**

   Visio displays a submenu that lists all pages in the drawing.

2. **Click the Page option at the bottom of the submenu.**

   Visio displays the Page dialog box, which lists all pages in the drawing.

3. **Click the page that you want to view.**

4. **Click the Open Page in New Window option at the bottom of the dialog box.**

5. **Click OK.**

   Visio opens the page in a new window.

Repeat these steps to open additional page windows. Each time you open a new page, it becomes the current page on your screen. Pages you previously opened are still open; if you click on the Window menu, you see each page name listed at the bottom of the menu.

Choose Window⇨Tile or Window⇨Cascade to arrange all open windows on your screen.

Reordering pages

When you add pages to a drawing, Visio automatically adds them to the *end* of the drawing (even though the menu name is Insert). Since Visio doesn't let you *insert* pages in a drawing (such as between Pages 3 and 4), the only way to put added pages in the order that you want them is to *reorder* them. If you use the default page names that Visio suggests (such as Page-2, Page-3, and so on) Visio can automatically update page names when you reorder pages.

To reorder pages, use these steps:

1. **Check your drawing to see which page you need to move where (for example, move Page 3 to before Page 2).**

2. **Choose Edit➪Drawing Page➪Reorder Pages.**

   Visio displays the dialog box shown in Figure 8-7. Pages are listed in the dialog box in the order that they are stored in the file.

Figure 8-7:
Use the
Reorder
Pages
dialog box
to rearrange
pages and
update their
names.

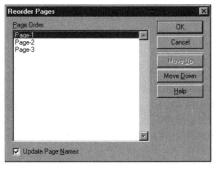

3. **In the Page Order box, click the page that you want to move (such as Page-3).**

4. **Click the Move Up or Move Down button until the page appears in the list where you want it (for example, Page-3 appears before Page-2).**

5. **If your pages use default page names, click the Update Page Names check box at the bottom of the dialog box to have Visio update the pages with the correct page names.**

   (For example, use this check box to change the name "Page-3" to "Page-2" and vice versa. If you use unique page names, this option has no effect on your page names.)

6. **Click OK.**

Viewing on the Big Screen

You already know how to use the Preview Tool button to see how your drawing will look on the printed page. (If you don't remember, see Chapter 2!) Now I show you how you can use your *entire* screen to display a drawing, without title bars, menu bars, status bars, scroll bars, or any other Windows trimmings. And if your drawing has multiple pages, you can move from page to page on the big screen. This is a great way to create a mini slide show for a small group of viewers — and you don't even need a slide projector!

Use these steps to view pages in full-screen mode:

1. **Display the first page of your drawing on the screen.**

2. **Choose <u>V</u>iew⇨<u>F</u>ull Screen.**

   Visio switches to full-screen mode and displays the first page of your drawing.

3. **To move to the next page, press N (for next), Page Down, or the right-arrow key.**

4. **To move to a previous page, press P (for previous), Page Up, or the left-arrow key.**

5. **Optional: If you prefer to use the mouse, click the left mouse button to move forward from page to page.**

   Click the right mouse button to pop up a shortcut menu with Previous, Next, and Go To options. (Right-clicking is an important method to remember if you're on Page 3 and you want to go quickly to Page 42!)

6. **Press Esc to return to the Visio screen.**

Hyperlinks are a really cool feature of Visio. If your drawing contains *hyperlinks* — jumps from one page to another — you can click a hyperlinked shape to jump to the link. For detailed steps about adding hyperlinks to a drawing, see Chapter 13.

What's in a Background?

As if you didn't have enough pages in your drawing already, now you can add *background* pages! Why would you want to do that, you ask? The best answer to that question is that they offer you *flexibility.* If you want a file name, date, company name, logo, page number, or any other type of information on a drawing — but you don't want it to be *part of* the drawing — you can put all that information on a background page. Using a background page is sort of like printing your drawing on a transparency and slipping the background page underneath. The information on the background page "shows through" the transparency — visible and printable — but the drawing itself doesn't get mucked up with all sorts of extraneous information.

The technical term for a drawing page is a *foreground* page because it appears on top of a background page.

You can create as many background pages as you want in a drawing file. What can you do with them? You can:

✔ Assign a single background page to a single foreground page

✔ Assign a single background to several foreground pages

✔ Assign a different background page to each foreground page

✔ Assign a background page to another background page

The most important thing to realize is that you *can't* assign more than one background page to any other page. So what do you do if you want a foreground page to have more than one background? You can piggyback background pages on a foreground page by assigning a background to a background and then assigning those to a foreground. Clear as mud yet? Figure 8-8 illustrates how pages can be assigned to one another and the results.

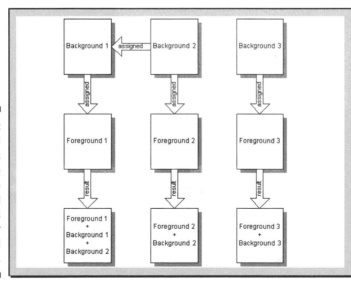

Figure 8-8:
Background
pages
can be
assigned to
foreground
pages
or other
background
pages.

Creating and assigning a background page

Background pages aren't very useful by themselves. To use a background page, you must create it and then *assign* it to another page. Unassigned, you can still print a background page, but it prints entirely by itself (without any foreground information).

To create a background page, follow these steps:

1. **Display the page in your drawing with the attributes that you want the background page to have.**

2. **Choose Insert⇨Page.**

   Visio displays the Page Properties tab in the Page dialog box (see Figure 8-9).

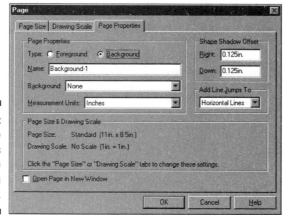

Figure 8-9:
The Page Properties tab in the Page dialog box.

3. **For Type, click the Background radio button.**

4. **In the Name field, a name for the page (Background-1, Background-2, and so on) is suggested. Use the suggested name or enter a new one.**

   You can now click the Page Size or Drawing Scale tabs in this dialog box if you want to change any attributes of the page size or drawing scale for this page.

5. **Click OK.**

Your background page is created. The next step is to assign it to the page (foreground or background) that you want it to go with. To assign the background to another page, follow these steps:

1. **Display the page that you want to assign the background page to (think of this as the parent page).**
2. **Choose File⇨Page Setup to display the Page Setup dialog box.**
3. **Click the Page Properties tab (refer to Figure 8-9).**

   The Name field displays the name of the current page.
4. **Click the down arrow for the Background drop-down list.**

   All background pages that you created are listed here. Click the one that you want to assign to this page (the page you selected in Step 1).
5. **Click OK.**

Displaying a background page

After you assign a background page to another page, its shapes are visible on the screen whenever its foreground (parent) page is displayed. If you don't want the background page shapes to be displayed when the foreground page is displayed, you must unassign the background from the foreground. Remember that unassigning doesn't delete the background page; it just leaves it sitting unassigned until you choose to assign it.

Editing a background page

Because a background page is just a type of page, you edit it just as you do a foreground page. If your Page toolbar isn't on your screen, display it by choosing View⇨Toolbars⇨Page. Click the down arrow on the Go To Page tool and then click the page that you want to edit. Visio displays the page that you select.

Are you driving yourself crazy by trying to select a shape on a page that just refuses to be selected? That's because the shape is on the *background* page assigned to your foreground page. It *appears to be* on the foreground page, but if you can't select it, it isn't. The only page it can possibly belong to is the background page. It's hard to tell because Visio makes no distinction between the two on the screen.

Rotating Pages

The best computer software program is one that is designed to work the way people worked before they had the program. Think about the following example for a minute. If you draw (with pencil and paper) a map of a section of a city where streets fall at odd angles, you'd probably take the following approach. You'd draw all the streets that run parallel to the edges of your paper and then *turn the paper at an angle* and draw in the angular streets, right? Well, that's exactly what happens when you rotate a drawing page in Visio: The program thinks the way you work on paper.

When you rotate a page, all the shapes that you have in the drawing rotate along with it. That includes *guides,* those vertical and horizontal lines you drag into your drawing from the rulers to help you position shapes. (To review creating and using guides, see Chapter 6.) When you know that you're going to rotate a page, you can use guides sort of like a custom grid.

The elements that *don't* rotate when you rotate a page are the rulers and drawing page grid. This is a good thing because you can always maintain a horizontal and vertical baseline from which to work, regardless of the angle of the paper.

Figure 8-10 shows a map of city streets with streets at 45-degree angles. All the streets are perfectly aligned and spaced because the page was rotated when they were drawn.

In Figure 8-11, you see a drawing page rotated 60 degrees. You can also see the *guides* that were drawn to make it easy to lay out these shapes. Notice that the *grid* remains parallel and perpendicular to the rulers bordering the drawing area. The guides are pulled from the vertical ruler to set them at a 60-degree angle to the grid.

To rotate a page, you must first enable page rotation (unless you're using Visio Technical, in which case page rotation is automatically enabled).

1. **Choose Tools⮕Options.**

    Visio displays the Options dialog box.

2. **Click the Advanced tab.**

3. **Click on the Enable Page Rotation check box.**

4. **Click OK.**

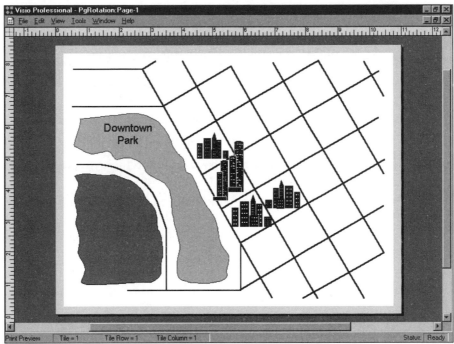

Figure 8-10:
Using page
rotation
makes it
easy to
draw a map
like this.

Grid parallel to rulers   Guide lines

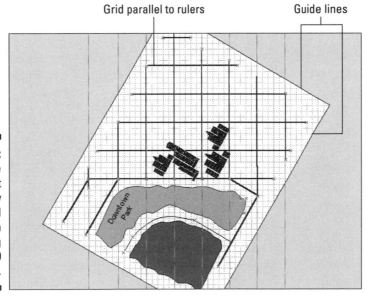

Figure 8-11:
You can see
how easy it
is to draw
the angled
streets with
the drawing
rotated to 60
degrees.

To rotate a page, drag it from one corner in either a clockwise or counter-clockwise direction. If you want to rotate to a specific angle, watch the status bar as you drag the page; it tells you the exact angle (in degrees) of the page as you rotate it. Use these steps to rotate a page.

1. **Click the Rotation Tool button (it looks like a dot with an arrow circling around it) on the Standard toolbar.**

2. **Move the mouse pointer over any corner of the page.**

   The pointer changes to a round rotation pointer.

3. **Drag the mouse clockwise or counterclockwise, depending on the direction that you want to rotate the page.**

   The farther you move the mouse pointer away from the page corner, the more precise the angle you're able to choose.

4. **Release the mouse button when the page is rotated to the angle that you want.**

Chapter 9

Love That Layered Look

● ●

In This Chapter

▶ Discovering what layers are and why you may want them

▶ Creating, removing, renaming, and hiding layers

▶ Assigning (and reassigning) shapes to layers

▶ Creating layers on background pages

▶ Protecting shapes on a layer from changes

▶ Changing the color of shapes on a layer

▶ Printing layers — only the ones you want!

● ●

*V*isio defines a *layer* as a *named category of shapes*. Huh? How about a more vivid description? When you were a kid, did you ever have one of those cool anatomy books with the transparent sheets? The bottom sheet had the skeletal structure, the next sheet had internal organs, and then you added the nervous system, the muscular structure, and finally the skin? Well, the layer system in Visio works much the same way. You can create layers in a Visio drawing for the same purpose as your old anatomy book: to show groups or categories of shapes independently of others or as part of the whole. Think of layers in a Visio drawing as being transparent, just like the transparent sheets in an anatomy book.

How can you use layers? In a landscape drawing, you may want to include structural walls and pathways on one layer; grass, ground cover, and small shrubs on another; trees on a separate layer; and ornamental flowers on another layer. Another example is a layout for a building or home in which the walls, doors, and windows appear on one layer, and the wiring, electrical system, plumbing, and HVAC system (heating, ventilation, and air conditioning) appear on individual layers. You can display just one layer to view the shapes in a particular group or display all layers to view the complete plan.

Some Essential Facts about Layers

Okay, some of this may seem confusing because Visio gives you so many options! I try to make it as straightforward as possible with the following list:

- ✔ A Visio drawing can have more than one page.

- ✔ Each page can have its own set of layers.

- ✔ Visio automatically assigns some shapes to predefined layers (based on the template that you choose).

- ✔ A shape can be assigned to (and therefore, appear on) one or more layers. (This is the only point for which our anatomy book example doesn't hold true: A liver or spleen only appears on the internal organs sheet; you don't find it duplicated on the skeletal structure sheet or the nervous system sheet.)

- ✔ A Visio page (with or without layers) can have one or more background pages.

- ✔ Although similar in behavior, a background page is not the same as a layer! A background page can have its own layers.

Confused yet? It becomes clearer if you keep in mind an image of one transparent sheet as a *layer,* a stack of transparent sheets as a *page,* and multiple stacks as separate pages in a drawing. Although a Visio background page is also transparent, its purpose is to display repetitive information (such as a company logo or document title and date) rather than a category of shapes, as a layer does. If the bottom transparent sheet of the anatomy book had only a title, such as "The Human Body," it would be analogous to a Visio background page (see Figure 9-1). Check out Chapter 8 to find out how to create multiple pages and background pages in a Visio drawing.

The bottom line: When you want to group and display categories of shapes in a drawing, use layers. When you want repetitive information to appear on each page of a drawing, use a background page.

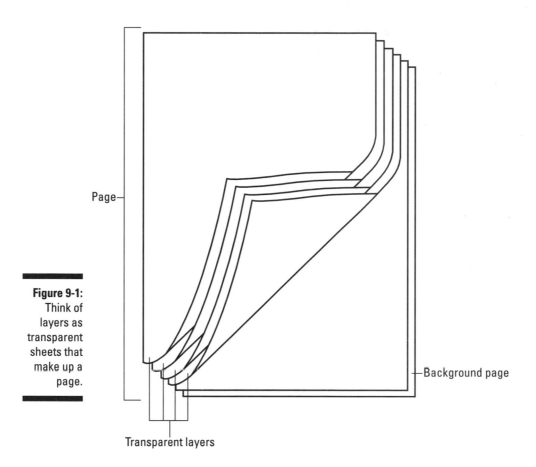

Figure 9-1:
Think of
layers as
transparent
sheets that
make up a
page.

Page—

—Background page

Transparent layers

How Layering Works

In general, you *assign* shapes to a specific layer or to more than one layer. However, some Visio templates include predefined layers. In these cases, the shapes in the template's stencils are preassigned to a particular layer. This means that Visio has done some of the work for you already; you don't have to create layers for your drawing. When you drag a shape onto the drawing page, Visio automatically creates the layer to which that shape is preassigned. When you drag another shape that is preassigned to a different layer, Visio adds that layer to the drawing. The layers aren't added to your drawing, how-ever, until you use the shapes in your drawing. The Office Layout template is a good example of a template with predefined layers. Its layers include:

- **The building envelope** (walls, doors, windows)
- **Equipment** (computers, copy machines)
- **Movable furnishings** (desks, chairs)

> ✓ **Non-movable furnishings** (corner work surfaces, panels)
>
> ✓ **Power/communications** (telephone jacks, power outlets)

A layer (preassigned, or one that you add) applies to a single page in a drawing. If you add a page to your drawing, it doesn't contain any layers until you either drag a shape into the drawing that's preassigned to a layer, or until you create a new layer, as I describe in the following section.

Using the View Toolbar

Visio has a total of seven toolbars, some of which you display all the time, others that you display only when you need them. When you work with layers, snap, or glue, I recommend that you use the View toolbar. It contains the Layer Properties Tool button, which displays the Layer Properties dialog box, and the Shape Layer Tool button, which lists the layer (or layers) a selected shape is assigned to. To display the View toolbar, choose View⇨Toolbars⇨View. Table 9-1 shows you some of the tools on the View toolbar.

Table 9-1	Tools on the View Toolbar
Button	*Tool*
⊞	Grid tool
⊤	Guide tool
⌗	Connector tool
▤ {No Layer} ▼	Layer Properties tool
◀ ▶ Page-1 ▼	Shape Layer tool

Adding a Layer or Removing One?

When the template that you're using doesn't include predefined layers (or if you're not using a template at all), you can create layers of your own to help you organize your shapes. Even if you are using a template that includes layers, you can add to them if you need to.

Follow these steps to add a layer:

1. **Choose View⇨Layer Properties, or click the Layer Properties Tool button (refer to Table 9-1) on the View toolbar.**

   Visio displays the Layer Properties dialog box showing a list of layers for the current page (see Figure 9-2).

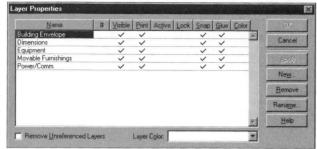

Figure 9-2:
The Layer
Properties
dialog box
lists all
layers by
name.

If your Layer Properties dialog box is empty, it doesn't necessarily mean that the template you're using doesn't include predefined layers. The layers show up in this dialog box only after you've dragged preassigned shapes onto your drawing page.

2. Click New.

Visio displays the New Layer dialog box. (See Figure 9-3.)

Figure 9-3:
Type a
name for
the new
layer in the
Layer Name
box.

3. In the Layer Name box, type the name that you want for a new layer and then click OK.

Your new layer is added to the list in the Layer Properties dialog box.

4. If you want to add more layers, click Apply and then repeat Steps 2 and 3.

5. Click OK to close the Layer Properties dialog box.

When you add or remove layers, they are added to or removed from *the current page only*. If your drawing has multiple pages and you want to add or remove layers, you need to do so individually for each page.

At some point, you may decide to remove a layer. *If so, make sure that you reassign all shapes on that layer to another layer.* Otherwise you may lose all shapes on that layer.

To remove a layer, follow these steps:

1. **Choose View⇨Layer Properties, or click the Layer Properties Tool button (refer to Table 9-1) on the View toolbar.**

   Visio displays the Layer Properties dialog box showing a list of layers for the current page.

2. **Choose the layer name that you want to remove and then click Remove.**

   If the layer contains shapes, you see a warning asking whether you really want to remove the layer. If you're willing to sacrifice the shapes on the layer, that's fine; go ahead and click Yes. If not, click No, click Cancel, and then reassign the shapes to a different layer before removing the layer. (See the section, "Assigning Shapes to Layers," later in this chapter.)

3. **Click OK.**

If you respond "No" to the warning message and then immediately try to remove the same (or another!) layer without closing the Layer Properties dialog box first, you don't receive the warning message again, and Visio deletes the layer even though it contains shapes. (Edit⇨Undo doesn't bring the layer back.) This appears to be a not-so-minor glitch in Visio! If you want to keep the shapes on the layer, be sure to reassign them to a different layer before trying to remove the layer again.

Renaming a Layer

You may want to change the name of a layer, perhaps to something more descriptive of the shapes that you use, or just because you *feel* like it. It's best to use this option when you're working with layers that you create.

I don't recommend renaming a predefined layer. Here's why: As soon as you drag another shape into a drawing that's assigned to the original, predefined Visio layer, that layer name appears on the list again in the Layer Properties dialog box, and your drawing page includes both the predefined layer and the layer you renamed. This can be confusing if you want all your shapes to appear on a single layer.

To rename a layer, follow these easy steps:

1. **Choose View⇨Layer Properties, or click the Layer Properties Tool button (refer to Table 9-1) on the View toolbar.**

   Visio displays the Layer Properties dialog box.

2. **Choose the layer that you want to rename and then click Rename.**

   Visio displays the Rename Layer dialog box.

3. **Type the new name in the Layer Name box and then click OK.**

   Visio displays the new layer name in the Layer Properties dialog box.

4. **Click OK.**

Hiding a Layer

One of the big advantages of using layers in a drawing is that you can turn them off when you don't want to display their shapes. Return for a moment to the building layout example I use earlier in the chapter. If you want to work on the plumbing layer of the building, you also want to display the layer that contains the building walls (that is, the Building Envelope), but you don't need furniture cluttering your view. Or, if you want to distribute the drawing to employees so that they can decide how they want their furniture arranged in their offices, it's not important for them to see the plumbing and HVAC layers. They do, however, need to see the Building Envelope and Electrical layers so that they know where walls and electrical outlets are located in their offices.

To hide a layer, follow these steps:

1. **Choose View⇨Layer Properties, or click the Layer Properties Tool button (refer to Table 9-1) on the View toolbar.**

   The Layer Properties dialog box appears (see Figure 9-4).

2. **Find the name of the layer that you want to hide. Click the check mark that appears in the Visible column.**

   The check mark is removed, making the layer invisible.

Figure 9-4:
Layers that
are not
checked in
the Visible
column are
hidden in
the drawing.

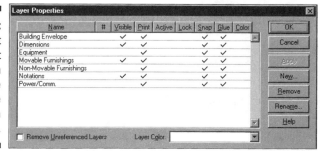

To display or hide all layers at the same time, click the Visible button (the column header is a button). This button toggles every item in the column on and off.

3. **Click OK or Apply.**

   If you want to hide just one layer, click OK. If you want to hide other layers, click Apply; then follow Step 2 again until all layers that you want hidden are hidden.

TIP: To redisplay a hidden layer, use the same steps and add a check mark to the Visible column in the Layer Properties dialog box.

Assigning Shapes to Layers

You know that some templates automatically assign some shapes to predefined layers, but what happens when you use a template that doesn't have predefined layers? If you create your own layers, you assign shapes to the layers that you choose. (Yes, it's more work than using a template with predefined layers, but think of the fun you'll have!)

Follow these steps to assign a shape to a layer:

1. **Select the shape to assign.**

   If the shape is part of a group, click the group and then click the shape to select it by itself (it's displayed with gray handles).

2. **Choose View➪Shape Layer, or click the Shape Layer Tool button (refer to Table 9-1) on the View toolbar.**

   The Shape Layer dialog box, shown in Figure 9-5, appears.

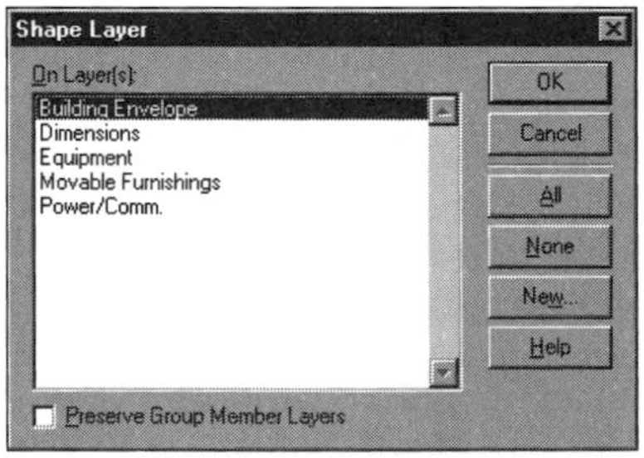

Figure 9-5: The Shape Layer dialog box lists all layers for the drawing on the current page.

3. **Click the layer that you want to assign the shape to.**

   TIP: Sometimes you may want a shape to appear on two or more layers so that it's always visible, even when other layers are hidden. To assign a shape to more than one layer, follow Steps 1 and 2 above. In this step, hold down the Ctrl key as you click all the layers you want to assign the shape to.

4. **Click OK.**

Curious which layer a particular shape is assigned to? To find out, select the shape and then choose <u>V</u>iew➪<u>Sh</u>ape Layer. The Shape Layer dialog box appears, and the layer the shape belongs to is highlighted. Even easier, if the View toolbar is displayed (View➪Toolbar➪View), just look at the Shape Layer tool on the View toolbar. It displays the layer the selected shape is assigned to. (If the shape is unassigned, the Shape Layer tool on the View menu says {No Layer}. If the shape is assigned to multiple layers, the Shape Layer tool on the View menu shows {Multiple Layers}. I show you more about activating layers in the next section, "Activating Layers.")

Activating Layers

When you drag a shape that isn't preassigned to a layer into your drawing, or when you create a new shape, the shape goes unassigned. When you *activate* a layer, all unassigned shapes that you use in your drawing are automatically assigned to the active layer. You can activate a single layer, or you can activate multiple layers. The advantage of activating multiple layers is that the unassigned shapes you use in your drawing are automatically assigned to *all* the active layers.

To activate a layer or layers, follow these steps:

1. **Choose <u>V</u>iew➪<u>L</u>ayer Properties, or click the Layer Properties Tool button (refer to Table 9-1) on the View toolbar.**

   The Layer Properties dialog box appears (refer to Figure 9-4).

2. **In the Active column, click the layer or layers that you want to make active.**

3. **Click OK.**

Using shapes on many layers

Why would you want a shape to appear on more than one layer? One reason is that when a particular layer is hidden, the shape is still visible on other layers. Another reason is that you can track a group of shapes on one layer and component shapes on individual layers. For example, suppose you're diagramming a computer network that contains components from multiple manufacturers. You would have an IBM layer, an HP layer, a Dell layer, a Compaq layer, and so on. But you would also have a layer called Network Components, which would include shapes from *all* the manufacturer layers. This gives you an easy way to track all network shapes, or shapes by manufacturer.

Using Layers on Background Pages

A background page appears behind another page; its contents "show through" the page to which it is assigned. (Remember, earlier I said that you should think of all pages and layers as being transparent.) Background pages are designed to contain repetitive information — text or graphics that you want to appear on one or more pages in a drawing. A company name, logo, or document name are examples of information that you may want to put on a background page. Individual pages in a drawing can have their own or the same background page; you determine to which page (or pages) a background is assigned. See Chapter 8 for information on creating and assigning background pages.

Just as pages can have layers, so can background pages. To create layers on a background page, you first need to create the background page! See Chapter 8 for step-by-step instructions.

After your background page is created, follow these steps to create layers for your background page:

1. **Display your background page by choosing Edit⇨Go To.**

2. **Choose View⇨Layer Properties, or click the Layer Properties Tool button (refer to Table 9-1) on the View toolbar.**

3. **Click New to display the New Layer dialog box (refer to Figure 9-3).**

4. **In the Layer Name box, type a new name and then click OK.**

   Visio adds the name to the Layer Properties list.

5. **Click OK or Apply.**

   If you want to add other layers, Click Apply and then repeat Steps 3 and 4. If you want to add just one layer, click OK.

Protecting Layers from Changes

After you go to all the trouble of defining layers and adding shapes to them, nothing is worse than having another user (or yourself) accidentally delete or change them. How can you avoid this? You can protect a layer from changes by *locking* it. When a layer is locked, you can't move, change, or delete shapes. You also can't add shapes to the layer.

To lock a layer, follow these steps:

1. **Choose View⇨Layer Properties, or click the Layer Properties Tool button (refer to Table 9-1) on the View toolbar.**

   Visio displays the Layer Properties dialog box (refer to Figure 9-4).

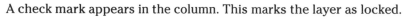

2. **Locate the layer that you want to lock and then click in the Lock column across from the layer name.**

   A check mark appears in the column. This marks the layer as locked.

   If you want to lock all layers quickly, click the Lock button (the column header for the Lock column is a button). To unlock all layers at the same time, click the Lock button again.

3. **Click OK or Apply.**

   To lock just one layer, click OK. To lock other layers, click Apply and then repeat Step 2 and this step for each layer that you want to lock. When you finish, click OK.

If you doubt that this method works, you can test it easily. Just try to move, delete, or copy a shape on the locked layer. You can't do any of these things because Visio doesn't even let you *select* the shape. When you're ready to work on the layer again, you can unlock it easily by removing the check mark from the Lock column.

For obvious reasons, you can't lock a layer that's marked as an active layer. Not so obvious? Remember that all unassigned shapes are automatically assigned to the active layer or layers. If you could lock the active layers, your shapes wouldn't be assigned to any layer.

Locking a layer isn't foolproof protection from changes. After all, you can unlock a layer just as easily as you can lock one. Think of a locked layer more as an alert or a reminder — to yourself or other users — that shapes on a locked layer *shouldn't* be changed. If you want a file to be fully protected from changes, open it or distribute it to other users as a read-only file. For more information on read-only files, see Chapter 12.

Assigning a Color to a Layer

Why would you want to assign a color to a layer, you ask? Well, suppose that your drawing has a half dozen layers and you're beginning to get confused about which shapes belong to what layer. Assigning a color to each layer lets you quickly determine which shapes belong to a particular layer. Another idea is to assign a color to all layers that are locked. This reminds you immediately which shapes can't be altered. Or, if you're distributing the drawing to other users for review and comment, you may want to assign a color to the layer that each user is allowed to change. Get the idea?

To assign a color to a layer, follow these steps:

1. **Choose View⇨Layer Properties, or click the Layer Properties Tool button (refer to Table 9-1) on the View toolbar.**

   Visio displays the Layer Properties dialog box (refer to Figure 9-4).

2. **Find the layer that you want to assign a color to and then click in the Color column across from the layer name.**

   A check mark appears in the column.

3. **At the bottom of the dialog box, choose a layer color from the Layer Color drop-down list.**

   Visio offers a dozen or so colors and ten shades of gray. If these options aren't enough for you, you can create a custom color by clicking Custom at the bottom of the list. When you click Custom, the Color dialog box, shown in Figure 9-6, appears.

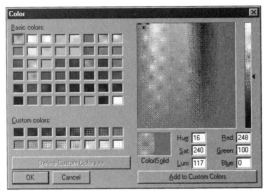

Figure 9-6:
Use the
Color dialog
box to
create a
custom
color.

To create a custom color, follow these steps:

1. **Find the layer that you want to assign a color to and then click in the Color column across from the layer name.**

   A check mark appears in the column.

2. **At the bottom of the dialog box, click Custom.**

   The Color dialog box appears (refer to Figure 9-6).

3. **Click an empty Custom Colors dialog box (in the lower-left part of the dialog box).**

4. **On the left side of the dialog box, click one of the Basic colors closest to the color that you want to create.**

5. **Move the pointer in any direction in the large color box area on the right side of the dialog box to customize the color.**

   • **To change the intensity of the color:** Move the small, black arrow up and down the vertical slide bar at the far-right side of the dialog box.

- **To adjust the Hue, Sat (Saturation), and Lum (Luminosity) of a color:** Enter a number in one of these boxes.

- **To adjust the amount of Red, Green, or Blue in a color:** Enter a number in one of these boxes.

6. **Click the Add to Custom Colors button.**

To create more custom colors, repeat Steps 1 through 4.

To use one of your custom colors for the selected layer:

1. **Click your custom color in the Custom Colors box (refer to Figure 9-6) and then click OK.**

   The Color dialog box closes. The Layer Properties dialog box is still open. Your custom color now appears at the bottom of the list.

2. **Click your custom color to apply it to the layer that you want to add the color to.**

3. **Click OK or Apply.**

   Visio displays all the shapes on the layer in the color you choose.

4. **To remove the color, choose View⇨Layer Properties again, or click the Layer Properties Tool button (refer to Table 9-1) on the View toolbar. Remove the check mark from the Color column.**

   Removing a color from a layer doesn't remove any custom colors that you create. They are still available in the Color dialog box.

   If you have a color printer and you assign colors to layers, the layers print in their designated colors.

Selecting Layers to Print

What good are layers if you can't print them selectively? In a building layout, for example, you probably want to print only the Building Envelope (walls) and Plumbing layers for the plumber. The plumber doesn't want or need to see the wiring, HVAC, and furniture layouts. And your employees, who need to place their furniture in their offices, certainly don't need to see the technical parts of your drawing. The only layers they need to see are the walls, nonmovable furniture, and the electrical outlets.

Visio automatically assumes that you want to print all layers, but you can change this easily by following these steps:

1. **Choose View⇨Layer Properties, or click the Layer Properties Tool button (refer to Table 9-1) on the View toolbar.**

2. **For the layers that you don't want to print, remove the check mark in the <u>P</u>rint column by clicking it.**

3. **Click OK.**

Don't be deceived by the Visible column in the Layer Properties dialog box! You can't keep a layer from printing by making it invisible. The Print column is the only setting that affects printing; the Visible column affects only what you see on the screen. If a layer isn't visible, but a check mark appears in the Print column, it prints!

Snap and Glue Options for Layers

If you followed some of the steps in this chapter, you've seen the Layer Properties dialog box, and you're probably wondering what the Snap and Glue columns are for. What are snap and glue, you say? *Snap* is a feature that works like a magnet to let you align and position shapes accurately in a draw-ing. You can specify that shapes automatically snap to other shapes, to grid lines, to guide lines, ruler divisions, and so on. *Glue* is a feature that keeps shapes connected even when you move them. Connection lines between shapes either stay connected at the same point on the shape, or move to a more convenient connection point, depending on the glue options that you specify. If you want to review these concepts, see Chapter 5 for more informa-tion about glue, and Chapter 6 for the scoop on snap.

Although the concepts of snap and glue are simple enough in and of them-selves, they seem a bit more confusing than necessary when it comes to layers. The following rules apply to the Snap and Glue options in the Layer Properties dialog box:

✔ **Snap:** When Snap is checked for a particular layer, shapes on that layer can snap to shapes on other layers and vice versa. (In other words, Snap is enabled in both directions.) When Snap is not checked for a par-ticular layer, shapes on that layer can still snap to shapes on other layers, but not vice versa.

✔ **Glue:** When Glue is checked for a particular layer, shapes on that layer can glue to shapes on other layers and vice versa. (In other words, Glue is enabled in both directions.) When Glue is not checked for a particular layer, shapes on that layer can still glue to shapes on other layers, but not vice versa.

All this snapping and gluing boils down to the simple fact that if you want shapes on other layers to steer clear of shapes on a particular layer, uncheck both options (snap and glue) for that layer.

Chapter 10

Save Time with Visio Wizards

· ·

· ·

*I*f you're like me, any time you learn a new application you always appreciate some extra help. A little magic here or there can't hurt. Well, wizards aren't exactly magic, but they're the next best thing.

What's a Wizard and Why Do I Want One?

A wizard is something that understands the task you need to accomplish — maybe even better than you do. A wizard picks your brain. A wizard asks you important questions about the task and makes you think. A wizard is logical, organized, and objective. A wizard is a dutiful and obedient servant; it does exactly what you tell it to do. Although mysterious, a wizard is your loyal and faithful assistant.

Okay, okay! What's a wizard, really? A *wizard* is a special kind of mini-program in Visio that helps you accomplish a specific task, like creating an organization chart, an office layout, or maybe a project timeline. I call a wizard a mini-program because it displays dialog boxes that ask you a series of questions, each designed to lead you one step closer to your goal. The wizard records all the information that you give it and, after asking its last question, does what it was designed to do, whether that's creating a drawing or compiling a report.

Essentially, a wizard is a macro. In its simplest form, a *macro* is nothing more than a series of recorded steps. The steps can include choosing menu commands; entering text or dragging shapes; or more complex operations, such as performing mathematical calculations or exporting data to other files. A macro automates a task by letting you play back the macro instead of performing the steps manually.

A wizard is designed to make things quick and easy for you. Wizards are especially helpful if you're trying to accomplish a particular task for the first time. A wizard can also ensure accuracy and consistency in a drawing, leaving you to worry about more important details. Before you get too excited about wizards, though, let me make it clear that some wizards accomplish very simple tasks whereas others accomplish complex ones. Sometimes a wizard is nice to use just because you're feeling lazy. If you just don't feel like hunting through menu commands and dialog boxes and would rather sit back and have a wizard ask you all the questions, feel free. That's what they're there for. The best way to discover wizards is to experiment with them.

Visio contains some additional tools that perform tasks for you as well. I include them throughout this chapter even though, technically, they're not wizards. But you can think of them as wizards because they *are* mini-programs that perform a task for you.

Discovering What Wizards Can Really Do

Visio Standard, Visio Technical, and Visio Professional all include wizards. Technical and Professional include all the wizards that Standard offers, in addition to some specialized wizards. You can find all the wizards that I discuss in this chapter in all the three products.

I describe the simple ones first:

- ✔ **Build Region.** This is a tool that gathers shapes (like states, provinces, countries) that you've dragged into your drawing and pulls them together into a geographically correct map. For example, you can drag Washington, Oregon, Idaho, California, and Utah shapes (from the Maps of the U.S. stencil) onto the drawing page and place them anywhere. Build Region positions them correctly in relation to one another.

- ✔ **Chart Shape Wizard.** When you're creating a chart and want to use multiple shapes to depict quantity, this wizard creates the additional shapes for you and stacks them (horizontally or vertically). For example, if you're creating a bar chart to show numbers of people who own personal computers at home, you can choose a personal computer shape to represent quantity. The higher the quantity, the more shapes the wizard adds to the chart. You can also use this wizard to stretch 2-D shapes to represent increasing or decreasing quantity. For example, a stretchable pencil would be a great shape for a teacher to use for a chart that shows average hours of homework for each grade in school.

✔ **Page Layout Wizard.** If you're not using a template, this wizard is a good one to use to help you set up your drawing page size, orientation (landscape or portrait), and drawing scale. The wizard also prompts you for information about adding a title or page border to your drawing. For more information about using templates, refer to Chapter 1.

✔ **Organization Chart Wizard.** This wizard lets you create a generic organization chart (to which you can add data later) or create an organization chart based on data that you have in a Microsoft Excel file (.xls), Org Plus (.txt) file, a text file (comma-delimited or tab-delimited), or an ODBC-compliant (Open Database Connectivity) database table. See Chapter 15 for examples and more details on this wizard.

✔ **Shape Explorer.** Here's another tool that can help you out. Looking for a particular shape but don't remember which stencil it's on? Shape Explorer helps you find it. You don't even have to know the name of the shape; just type in a description of the shape and Shape Explorer searches for it.

✔ **Stencil Report Wizard.** Want a Visio drawing of all the shapes on a stencil? This wizard gives you an example of every shape on a stencil, and their names and descriptions. If a shape is as simple as a star, the description "six-pointed star" may seem rather obvious. But what if the shape is a Catalyst 3000B Switch with the description "Cisco - 16-Port Catalyst 3000 Switch w/ 10K addr, SNMP, Address Filter, Spanning-Tree Protocol w/ VLAN suppt, Full Duplex"? This description isn't so obvious. A stencil report serves as a great reference guide for a stencil. For a quick glance at the shapes in many of Visio's stencils, see Appendix A, the Stencil Gallery.

✔ **Print ShapeSheet.** The ShapeSheet spreadsheet describes shapes in Visio in every way imaginable. The ShapeSheet contains mathematical and geometric information about the shape, as well as the x,y coordinates of its vertices and connection points, text box characteristics, line and fill characteristics, protection, glue, and layer characteristics, and much more. The Print ShapeSheet tool displays a Print dialog box in which you can select the ShapeSheet characteristics that you want to print. You can print to your printer, to a file, or to the Windows clipboard.

✔ **Flowchart-TQM (total quality management) Diagram Wizard.** This wizard helps you create various types of flowcharts or TQM diagrams. You can use existing data, enter new data, or create a generic flowchart or diagram structure and add data later.

Some of the more advanced wizards include:

- ✓ **Property Reporting Wizard.** In case you haven't noticed by now, a shape in Visio is much more than just a shape. A shape is not only "smart" (in that its behavior changes based on the circumstances in which you use it), but it stores data such as inventory numbers or cost data as well. The Property Reporting wizard compiles data from the shapes that you select into a report that you can store in a spreadsheet.

- ✓ **Custom Properties Editor.** Use this tool to edit the data stored in shapes by adding data fields or deleting existing data fields. Now you can get rid of data fields that you don't use and add data fields that are particularly important to you.

- ✓ **SmartShape Wizard.** This is one of Visio's coolest wizards because it lets you change the way a shape looks and behaves. For example, you can reposition a shape's text box, add a built-in connector to a shape, add a hidden note to a shape, or change the attributes of the shape that are locked (protected from change).

- ✓ **Project Timeline Wizard.** This wizard helps you create a project time-line using a Gantt chart, a type of chart that shows a list of project tasks on a calendar timeline. If your project data already exists, you can use it; if not, you can create it in an Excel file or a text file. Or, you can create a blank Gantt chart and enter your data later.

- ✓ **Database Wizard.** Want to link data stored in your shapes to a data-base? Use the Database Wizard to do it. This wizard links data to ODBC-compliant databases like Microsoft Access and Oracle SQL Server. (*Linking* makes a connection between the data stored in Visio shapes and data stored in a database so that when one is changed, the other is updated.)

- ✓ **Database Export.** This tool lets you export (transfer out of Visio) data that is stored in a drawing's shapes. Where do you export it to? An ODBC-compliant database file, which saves you the work of recreating a database table from data that already exists in the Visio Custom Properties and ShapeSheet spreadsheets.

Finding the Wizard That You Want

Because a wizard is a macro, you can always find wizards listed under Tools➪Macro. This command leads to a submenu that lists categories of macros, then finally, the names of individual wizards and tools (see Figure 10-1).

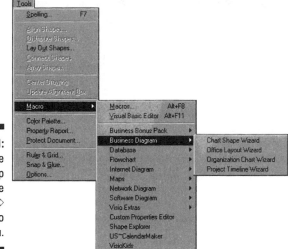

Figure 10-1:
Wizards are
listed deep
on the
Tools⇨
Macro
menu.

The list shown in Figure 10-1 is from Visio Professional. If you're using Visio Standard, you may not see all these wizards on your screen. If you're using Visio Technical, you probably see more!

If you're not sure in which category a wizard is listed, you can always choose Tools⇨Macro⇨Macros (or click Alt+F8), which displays a dialog box listing all tools and wizards in alphabetic order. To use one of these wizards, click the wizard that you want (to highlight it); then click Run.

Visio lists wizards in other locations as well. For example, suppose you start Visio using the Office Layout template and then decide that you want to use the Office Layout Wizard. When you open the Tools menu, the Office Layout Wizard appears as the first item on the Tools menu. This is true when you use other templates as well — open Visio using the Charts and Graphs template, and the ChartShape Wizard appears as the first item on the Tools menu. Keep in mind, though, that not every template has a wizard associated with it.

Wizards are also listed when you start Visio and the Choose A Drawing Template dialog box is automatically displayed (see Figure 10-2). When you choose a template category, you see wizards listed along with templates.

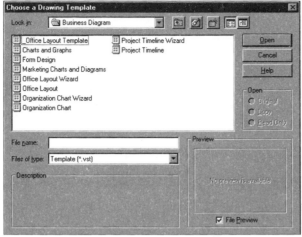

Figure 10-2:
Look for wizards in the Choose a Drawing Template dialog box when you start Visio.

Using a Wizard

Wizards are probably one of the easiest tools to use. When you start a wizard, a special dialog box is displayed describing what the wizard does and the tasks that you can perform using it (see Figure 10-3). At the bottom of the box are Back, Next, and Cancel buttons. The Next button takes you to the next screen in the wizard "script," which presents you with more questions or choices. If you ever want to change the choices that you've made, click the Back button. To exit the wizard without completing the task, click Cancel.

Some wizards have a More Information button like the one shown in Figure 10-3. When you click this button, the wizard displays helpful hints or information that may be essential for you to read before you can run the wizard.

I don't show you all the screens of a wizard because they are self-explanatory and incredibly easy to follow — really, they are! The last screen of the wizard replaces the Next button with a Finish button. After you click Finish, the wizard returns to your Visio drawing page and completes the task that it was designed for.

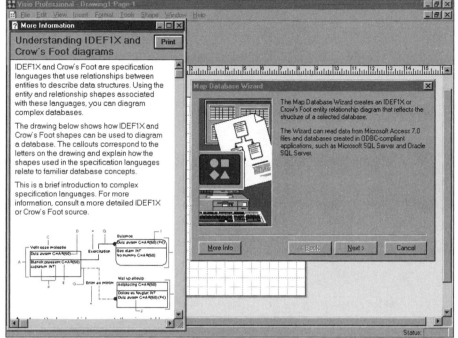

Figure 10-3:
Click the
More
Information
button to
pop up a
separate
window
about the
wizard.

Finding more help on the Web

Wizards are great helpers for particular tasks, but sometimes you have questions or problems that even a mighty wizard can't handle. The following list shows you where to turn for more help — the Visio Corporation Web site. You can access all three of these locations straight from your Visio product.

✔ **To Find Out about Visio Support and Service:** From Visio's Help menu, click Visio on the Web⇨Online Support, or go directly to www.visio.com/support/. From here, select one of Visio's support resources or get help on non-technical issues by clicking the Service and Support hyperlink, and then clicking Customer Service.

✔ **For Answers to Frequently Asked Questions:** From Visio's Help menu, click

Visio on the Web⇨Drawing Resources, or go directly to www.visio.com/support/drawing.html. Look under the Learn What Our Products Can Do heading and click The Knowledge Base hyperlink for answers to all kinds of questions from Visio's technical support group.

✔ **To Find Out about Available Training:** From Visio's Help menu, click Visio on the Web⇨Drawing Resources, or go directly to www.visio.com/support/drawing.html. This Web page offers sources for individualized or group training; information on Visio's Train the Trainer course; interactive, self-paced, computer-based training; and lists independent companies and trainers who offer Visio training.

Part IV

For the Die-hard Visio Junkie: Using More Advanced Stuff

The 5th Wave   By Rich Tennant

And tomorrow Daddy's going to teach you how to customize your own template.

In this part . . .

If you're a die-hard Visio user, you may want to dig right in to this part! See how to go one step beyond using Visio shapes, stencils, and templates by finding out how to create your own. Discover how storing information in shapes can help you create reports and find out how to protect your work from changes. And there's more! See how to incorporate elements of Visio into other programs, use Visio drawings on the Net, and add hyperlinks to drawings.

Chapter 11

Creating Stencils, Masters, Templates, and Styles

● ●

In This Chapter

▶ Using local and standalone stencils

▶ Working with master shapes

▶ Creating and saving custom templates

▶ Applying styles to shapes

● ●

*Y*ou're ready to start customizing Visio by creating your own Visio stencils, master shapes, templates, and styles. The flexibility that Visio offers is a great asset, and it also makes Visio that much more useful to you because you can tailor it to suit your unique needs.

Working with Stencils

In Chapter 1, I cover the basics of using templates and stencils. In this chapter, I go beyond the basics and discuss two different types of stencils: standalone and local.

✔ **Standalone stencils:** You work with standalone stencils all the time. *Standalone stencils* are the stencils that open automatically when you use a template. In the Visio file directories, standalone stencils have a .vss file extension. As long as you open the stencil first, you can use shapes from any standalone stencil in any drawing.

If the template that you're using doesn't contain all the shapes that you need, choose File⇨Stencils to open additional stencils.

✔ **Local stencils:** Visio creates a *local* stencil automatically whenever you create a drawing, but you haven't been aware of it until now. A local stencil stores all the shapes that you use in a drawing (from all the stencils you use), even if you delete the shapes from your drawing. Think of it as a type of shape history log for your current drawing. The local stencil is automatically saved with your drawing file, but unless you call it up, you never see it.

To open a drawing's local stencil, choose <u>W</u>indow⇨Show M<u>a</u>ster Shapes. The stencil is shown in its own window next to the drawing and carries the same name as the drawing file followed by `:Stencil`. Notice that all open toolbars are replaced by the Stencil toolbar. (See Figure 11-1.)

So what's the point of having a local stencil, you ask? Suppose you open and close a dozen or more stencils on a quest for a particular shape. After you drag the shape into your drawing, you delete it and close all the open stencils. Later, you want to use that shape again, but now you can't remember what stencil it was on. A local stencil saves you the hassle of opening a dozen stencils again looking for it; you simply drag the shape into your drawing from the local stencil.

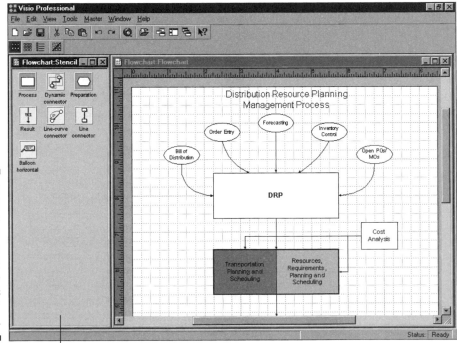

Figure 11-1:
A local stencil is displayed in its own window and mirrors the name of its "parent" drawing.

Local stencil

As you work with stencils, you'll probably use the buttons on the Stencil toolbar. Table 11-1 shows you some of these buttons and the corresponding tools.

Table 11-1	Tools on the Stencil Toolbar
Button	**Function or Tool**
✂	Cut
📑	Copy
📋	Paste
⊞	Icons Only tool
⊞	Icons and Names tool
☰	Names Only tool
▦	Arrange Icons tool

Saving a local stencil as a standalone stencil

A local stencil is available only to the current drawing; other drawings have their own local stencils. But what if you want to save a local stencil as a standalone stencil? Can you do it? What would be the advantage?

Yes, you can do it, and the advantage is that the stencil then becomes available to any other drawing that you create, not just the original drawing. Say you go through dozens of stencils to find the perfect shape. If you need to create a similar drawing (using the same shapes), are you going to want to open all of those stencils again? Probably not. Saving the local stencil as a standalone stencil lets you use the standalone stencil to create your new drawing, which saves you a lot of time.

Use these steps to save a local stencil as a standalone stencil:

1. **Open the drawing that contains the shapes that you want to store on a standalone stencil.**

2. **Choose Window⇨Show Master Shapes.**

   Visio displays and selects the local stencil on the left side of the screen in its own window. The name in the title bar is your drawing file name followed by :Stencil (refer to Figure 11-1).

3. **Choose File⇨Save As.**

   Visio displays the Save As dialog box, shown in Figure 11-2.

Figure 11-2:
Save your
stencil as a
.vss file in
the
Solutions
subfolder.

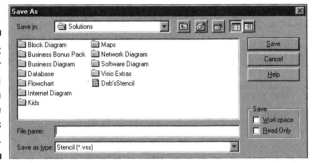

4. **In the Save In box, choose the Visio Solutions folder.**

   (Naming and saving the stencil in the Visio Solutions subfolder adds it to the submenu that's displayed when you choose File⇨Stencils.)

5. **In the Save As Type box, choose Stencil (*.vss).**

6. **In the File Name box, type a name for your stencil.**

7. **In the Save area, be sure the Workspace option isn't checked.**

8. **Click Save.**

9. **In the Properties dialog box, type any information that you want to store with the file (subject, company, keywords, description, and so on); then click OK.**

   With the stencil still selected, Visio changes the name to the name you entered in Step 6.

10. **Choose File⇨Close to close the new stencil.**

Creating a standalone stencil from scratch

If you create a bunch of custom shapes, storing them all in one place is very handy. A standalone stencil is a good place to store your shapes; the stencil you create becomes your "custom" stencil. And because it's a standalone stencil, it's available to any drawing you create, not just the current one.

To create a standalone stencil, follow these steps:

1. **Choose File⇨Stencils⇨Blank Stencil.**

   Visio opens a separate stencil window next to your drawing window named StencilX (where X is a number that's incremented each time you create a new stencil).

2. **Make sure that the stencil window is active (click on the window's title bar), and then Choose File⇨Save As.**

   Visio displays the Save As dialog box (refer to Figure 11-2).

3. **In the Save In box, choose the Visio Solutions folder.**

   (Naming and saving the stencil in the Visio Solutions subfolder adds it to the submenu that's displayed when you choose File⇨Stencils.)

4. **In the Save As Type box, choose Stencil (*.vss).**

5. **In the File Name box, type a name for your stencil.**

6. **Be sure the Workspace option isn't checked.**

7. **Be sure the Read Only option isn't checked so you can add shapes to the stencil later.**

8. **Click Save.**

Now when you choose File⇨Stencils again, your new stencil is listed on the submenu and you can open it just like any other stencil. To see how to add shapes to the stencil, refer to "Adding master shapes to stencils" later in this chapter.

Creating a standalone stencil from a Visio stencil

Of course, you may not always want to start from scratch when it comes to creating a stencil. Suppose one of the Visio stencils contains a lot of shapes that you typically use, but you want to delete some and add others. You can do this, too. You save the stencil with a new name and then make whatever changes you want to it.

You can permanently alter a Visio stencil by opening the original stencil and making changes to it. However, I don't recommend doing this unless you're absolutely, positively sure that you don't need whatever you're deleting. (Is anyone ever absolutely, positively sure of anything?) If you decide later that you want to restore the original stencil, the only way to do it is to reinstall Visio on your computer, which is a lot of bother you can do without!

To create a new stencil from a Visio stencil, use these steps:

1. **Choose File⇨Stencils⇨Open Stencil.**

   Visio displays the Open Stencil dialog box (see Figure 11-3).

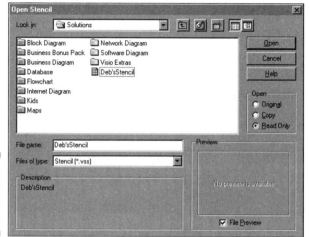

Figure 11-3:
The Open
Stencil
dialog box.

2. **In the dialog box, select the Visio stencil that you want to open.**

3. **In the Open area of the dialog box, click the Copy radio button; then click Open.**

   Visio opens the stencil in a format that lets you change it.

4. **With the title bar of the stencil selected, choose File⇨Save As.**

5. **In the Save In box, choose the Visio Solutions folder.**

   (Saving the stencil here adds it to the submenu that's displayed when you choose File⇨Stencils.)

6. **In the Save As Type box, choose Stencil (*.vss).**

7. **In the File Name box, type a name for your stencil.**

8. **Be sure the Workspace option isn't checked.**

9. **Click Save.**

Now the original Visio stencil is protected from change, and your new stencil, along with the drawing that you opened in Step 1, is still displayed on your screen. You can begin making changes to your new stencil by deleting and adding shapes (see "Deleting master shapes from stencils" and "Adding master shapes to stencils," later in this chapter).

Working with Master Shapes

When you take the time to create new shapes (see Chapter 7), your hard work and time aren't wasted. You can convert all of those wonderful shapes into master shapes. *Master shapes* are shapes that are stored on stencils so you can use them in any drawing.

Adding master shapes to stencils

If you create a custom, standalone stencil, you can store your custom shapes on that stencil or on a Visio stencil. (Yes, you can add to or delete shapes from a Visio stencil. But be careful, because the only way to get the original stencil back is to reinstall Visio.) See "Working with Stencils" earlier in this chapter for more on creating, editing, and storing stencils.

To store a shape on a stencil, you need to open the stencil to make it "writable." (When you use a template, Visio opens read-only versions of stencils so that you don't accidentally change them.) To make a stencil writable, open either the original stencil or a copy of it. (If you open a copy of it, you preserve the original stencil and save the copy under a new name. If you open the original, you change the original stencil, which you probably don't want to do.)

To add your custom shapes as masters to a stencil, follow these steps:

1. **In the drawing area, display the drawing that contains the shape that you want to save as a master shape.**

2. **Choose File⇨Stencils⇨Open Stencil.**

   Visio displays the Open Stencil dialog box (refer to Figure 11-3).

3. **Highlight the stencil that you want to open, and then choose Copy to open a copy of it or Original to open the original stencil.**

4. **Click Open.**

5. **In your drawing, select the shape that you want to add to the stencil; then press and hold the Ctrl key as you drag the shape from the drawing page onto the stencil.**

   Visio places a copy of the shape on the stencil as a master shape.

   If you don't hold the Ctrl key as you drag, you *move* the shape from the drawing onto the stencil instead of copying it.

6. **With the shape still selected on the stencil, choose Master⇨Properties.**

   Visio displays the Properties dialog box shown in Figure 11-4.

Figure 11-4:
Give your
new master
shape a
name.

7. **In the Master Name box, type the name that you want to appear with the master shape.**

8. **Click OK.**

9. **(Optional) In the Prompt box, type the phrase or description that you want to appear on the Visio status bar when you select the shape.**

10. **When you're finished adding shapes to the stencil, click the stencil title bar to make sure that the stencil window is selected.**

11. **Choose File⇨Close.**

   Visio displays a dialog box asking if you want to save the changes to the stencil.

12. **Click Yes.**

Closing the file in Step 11 protects the stencil from accidental changes. When you want to use the stencil again, reopen it in the usual way (using File⇨Stencils), which reopens the stencil as read-only.

Deleting master shapes from stencils

Although you probably won't do it often, you may want to delete a shape from a stencil. If you never use a shape (and don't anticipate ever needing it), if you accidentally make two copies of it, or if the shape is no longer accurate, deleting the shape is probably better than having it clutter up your stencil.

To delete a shape from a stencil, use these steps:

1. **Choose File⇨Stencils⇨Open Stencil.**

   Visio displays the Open Stencil dialog box (refer to Figure 11-3).

2. **Highlight the stencil that you want to open; then choose Original to open the original stencil.**

3. **Click Open.**

4. **Select the shape that you want to delete.**

5. **Click the Cut button on the Stencil toolbar (refer to Table 11-1), and then choose Edit⇨Cut or press the Delete key.**

   Visio removes the shape from your stencil.

Moving master shapes from one stencil to another

Sometimes you just can't make up your mind where you want to store a master shape. Or maybe you just decide that a particular shape belongs on a different stencil. Fortunately, you can move a master shape from one stencil to another. If you're really undecided, you can copy a shape from one stencil to another.

To move or copy a shape:

1. **Choose File⇨Stencils⇨Open Stencil.**

   Visio displays the Open Stencil dialog box (refer to Figure 11-3).

2. **Highlight the first stencil that you want to open, click the Original option (in the Open section of the dialog box), and then click the Open button.**

3. **Repeat Steps 1 and 2 to open the second stencil (be sure to choose Original again).**

4. **Select the shape that you want to move (or copy).**

   To *move* the shape, hold down the Shift key, and then drag the shape from its stencil to the other stencil.

   To *copy* the shape, drag the shape without using the Shift key.

5. **Choose File⇨Close to close each stencil individually, saving the changes.**

Viewing and arranging shapes on a stencil

After you've added, copied, and moved shapes around between stencils, you'll probably want to spend a little time putting them in some sort of order. Luckily, the Auto Arrange command on the View menu is set by default for all stencils you open. *Auto Arrange* is the feature that snaps your shapes into a nice, neat order when you copy, add, or move shapes onto a stencil. When Auto Arrange is turned off (it toggles on and off when you select it) and you drag shapes around, your stencil may look like the one shown in Figure 11-5.

Visio gives you other ways to view stencils as well. Take a look at the stencil tools shown in Table 11-1. It contains four tools for viewing and arranging stencils:

- ✓ **Icons and Names** displays shapes and their names in the stencil. This is the arrangement that you typically see.(Refer to Figure 11-1.)

- ✓ **Icons Only** displays shapes without their names in the stencil. This compresses the shapes and lets you see more of them at one time when the stencil contains a lot of shapes. (For an example of what Icons Only looks like, see Figure 11-6.)

- ✓ **Names Only** displays only the names and hides the shapes (see Figure 11-7).

- ✓ **Arrange Icons** arranges shapes on the stencil automatically (which has the same affect as View➪Arrange Icons).

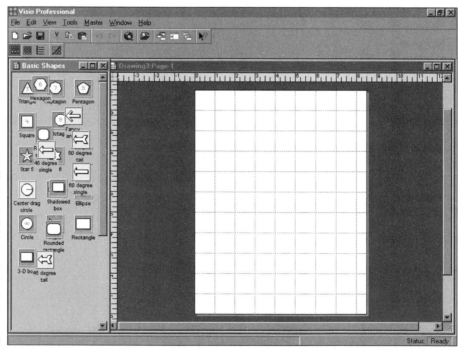

Figure 11-5:
If you drag shapes onto a stencil when Auto Arrange is turned off, it can get really messy!

Figure 11-6:
When you click Icons Only, a stencil displays only the shapes (no names).

Figure 11-7:
When you click Names Only, a stencil displays only the shape names.

Working with Templates

A template is like a model for a drawing; it sets up the page size, orientation, drawing scale, grid, and text and font styles for your drawing area, and then opens up appropriate stencils for the type of drawing that you're creating. The biggest advantages templates offer are consistency and efficiency. And that's why creating and saving custom templates is a good idea.

If you're going to create a series of related drawings, you want them to be consistent from the first to the last. While it's possible that none of the Visio templates meet your needs exactly, you can create a custom template that does. You can base your custom template on an existing Visio template or drawing and then make changes to it, or you can create the custom template from scratch.

If you save your template in the Visio Solutions folder, the new template name is listed on the submenu along with other Visio templates when you start a new drawing.

To create a custom template from a Visio template or an existing drawing, follow these steps:

1. **Start Visio selecting the template that you want to use.**

    If Visio is already running, choose File⇨New and then choose a template. If you want to base your new template on an existing drawing, choose File⇨Open.

2. Choose File⇨Stencils to open any other stencils that you want to include in your new template.

3. Choose File⇨Page Setup.

    Visio displays the Page Setup dialog box.

4. Click the appropriate tab to change anything about the template (page size and orientation, drawing scale, page properties, and so on).

5. If you want your template to include a background page, create it now (see Chapter 8 for details).

6. Choose File⇨Save As.

    Visio displays the Save As dialog box.

7. In the Save In box, choose the folder that you want to save your new template in.

    Choose the Visio Solutions folder if you want the template to appear on the submenu when you choose File⇨New and in the Choose a Drawing Template dialog box when you start Visio.

8. In the File Name box, type a name for your new template.

9. In the Save As Type box, choose Template (*.vst).

10. In the Save area of the dialog box, make sure the Workspace option is checked.

11. Click Save.

To create a custom template from scratch, the best way to do it is to set up a drawing with all the settings that you want the template to have. Choose File⇨Page Setup to set the page size, drawing scale, and page property settings that you want for the new template. And don't forget about background pages (see Chapter 8) and layers (see Chapter 9). When the drawing is the way you want it, follow Steps 6 through 11 in the preceding numbered list.

Working with Styles

In Chapter 4 (on working with text) and Chapter 7 (on creating and jazzing up your shapes), I discuss working with the *components* of style. A *style* is a collection of attributes that apply to a shape, such as a green and yellow striped fill, a purple outline, and bold orange text in the Haettenschweiler font. The style has a name (such as Disgusting) and is saved along with a template or a drawing file.

What's the point of having a style? A style saves you the time of applying all Disgusting's attributes individually to a shape. You simply apply the style to as many shapes as you want, and — voila! — you have multiple Disgusting shapes. Using styles not only saves you time, but it ensures consistency when you want shapes to be formatted exactly alike, too.

A style can contain just one attribute or dozens of attributes. It can contain text attributes, line attributes, or fill attributes, or any combination of the three. Most Visio templates contain at least a few predefined styles (with one, two, or all three attributes). To see examples of styles, open any sample Visio file from the Visio/Samples folder. Make sure that the Text and Shape toolbars are displayed on your screen. (If not, right-click anywhere in the toolbar area to select these toolbars.) The Text toolbar contains a Text Style box; the Shape toolbar contains Line and Fill style boxes (see Figure 11-8). To see how different styles are applied in the drawing, click a shape and look at the style boxes on the toolbar. Now click several other shapes, watching the style boxes each time you click another shape. You see that some shapes have a style assigned to them while others don't.

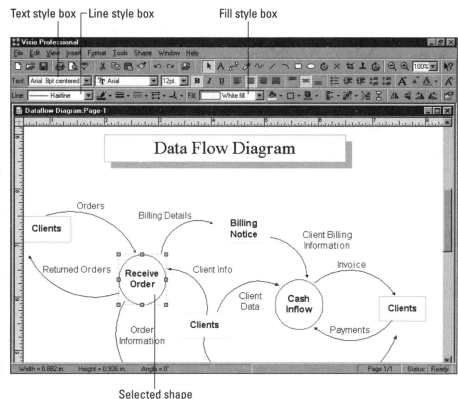

Figure 11-8: The Text and Shape toolbars contain style boxes that tell you the style that's applied to the selected shape.

Creating and saving a style

You can base a new style on an existing one or create it from scratch. If the style that you want to create is similar to another style, begin with the existing style, make the changes that you want, and then save the new style under a different name.

Use these steps to create a style:

1. **Choose Format⇨Define Styles.**

   Visio displays the Define Styles dialog box, shown in Figure 11-9.

2. **In the Style box, type a name for the new style.**

   If you're basing the new style on an existing one, choose it in the Based On box.

3. **In the Includes box, check all the characteristics that your new style includes (Text, Line, Fill).**

4. **For each option that you chose in Step 3, click the appropriate button in the Change box (Text, Line, Fill).**

   In the dialog boxes that appear, choose the attributes that you want; then click OK to close each box.

5. **In the Define Styles dialog box, click Apply.**

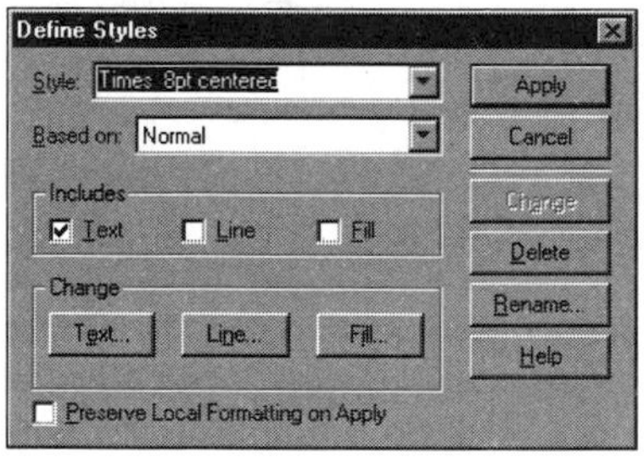

Figure 11-9:
The Define
Styles
dialog box.

You can also use the Define Styles dialog box to rename existing styles or delete styles that you don't want to use anymore (see the Delete and Rename buttons in Figure 11-9).

Typically when you define a style, that style is available only to the current drawing. However, if you save the style with your template (see "Creating and saving a template"), the style is available in all drawings that you create using that template.

Applying a style to a shape

After you created a style, you simply apply it to a shape to assign all the style's attributes to the shape at once. If you want to apply the style to more than one shape, you can save yourself some time by applying the style to all the shapes at the same time. Here's how:

1. **Select the shape that you want to apply a style to.**

   To select more than one shape, press and hold the Shift key as you click several shapes.

2. **To apply text, line, and fill styles:**

   Separately, click the down arrow for the style box in the appropriate toolbar (for example, the Fill style box in the Shape toolbar).

   To change several styles at the same time, choose Format⇨Style. In the Style box that appears, choose the appropriate styles from the drop-down boxes by clicking the down arrows; then click OK.

Chapter 12

Storing, Using, and Protecting Information in Your Shapes

● ●

● ●

*I*f you consider yourself a *techie,* you may look at the topics in this chapter and wonder what's so techie about it. If you don't consider yourself a techie, you may look at the topics and scratch your head wondering whether any of this applies to you.

Chapter 12 is sort of a catchall chapter of advanced features that the average Visio user may not think about, want to use, or care about. But you certainly don't have to be a techie to understand or do any of the tasks described here!

Storing Data in Visio Shapes

Shapes are more than what they appear to be. Some are "smart" because their behavior changes depending on the circumstances in which they're used. Others have very sophisticated geometry. And all shapes are able to store data.

Why would you want to store data in a shape, you ask? Well, you may not if your drawing illustrates a simple workflow process like Get bills⇨ Enter in payables⇨Pay bills⇨Record in register⇨File paperwork. However, if this process is more complex, with costs associated with each task in the process, you may very well want to store cost data, resources required to complete the task, and the duration of time involved in each task.

Now, pretend that you're a property manager in charge of distributing and tracking computer equipment for your company. (Okay, it may not sound as exciting as whale watching, but it pays!) In an office layout plan, you can store inventory numbers and owner information for each computer component shape shown in a drawing. You may want to store additional information like serial numbers, acquisition dates, and manufacturer names or model numbers. Visio calls any type of custom data that you store in a shape *custom properties* data. The data is entered in a shape's custom property *fields* under field names like Inventory Number or Owner. Many Visio shapes have built-in custom property fields. For example, all office layout shapes include inventory number and owner fields. Flowchart shapes contain fields for recording cost, duration, and resources.

Surprise! Some Visio shapes don't have custom properties fields. (Some shapes are too ordinary for you to care about storing data in them.) To find out if a shape has custom property fields, select the shape; then choose Shape➪Custom Properties. Or you can right-click the shape and then click Shape➪Custom Properties. If the shape contains custom property fields, Visio displays a Custom Properties dialog box like the one shown in Figure 12-1. If not, a message appears saying no custom properties exist.

Figure 12-1: When a shape has custom properties, the data is displayed in the Custom Properties dialog box.

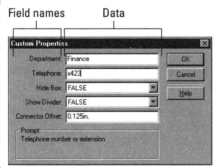

Entering custom properties data

When a Visio shape already contains custom properties fields, entering the data is easy:

1. **Open the drawing where you want to store data in shapes.**

2. **Click the shape where want to store data.**

3. **Choose Shape➪Custom Properties or right-click the shape, and then choose Shape➪Custom Properties.**

   Visio displays a Custom Properties dialog box like the one shown in Figure 12-1. The fields in the box are different depending on the shape you select in Step 1.

4. **In each field, enter the data that you want to store.**

5. **Click OK.**

Editing custom properties fields

The custom properties fields for Visio shapes are predefined, but that doesn't mean that you can't change them. You can, with the Custom Properties Editor. Visio lets you do this so that the fields are meaningful to your particular situation. If "materials" better describes what you want to track than "resources," why not change the field name? Or suppose that you want to create an office layout drawing, but for each equipment shape, you want to store data on serial numbers, manufacturers, and acquisition dates in addition to the fields already provided. You need to add custom property fields.

Use the Custom Properties Editor to change, add, or delete fields in a Visio shape. Or use the editor to add fields to a custom shape you created. In either case, you edit the custom property fields for each shape individually in either the local stencil or the standalone stencil. When you edit the fields of shapes in the standalone stencil, the changes affect the shapes in the current drawing and every other drawing you create using that stencil. If you edit property fields of shapes in the local stencil instead, only the shapes in the current drawing are affected. (Aha! Don't remember what local and stand-alone stencils are? Refer to Chapter 11.)

Although deleting custom property fields is possible, it's best not to do this with Visio-created shapes because doing so may affect other aspects of the shape's behavior that you're not aware of. Feel free, however, to add, change, or delete fields from custom shapes that you create.

The Custom Properties Editor is actually a wizard, so using it is very easy. (Refer to Chapter 10 for more information on using wizards). Follow these steps:

1. **Choose Tools⇨Macro⇨Macros⇨Custom Properties Editor.**

   Visio displays the Custom Properties Editor Wizard.

2. **In the first screen, choose the stencil or drawing where you want to edit custom properties; then click Next (see Figure 12-2).**

   The choice you make determines which wizard screens you see next.

3. **Follow the rest of the screens until the end; then click Finish.**

As you work through the stencil screens, be prepared to provide the name of the drawing or stencil whose shapes you want to edit. If you're adding custom properties fields to a shape, choose names for the fields that you want to add before you start the wizard. Be sure to click the More Info buttons in the wizard to get details on the information that the wizard asks for.

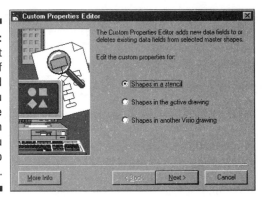

Figure 12-2:
The first
screen of
the wizard
lets you
choose
which
shapes you
want to
change.

Want to test whether your custom property fields have really changed? Drag a shape into your drawing from the stencil you edited (either the local stencil or a standalone stencil). Right-click the shape, and then choose Shape⇨ Custom Properties. The Custom Properties dialog box appears, and the changes you made to the field names are shown in the dialog box. Now you can enter the data to be stored.

Reporting on Data Stored in Visio Shapes

What would be the point of storing data in shapes unless you could report on it somehow? Data just sitting in a shape is of limited use as reference information; it's much more useful as a report of some kind. Visio provides the tools that you need to generate inventory reports and numeric reports from the data stored in your drawing's shapes. An inventory report typically counts items (or counts and totals duplicate items). For a numeric report, you can add simple calculations (such as totals, averages, maximums, minimums, and so on), or you can include more complex calculations using spreadsheet formulas.

Now add one more dimension to the picture. When you use layers in your drawing, you can report more precisely on the data stored in shapes. For example, in a space plan drawing, you may have plumbing on one layer, electrical on another, structural walls on another, and cubicle walls, dividers and fixed furniture on another layer. Now you have the flexibility to create reports for one layer at a time, a combination of layers, or all layers.

Creating a report

When you're ready to create an inventory or numeric report from data stored in shapes, choose Tools⇨Property Report. This command starts the Property Reporting Wizard, which guides you step-by-step through the process of creating a report. Wondering how to specify mathematical calculations for a report? Don't worry, the wizard asks you. Or maybe you want to know how to select shapes or layers to report on? The wizard asks you this, too. I encourage you to experiment with the wizard until you get the results that you want. Remember, each screen in a wizard has a Back button in case you change your mind about any choices you make.

Midway through the wizard screens, Visio creates and displays the report in a spreadsheet-type format. Think of it as sort of a trial report because you can always change it. If you're happy with the report and want to save it outside of Visio, you can save it as a spreadsheet in a Microsoft Excel (.xls) file or as a text (.txt) file by clicking the Save tool on the wizard screen just above the spreadsheet grid. (This looks like a disk, just like the Save button on the Standard toolbar.) If you want to change anything about the report, click the Back button to go back to the wizard and make changes to the spreadsheet/report data.

When the report is the way that you want it, the wizard asks you more questions about how you want the report formatted (add a title, column headings, filename, other explanations, and so on). When you click Finish on the last wizard screen, the data is pasted into your drawing, not as a spreadsheet, but in a special report shape that looks similar to the table shown in Figure 12-3.

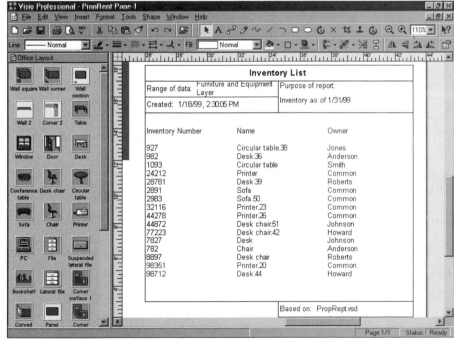

Figure 12-3:
This
furniture
and
equipment
inventory
was
generated
by the
Property
Reporting
Wizard.

Updating reports

After you spend time creating reports, do you want to re-create them every time your data changes? I'm guessing not. Fortunately, Visio understands this, so it lets you update existing reports with new data using — you guessed it — the Property Reporting Wizard. The wizard can update a report as long as the report is complete and pasted into your drawing in a report shape like the one shown in Figure 12-3. If you saved the report data as a spreadsheet when you originally created the report, the Property Reporting Wizard generates a new spreadsheet when you update the report. When the new spreadsheet appears, you can save it under a new name or overwrite the previous file.

To update a report, use these steps:

1. **In your drawing, right-click the report shape.**

   The shortcut menu appears. (See Figure 12-4.)

2. **Choose Update Property Report.**

   The Property Reporting Wizard begins loading and updates your report data.

3. **If you originally saved the report data as a spreadsheet, the wizard displays a new spreadsheet reflecting the updated data. To save the spreadsheet, click the Save tool above the spreadsheet.**

Voilà! The wizard finishes its task and updates the report shape in the drawing.

Figure 12-4:
Choose
Update
Property
Report from
the shortcut
menu.

Customizing Shape Behavior

Are you tired yet of hearing about how smart the Visio shapes are? Well, don't go to sleep on me yet, because there's more. Visio lets you set a shape's behavior. You can pick and choose how you want a shape to behave and choose the characteristics that you want it to have.

You can define the behavior and attributes of any shape: a Visio shape or a shape that you create. After you change the behavior of a shape on a drawing, the drawing's local stencil (a sort of "history log" stencil that's stored with your drawing) contains the shape so that you can use it again and again in that drawing. If you want to use the shape in other drawings, you need to save the shape as a master on a standalone stencil — a Visio stencil or one that you create. (For details on saving a shape as a master, see Chapter 11.)

Using the SmartShape Wizard

If you want to change several aspects of a shape's attributes all in one place, using the SmartShape Wizard is the best way to do it. This wizard addresses four major areas of shape behavior and appearance:

- ✔ **Text:** You can decide where a shape's text box is located, choose whether text rotates when you rotate the shape, and decide whether the font size adjusts automatically based on the amount of text in the text box.

- ✔ **Built-in connectors:** For shapes that have none, you can add built-in connectors so that you can pull a connector from a shape.

- ✔ **Hidden note:** You can add to a shape a hidden note or comment that you can show or hide using a command on the shortcut menu.

- ✔ **Protect shape attributes:** You can lock certain attributes (like the size, position, or formatting style) of a shape so that it can't be changed.

In the following section ("Setting shape behavior with a menu command") you see that the Visio Format menu has commands for controlling shape behavior, shape protection, and double-click behavior. If you compare the options available on these commands to the SmartShape Wizard, you notice that some of the options are the same; some are different. So, how do you know whether to use the SmartShape Wizard or the menu commands? As a general guideline, using the SmartShape Wizard is best when you want to make more global changes to a shape — changes that you may want to save and apply to a master shape that you can use in many drawings. Use the commands on the Format menu when you want to make changes to selected shapes.

To use the SmartShape Wizard, follow these steps:

1. **Open the drawing that contains the shape that you want to change.**

2. **Click the shape whose behavior you want to define.**

3. **Choose Tools⇨Macro⇨Macros⇨SmartShape Wizard, which displays the screen shown in Figure 12-5.**

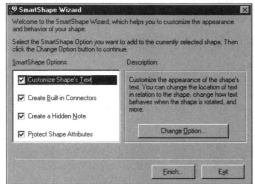

Figure 12-5:
Choose any
of the four
options on
the
SmartShape
Wizard's
first screen.

4. **On the left side of the first screen of the wizard, click all the options that you want to change.**

5. **Click the Change Option button.**

   Visio displays a screen with questions about the first option that you checked.

6. **Click Next.**

   When you've answered all the questions for the first option that you checked, the wizard returns to the first screen. (For some options, the wizard may display two or three screens of questions.)

7. **Repeat Steps 5 and 6 until you complete all options that you checked.**

8. **Click Finish.**

Setting shape behavior with a menu command

The Visio format menu also has a command for changing shape behavior. Format➪Behavior lets you choose how a shape behaves (as a one-dimensional or two-dimensional shape), how a shape is displayed on the screen, how the shape is resized when it's part of a group, and how its connectors behave — that is, whether its connectors are routable or not. For more information about routable connectors, refer to Chapter 5.

If these are the attributes that you want to set, use the Format➪Behavior command rather than the SmartShape Wizard.

Here's how to use the Format⇨Behavior command:

1. **In your drawing, select the shape or shapes that you want to change.**

2. **Choose Format⇨Behavior.**

   Visio displays the Behavior dialog box shown in Figure 12-6.

3. **In the Interaction Style box, choose whether you want the selected shape to behave as a 1-D or 2-D shape.**

4. **In the Selection Highlighting box, choose the shape attributes that you want to be visible when the shape is selected in the drawing.**

5. **In the Resize Behavior box, choose how you want the selected shape to behave if it's grouped with other shapes.**

6. **In the Layout Behavior box, choose how you want the shape's connectors to behave when connectors cross.**

7. **If you want the selected shape to appear on the screen but not in your printed copy, click the Non-Printing Shape option.**

8. **Click OK.**

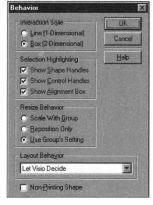

Figure 12-6:
Use the
Behavior
dialog box
to change
the behavior
of selected
shapes.

Use the commands on the Format menu when you want to make changes to selected shapes.

Setting a shape's double-click behavior

One of the coolest features of Visio is the ability to set how a shape behaves when you double-click it. Until now, you've only seen a shape's text box open when you double-click the shape, but you have a bunch of other choices. You can have it open a group of shapes, display a help screen, run a macro, jump to another page in the drawing, or do nothing.

Jumping to another page is a way to create what's known as a *drill-down* drawing. Figure 12-7 shows an overview diagram of a wide area network (WAN) covering China, Taiwan, and Japan. The map is impressive enough on its own, but the really slick feature is that you can drill-down to another page of the drawing that shows a detail map.

When you double-click the shape, Visio switches to the drawing called China LAN, shown in Figure 12-8. This map is the second page of the same drawing shown in Figure 12-7. Now that you're here, how to you get back? Check out the callout in the upper right of the drawing. When you double-click it, Visio returns to Page 1 of the drawing.

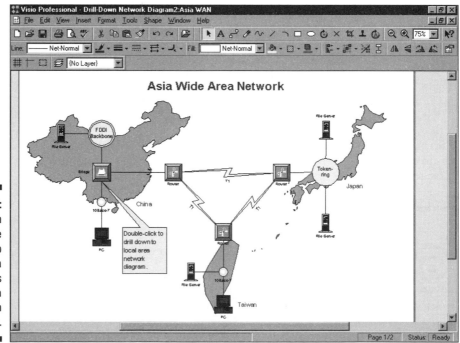

Figure 12-7:
An impressive map showing a company's wide area network in Asia.

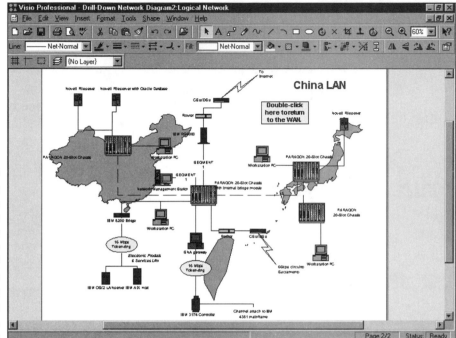

Figure 12-8:
A detail map
of China's
LAN is
actually
Page 2 of
the same
drawing
shown in
Figure 12-7.

Use these steps to set a shape's double-click behavior:

1. **In your drawing, select the shape that you want to change.**

2. **Choose Format⇨Double-Click.**

   Visio displays the Double-Click dialog box shown in Figure 12-9.

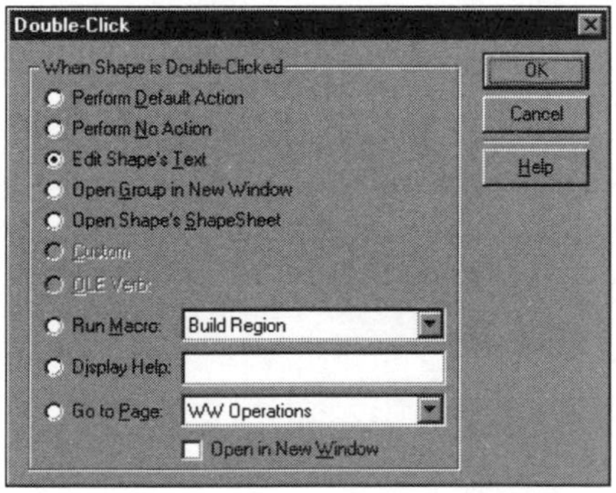

Figure 12-9:
Use the
Double-
Click dialog
box to set
what a
shape does
when you
double-
click it.

3. **Choose one of the options listed.**

   If you choose Run <u>M</u>acro, click the down arrow to select a macro from the list.

   If you choose Go to <u>P</u>age, click the down arrow to select a drawing page.

4. **For the Go to Page option, you can have Visio display the page in a new window by checking the Open in New <u>W</u>indow option.**

5. **Click OK.**

Protecting Your Work

When you create drawings that you're going to share with others, you want to protect your work from unwitting destroyers. You can protect entire drawings from change, or you can protect selected aspects of a shape from change. There are several methods for protecting your work, as you discover in this section.

Keeping shapes secure from change

Using either the SmartShape Wizard or a menu command, you can keep shapes in a drawing from being changed. When you use the wizard, you have more locking options than with the menu command. Both of these options are described in this section.

Securing with the SmartShape Wizard

Earlier in this chapter you saw how you can use the SmartShape Wizard to change many aspects of a shape, one of which is its *protection*. You protect a shape by "locking" it, or certain aspects of it. When you run the SmartShape Wizard and choose the Protect Shape Attributes option, the wizard displays the screen shown in Figure 12-10. You can use the SmartShape Wizard to set protection on any of the attributes shown in Figure 12-10.

The lock options listed in Figure 12-10 are self-explanatory. When an option is grayed out, it doesn't apply to the shape that's currently selected. For example, when you select a single, ungrouped shape to lock, the Prevent Ungrouping option doesn't apply, so it's grayed in the dialog box.

Figure 12-10:
Use the
SmartShape
Wizard
to set
protection
on one or
more shape
attributes.

To run the SmartShape Wizard for shape protection, use these steps:

1. **Open the drawing that contains the shape that you want to protect.**

2. **Select the shape or shapes that you want to protect.**

   To select more than one shape, hold down the Shift key as you click shapes.

3. **Choose Tools⇨Macro⇨Macros⇨SmartShape Wizard (refer to Figure 12-5).**

4. **Click the Protect Shape Attributes option.**

5. **Click the Change Option button. Visio displays the screen shown in Figure 12-10.**

6. **Click Next; then click Finish.**

If you want the protection to apply to the shape every time you use the shape, add the shape to a standalone stencil (see Chapter 11).

Using a menu command to lock your shape

Another way to lock aspects of a shape is by choosing Format⇨Protection, which displays the dialog box shown in Figure 12-11. Like the SmartShape Wizard, this command lets you lock aspects of a shape to prevent them from being changed. Notice that all the options listed in the Protection dialog box are available using the SmartShape Wizard as well, but the wizard includes additional lock options. If you want to lock only one aspect of a shape, using this command is quicker than using the wizard. Also, when you want to unlock an aspect of a shape, using the Format⇨Protection command may be quicker than the wizard.

Figure 12-11:
To protect
shapes,
choose
options
in the
Protection
dialog box.

To lock selected aspects of a shape using the Format⇨Protection command, follow these steps:

1. **Open the drawing that contains the shape that you want to protect.**

2. **Select the shape or shapes that you want to protect.**

   To select more than one shape, hold down the Shift key as you click the shapes.

3. **Choose Format⇨Protection, which displays the dialog box shown in Figure 12-11.**

4. **Click each shape aspect that you want to lock.**

5. **Click OK.**

If you choose to protect a shape from selection, be aware that you must also use the Tools⇨Protect Document command, and then choose the Shapes option to make a shape unselectable. The Tools⇨Protect Document command is described in the following section.

Keeping drawings secure

You have several options for protecting drawings from change. The method that you choose depends on the results that you want to achieve. All the methods make a drawing readable by others but not changeable (to whatever degree you define).

Password-protecting a drawing

Password protection probably isn't what you expect it to be. Password protection does *not* prevent a drawing from being opened without a password; rather, it protects certain *aspects* of the drawing from change. For example, when you password-protect a drawing, you can choose to protect styles, backgrounds, shapes, and master shapes, which means other users can't change these aspects of the file without knowing the password and unprotecting the file.

The Backgrounds option is a good solution for partially locking a drawing. For example, if you want other users to be able to edit the actual drawing but not the shapes on the background page, protect only the background. You can also protect shapes from change, but *beware!* To protect shapes, you must password-protect the drawing *in addition to* using the Format➪ Protection command to protect shapes from selection. If you do one without the other, shapes are *not* protected from change.

Use these steps to password-protect a drawing from specific changes:

1. **Open the drawing that you want to protect.**

2. **Choose Tools➪Protect Document.**

   Visio opens the dialog box shown in Figure 12-12.

3. **Enter a password in the Password box.**

   (*Don't* forget your password, and don't forget how you used uppercase and lowercase characters!)

4. **Check any or all of the drawing aspects (styles, backgrounds, shapes, or master shapes) that you want to protect.**

5. **Click OK.**

When you want to make changes to the drawing again, choose Tools➪ Unprotect Document and enter your password. This unlocks the file.

Figure 12-12:
The Protect
Document
dialog box.

Locking layers

A great way to protect parts of a drawing is to lock layers. If you want other users to be able to edit certain layers but not others, locking layers is a perfect solution. When a layer is locked, shapes on that layer can't be selected or changed in any way. Be aware, however, that if the other user knows how to unlock the layer, shapes on that layer can be changed. (You can't password-protect a layer.)

To lock one or more layers of a drawing, do this:

1. **Open the drawing whose layers you want to protect.**

2. **Right-click the toolbar area and select the View toolbar from the drop-down menu.**

3. **Click the Layer Properties tool (it looks like a stack of pages) on the View toolbar to display the Layer Properties dialog box.**

4. **In the dialog box, put a check mark in the Lock column for each layer that you want to lock.**

5. **Click OK.**

Saving files as read-only

If you truly want to keep other users from changing a drawing, the best way to protect it is to save the drawing as a read-only file. No matter what other protections are set in the drawing or the file, the file can't be changed. The only way another user can work around changing the file is to save a writable version of the file under a different name and then change that file, but in that case your file is still protected.

To save a file as read-only, follow these steps:

1. **Open the drawing that you want to save as a read-only file.**

2. **Choose File⇨Save As.**

   Visio displays the Save As dialog box shown in Figure 12-13.

3. **Click the drop-down arrow on the Save In box to select the folder where you want to save the file.**

4. **In the File Name box, type the name that you want to use to save the file.**

5. **In the Save box, click the Read-Only check box.**

6. **Click Save.**

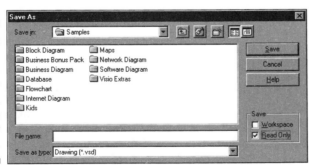

Figure 12-13:
To protect a drawing from any changes, choose the Read Only option.

Chapter 13

Using Visio with Other Programs

• •

• •

*I*t seems pretty rare that I ever use files from one computer program all by themselves anymore. This chapter shows you how to incorporate Visio drawings in other programs and how to create Visio drawings using data stored in other programs. I also show you how to e-mail Visio drawings and use them on the Internet.

Creating Drawings from Data in Other Programs

Hey, want to save yourself some work? If you have data stored in other programs such as Microsoft Excel, Microsoft Project, a database, or a simple text file, you can create drawings from your stored data. Why would you want to do that? Check out these three good reasons:

✔ **You can avoid re-entering data.** Maybe you have a lot of data that already exists in another program, such as an Excel database. Do you want to take the time to re-enter it all in Visio — just so that you can create a drawing? Probably not — and you shouldn't have to. If the data already exists, you can save yourself a lot of time by saving the file in a format that Visio can use to create a drawing for you.

✔ **You can enter the data in the program where you use it most.** If your data doesn't already exist, sometimes it can be faster to enter the raw data in another program — the program where you really need the data — and have Visio do the work of creating a drawing for you.

> ✔ **You can share drawings with other Visio users who may not have the same applications that you use to store and compile data.** Suppose that you're a project manager and rely on Microsoft Project to schedule and track large projects. Your site managers, however, don't have Project on site, but they do have Visio. You can use Project to generate daily or weekly Gantt charts (a type of chart that maps project tasks on a timeline) in Visio and e-mail them to your site managers to keep them up-to-date. They don't need to have Project or know how to use it; all they need to do is open a Visio drawing.

Creating organization charts

It's easy to create Visio organization charts from employee data stored in a database, Excel, comma separated variable (.csv) files, or text files. (You can create comma separated variable files and text files using any text editor or word processing program.) The data must be set up in a format that Visio can work with.

In database and spreadsheet files:

> ✔ Columns represent fields
> ✔ The first row represents column headings
> ✔ Remaining rows represent records

In a text file or comma separated variable (.csv) file:

> ✔ The first row represents column headings
> ✔ Remaining rows represent records

Because a comma separated variable (.csv) file has no columns, individual fields are separated by a comma. (This is known as a *comma-delimited* file; the comma is a *delimiter.*) Text files typically separate individual fields by a tab.

To generate a Visio organization chart from a data file, the file must include these three fields:

> ✔ A unique identifier for each employee; whether a name or number
> ✔ Employee name
> ✔ The person the employee reports to

Figure 13-1 illustrates how a comma separated variable file that's used as input for generating an organization chart should look.

```
Unique_ID,Name,Position,Reports_To,Department,Telephone,Master_Shape
F11,Ben Wyss,Corp Controller,F10,Finances,x300,Position
M11,Chris Klustner,Mkt Mgr-Mkt Dev,M10,Marketing,x269,Position
F12,Dave Vollan Cole,Customer Svc Mgr,F10,Finances,x304,Position
S10,Eric Philip,VP Sales,A10,Sales,x283,Manager
M10,Geraldine Gigot,VP Marketing,A10,Marketing,x285,Manager
A11,Jason Pinkston,Executive Assistant,A10,Operations,x340,Assistant
S11,Karl Collins,Dir-Channel Sales,S10,Sales,x343,Position
F13,Keri Myrick,IS Manager,F10,Finances,x301,Position
S12,Kristi Horsburgh,Mnging Dir-France,S10,Sales,x346,Position
D11,Matt DeWilliam,Doc Manager,D10,Product Development,x338,Position
S13,Michelle Habert,Mnging Dir-GB,S10,Sales,x345,Position
M12,Morgan Cormier,Demonst.Mktg Mgr,M10,Marketing,x267,Position
F10,Peter Chilberg,CFO & VP F&O,A10,Finances,x284,Manager
D10,Regis Johnson,VP Product Dev.,A10,Product Development,x286,Manager
A10,Susan Jaech,CEO & Pres,,x352,Executive
D12,Ted Mullen,VISIO Dev Mgr,D10,Product Development,x349,Position
F14,Tim Scoble,Mgr FP&A,F10,Finances,x302,Position
S14,Ursula Grosskreutz,Mnging Dir-Germany,S10,Sales,x344,Position
```

Figure 13-1:
A sample of
a comma
separated
variable
(.csv) file.

Unique identifier   Blank field   └─Person employee reports to

The fields don't have to appear in any particular order; the wizard finds the data it needs based on the column headings. To leave a field blank, enter a comma between the two commas used to separate entries (in an Excel file, leave the cell blank). Notice that in Figure 13-1 a final field, Master_Shape, is added to the data file. This is not required, but you can use it if you want to choose a specific Visio shape for your data. If you want, you can include more data fields in the organization chart, such as the employee's phone number or physical location.

TIP

A comprehensive database compiled by the human resources department of a large corporation may include 30 or more fields of data on each employee (department, address, home phone number, social security number, date of birth, and so on). If your data file is this large, just generate a subset comprised of the data that you want to use, and then use that file as input for Visio.

To create an organization chart from an existing data file, use these steps:

1. **Start Visio, using a blank drawing.**

2. **Choose Tools⇨Macro⇨Business Diagram⇨Organization Chart Wizard.**

   Visio displays the first screen of the wizard.

3. Click **N**ext to go to the second screen of the wizard (see Figure 13-2).

4. **Choose the source of your data; then click Next.**

   - **Click the No Source radio button** if you don't have a data file.

   - **Click the ODBC Data source radio button** if your data is stored in an ODBC (Open Database Connectivity) database file like Access, Oracle SQL Server, or Microsoft SQL Server.

   - **Click the Enter Data in a New Text File or Enter Data in New Microsoft Excel Workbook radio button** if your data doesn't exist yet and you want to create it. When you choose either of these options, the wizard creates a *template* Excel or text file that includes all the required column headings for your data.

   - **Click the Read Data From Existing File radio button** if your data exists in a spreadsheet file (like Excel), text file, or comma separated variable file.

5. **Follow the wizard (which asks questions about the design and layout of the organization chart) through to the last screen, and then click Finish.**

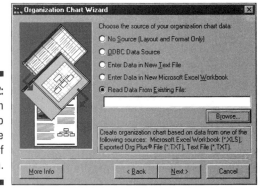

Figure 13-2:
This screen asks you to choose the source of your data.

Visio creates the organization chart based on your data file, the fields that you choose to include, and the format you specify. If the chart has some unexpected results, go back and check the format and content of your input file, and then run the wizard again. The wizard creates a new file each time you run it.

If you choose an option in Step 4 for creating new data, create and save the data; then run the wizard again, choosing Read Data From Existing File in Step 4.

The More Info button on most wizard screens is very helpful! If you ever need an explanation of the information the wizard's looking for, click this button to display a More Information dialog box.

Creating project timelines

A project timeline includes information about the tasks that you need to complete to accomplish a goal, the duration of each task, their dependent tasks, and the resources required to complete each task. If the data that you want to use exists in a text (.txt) file or comma separated variable (.csv) file, fields must be separated by a tab or a comma. You can also use data from Microsoft Excel in .xls format, or data from Microsoft Project in exchange format (.mpx). The data must include at least the following fields for each task:

- **Dependent task:** A task that can't be started until another task is completed; if the first task slips, the entire list of dependent tasks slip.
- **Duration:** The time allowed to complete a task.
- **End date:** The date that you want a task to be completed.
- **Resource:** The human resources or materials needed to complete a task.
- **Start date:** The date that you want a task to begin.
- **Task name:** The name that you give to a task that's part of a project.
- **Unique task number or identifier:** Any number or name that you give to a task to identify it uniquely from other tasks.

The Project Timeline Wizard can create a .txt or .xls template for you if your data doesn't exist yet. This saves you the time of setting up your text or Excel file with the required fields. Just use the template and fill in the data as I describe in the following steps.

To create a project timeline, use these steps:

1. **Start Visio, using a blank drawing.**

2. **Choose Tools➪Macro➪Business Diagram➪Project Timeline Wizard.**

   Visio displays the first screen of the wizard.

3. **Click Next.**

   Visio displays the second screen of the wizard.

4. **Choose the source of your data; then click Next.**

   - **Click the Enter Data in New Text File or Enter Data in New Excel Workbook radio button** if you want to create the data.

   - **Click the No Data radio button** if you don't have a data file.

- **Click the Enter Data in a New Text File or Enter Data in New Microsoft Excel Workbook radio button** if your data doesn't exist yet and you want to create it. When you choose either of these options, the wizard creates a *template* text or Excel file that includes all the required column headings for your data.

- **Click the Import MPX File radio button** if your data exists in a Microsoft Project Exchange (.mpx) file.

- **Click the Read Data From Existing File radio button** if your data exists in a spreadsheet file (like Excel), text file, or comma separated variable file.

5. **If you specified a data file in Step 4, finish the wizard. If you're entering new data, save the data file and then restart the wizard.**

When you finish the wizard, it creates a Gantt chart for you automatically. A Gantt chart is a type of chart that maps project tasks against a calendar or timeline.

Using Visio in Non-Visio Documents

The Windows object linking and embedding (OLE) feature makes it possible to share many different types of data and graphic images between Windows-compatible applications. You can insert Visio shapes or drawings into other documents, such as a Word document. Or you can do the opposite; insert data or images from another application into Visio. This section describes the different methods for sharing data and images between programs.

Dragging or pasting shapes

If you want to use one of the Visio shapes in another document, the easiest way is to drag it right in! If both programs support Windows OLE (Object Linking and Embedding, discussed in the sections "Linking shapes and drawings" and "Embedding shapes and drawings" later in this chapter), you can drag shapes from Visio into the program. Use these steps to copy a shape or an entire drawing to another document:

1. **Open the Visio drawing or stencil with the shape that you want to use.**

2. **Open the other application (such as Word or Excel) and the file where you want to insert a Visio shape.**

3. **Click the Maximize/Restore button (which looks just like the one in Windows) in Visio to make the Visio window smaller than full screen.**

4. **Click the Maximize/Restore button in the other application to make the window smaller than full screen.**

5. **Arrange the windows on the screen so that you can see the shape that you want to drag and a blank portion of the other document window.**

6. **To copy a shape (rather than just moving it), press and hold the Ctrl key, and then drag the shape from Visio into the other application's document area.**

    If you want to insert an entire Visio drawing in another document, choose Edit⇨Select All, press and hold the Ctrl key, and then drag so that the shapes are copied instead of moved.

    When you release the mouse button, the shape or shapes are pasted into your document.

You can also use the Cut, Copy, and Paste commands to accomplish the task of including a Visio shape in another document. The following steps show you how.

1. **Open the Visio drawing or stencil with the shape that you want to use.**

2. **Open the other application (such as Word or Excel) and the file where you want to insert a Visio shape.**

3. **Click the Maximize/Restore button (which looks just like the one in Windows) in Visio to make the Visio window smaller than full screen.**

4. **Click the Maximize/Restore button in the other application to make the window smaller than full screen.**

5. **Arrange the windows on the screen so that you can see the shape that you want to drag and a blank portion of the other document window.**

6. **In your drawing, select the shape or shapes that you want to paste in the other document.**

7. **To cut the shape or shapes from Visio, choose Edit⇨Cut or press Ctrl-X. To copy the shape from Visio, choose Edit⇨Copy or press Ctrl-C.**

8. **Click the other document where you want to paste the shape or shapes; then choose Edit⇨Paste or press Ctrl-V.**

    The shape or shapes are pasted into the other document.

Neither of the methods I just described (dragging or pasting shapes) makes any connection between the two files; these steps are similar to dropping a clip-art image into a document. No association or connection between the two files or the data in each file is formed.

Linking shapes and drawings

Another way to share data (text, shapes, or drawings) between programs is to *link* data from one file to another. I can show you how to link Visio data to other files and be done with it, but you need to understand the difference between linking and embedding, which I describe later in the section called "Embedding shapes and drawings."

Linking creates a special connection between two files: the *source file* (where the data is created and displayed) and the *destination file* (where the data is displayed only). When you link data to a destination file, the original data stays in the source file where you created it; it never really moves anywhere. The destination file makes a note of the *location* of the data, and looks to that location to display a *representation of the data.*

Still scratching your head? Think of it like this. Suppose you link a Visio drawing (the source file) to an Excel spreadsheet (the destination file). When you open your Excel spreadsheet, you see the Visio drawing displayed right before your eyes — like magic! But it isn't really there. It's as if Excel opened up a door in the spreadsheet, then moved your drawing right into the doorway. You see the drawing, but it isn't part of your Excel file. You still have only one drawing, and it's located in Visio.

So why do you care if the drawing is part of your destination file or not? Several reasons. When you update the drawing in Visio, the drawing is automatically updated in the other program, too. And, since the drawing isn't really part of the destination file, it doesn't increase your file size at all. One more thing. If you want, you can double-click the drawing in the other program and update it there. How is that possible, since the drawing isn't really in the other program? More magic. When you double-click the drawing, Visio actually starts up and opens your drawing in its own window so that you can update the drawing using Visio menus and toolbars. When you finish updating the drawing and save it, close Visio. Your screen returns to the other program, where the file is automatically updated if you saved the changes in Visio.

All of these reasons make linking a good option to choose when you want to use a drawing in several different files and keep it updated in all its locations. You can link an entire Visio drawing or selected shapes from a Visio drawing to a document in any program that supports OLE (Object Linking and Embedding). Most Windows programs support OLE.

To link data from a Visio drawing to another file, follow these steps:

1. **In Visio, open the drawing that you want to link to another file.**

   Note that the file must be saved first before it can be linked.

2. **To link the entire drawing, choose Edit⇨Copy Drawing. To link a portion of the drawing, select the shapes that you want to link, and then choose Edit⇨Copy.**

3. **Open the document in the other program where you want to link the Visio drawing.**

4. **Choose Edit⇨Paste Special.**

   (Some programs may use a different command for linking files. If this command is not on your menu, check the online help or user documentation for the program that you're using.)

5. **In the Paste Special dialog box, choose Visio 5 Drawing Object from the list box.**

6. **Click the Paste Link radio button; then click OK.**

   The drawing or shapes that you linked are now displayed in the other program's document.

Embedding shapes and drawings

Embedding offers another way to share data between files, but it's different from linking. In fact, in some ways you can think of it as the opposite of linking. When you embed data in another file, it actually becomes part of the destination file, which means that the size of the destination file increases. If you update the data in the source file, the data in the destination file is *not* automatically updated. (Likewise, if you change the data in the destination file, the data in the source file remains unchanged.) Embedding is a good option to use when you definitely want the data to be part of your destination file, when you know the data doesn't need to be updated, or if you aren't storing a copy of the source file on your computer.

You can embed a new file that you create, or you can embed an existing file. Use these steps:

1. **Open the document in the other program where you want to link the Visio drawing.**

2. **Choose Insert⇨Object, and the dialog box, shown in Figure 13-3, appears.**

   Notice that the Create New tab is selected.

Find an existing file   ⌐Create new file

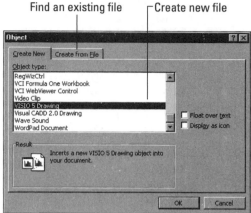

Figure 13-3:
Use the
Create New
tab in the
Object
dialog box
to create
a new
drawing
for your
document.

3. Embed your drawing in one of the following ways.

- **To create a new Visio drawing:** Choose Visio 5 Drawing from the list; then click OK.

    Visio starts up in its own window. Create your drawing; then click in the document window of the program that you're using. Visio automatically embeds the drawing in your document and closes the Visio window.

- **To embed an existing drawing:** Click the Create From File tab in the dialog box (see Figure 13-4), enter the file name, and click OK. (If you don't know the file name, click the Browse button to find the file.)

    Visio embeds the drawing in your document.

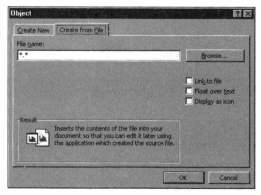

Figure 13-4:
On the
Create From
File tab in
the Object
dialog box,
choose an
existing
drawing.

When you use the Create New tab in the Object dialog box to create a new Visio drawing for your document, be aware that you can't save the drawing as a Visio file. If you want to save the drawing in Visio, create it first in Visio; then use the Create From File tab in the Object dialog box to embed the saved file.

Exporting shapes and drawings

When you want to use a Visio shape or drawing in another program that doesn't support OLE, your option is to *export* the file. Exporting converts the data in a Visio file to a non-Visio file format — one that you choose. In the other program, you then *import* the file as a picture.

The file type that you choose for exporting depends on the program that you want to use the drawing in and how you're going to use the drawing. For example, if you're creating a postscript document, you may want to export the Visio drawing in *.ps format. If you want to make changes to the drawing using Adobe Illustator, save the drawing in *.ai format. If you just want to insert the drawing into another file as a picture without editing it, use one of the more common graphics formats such as *.bmp, *.tif, or *.gif. If you want to give the drawing to a friend who uses a Mac, save the drawing in *.pct format. Table 13-1 lists all the file types that you can use to export a Visio drawing.

Table 13-1	File Formats for Exporting Visio Drawings
Format	**File Extension**
HTML	*.htm,*.html
Adobe Illustrator	*.ai
Computer graphics metafile	*.cgm
Encapsulated postscript	*.eps
Enhanced metafile	*.emf
Graphics interchange format	*.gif
IGES drawing file format	*.igs
Jpeg	*.jpg
Macintosh PICT format	*.pct
Portable network graphics format	*.png
Postscript file	*.ps
Tag image file format	*.tif
Windows bitmap	*.bmp, *.dib
Windows metafile	*.wmf
Zsoft PC paintbrush bitmap	*.pcx

To export a Visio drawing (or selected shapes from a drawing), follow these steps:

1. **Start Visio and open the drawing that you want to export.**

   If you want to export a few shapes rather than the whole drawing, hold down the Shift key as you click the shapes that you want to export.

2. **Choose File⇨Save As to display the Save As dialog box.**

3. **In the Save In drop-down menu, choose the folder where you want to save the drawing.**

4. **In the File Name box, type a name for the file.**

5. **In the Save As Type drop-down menu, choose a file format.**

6. **Click Save.**

In the other program, use the program's import command to bring the Visio drawing into the document. In many programs, the command is on the File menu (File⇨Import) and displays a dialog box.

Sending drawings via e-mail

If you use electronic mail and want to e-mail drawings to other Visio users, you can do so as along as your e-mail program supports the Messaging Application Program Interface (MAPI) protocol. (Check with your network administrator to see if your program supports MAPI protocol.) The message recipient must also have Visio running on his or her computer in order to view the Visio drawing.

To e-mail a drawing to another Visio user, use these steps:

1. **Start Visio and open the drawing that you want to send via e-mail.**

2. **Choose File⇨Send To⇨Mail Recipient.**

   If your mail program isn't running, it starts up automatically. A new e-mail message is created with a Visio icon and the Visio file name already placed in the file.

3. **Enter the recipient's e-mail address, subject, and any message that you want to appear with the file.**

4. **Send the message as you normally would.**

So, how do you view a Visio drawing sent to you by e-mail? Just start your e-mail program and display the e-mail message. The message contains a Visio icon for the drawing file. Double-click the icon to view the drawing.

If you're running Microsoft Office 97, you can use the Office features that let you route an e-mail message to more than one user (for instance, so all users in your group can review a Visio drawing). To add a routing slip to an e-mail message, follow these steps:

1. **Open Visio and the drawing that you want to send.**

2. **Choose File⇨Send To⇨Routing Recipient to display the Add Routing Slip dialog box shown in Figure 13-5.**

Figure 13-5:
Use the Add Routing Slip dialog box to send a Visio drawing to several people

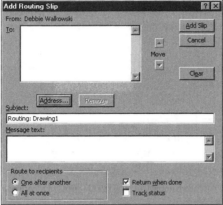

3. **Click the Address button to choose the recipients that you want to send the Visio drawing to. When you've added all the names that you want, click OK.**

4. **To route the drawing in a specific order, click a name in the list and then click the Move arrow (either up or down) to reorder the names.**

   Do this for all names until they are in the order that you want.

5. **In the Route to Recipients box, click the One After Another option if you're ordering the routing. If not, click the All at Once option.**

6. **Choose Return When Done to have the drawing sent back to you after everyone views it, or choose Track Status to receive an update after each person on the list views the drawing.**

7. **To add a message to the drawing, type the text in the Message Text box.**

8. **Click Add Slip to close this dialog box.**

9. **Choose File⇨Send To⇨Next Routing Recipient to send the message.**

To store a drawing in a Microsoft Exchange folder, open the Visio drawing, then choose File⇨Send To⇨Exchange Folder. Choose the folder that you want, then click OK.

Using Visio Drawings on the Internet

Okay, admit it. You're so proud of your Visio drawings that you're dying to publish them on your Web site, right? Well, now you can. You can save your drawings in HTML (Hypertext Markup Language) format when you create them, or you can convert existing files to HTML format. Either way, your drawings look as cool on your Web page as they do in Visio.

Adding hyperlinks to a drawing

A hyperlink is nothing more than a techie-sounding word for a *jump*. With just a click of the mouse, you can jump from the current page in your Visio drawing to another location. Using a hyperlink is sort of like setting a shape's double-click behavior, which lets you jump to another *page* in a drawing (I show you all about this in Chapter 12). But if you want to jump to another Visio drawing, a file in another program, or a Web site on the World Wide Web, follow these steps:

1. **Open the saved Visio drawing where you want to create a hyperlink.**

   Your Visio drawing must be a saved file because the link is created by referencing your drawing's file name.

2. **To create a hyperlink from a page in the drawing, make sure that no shapes in the drawing are selected. To create a hyperlink from a specific shape, select the shape.**

3. **Choose Insert⇨Hyperlink.**

   Visio displays the Hyperlink dialog box shown in Figure 13-6.

4. **In the Link to File or URL box, type the full path name for the file that you want to open, or type the URL.**

   The location you name is called the *linked file.*

   • **To enter a file path name:** Type the full directory name for a file on your own computer's hard disk or one that you have access to on a local network.

   • **To enter a URL (Uniform Resource Locator):** Type a Web site address on the World Wide Web, such as http://www.visio.com or http://www.microsoft.com. The http:// indicates the protocol used to access the site. It's important that you include this in the URL. (Some sites use ftp:// or other protocols.)

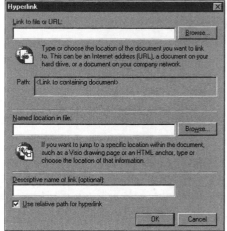

Figure 13-6:
In the
Hyperlink
dialog box,
tell Visio
where you
want to
jump to.

If you don't know the path or URL, click the Browse button. After you type your entry, the full path name appears in the Path box.

5. **In the Descriptive Name of Link box, you can type a name that describes the location that you're linking to.**

   This step is optional.

6. **Click OK.**

To use your hyperlink, right-click the shape or drawing page, choose Hyperlink, and then choose Open or Open in New Window. Open in New Window lets you see the hyperlink, as well as your Visio drawing.

Saving a drawing as an HTML page

If you want Visio to create a Web page for you and include your drawing in it, saving the drawing as an HTML page is the way to go. If you save a multi-page drawing as an HTML page, Visio creates a separate HTML page for each page in the drawing. If your drawing includes hyperlinks — pointers in your drawing to other locations in the drawing, to other files, or to other locations on the World Wide Web — saving it in HTML format preserves the links, making it an *image map,* another name for a graphic file that has hyperlinks.

To save a drawing as an HTML page use these steps:

1. **Start Visio and create or open the file that you want to save.**

2. **Choose File⇨Save As to display the Save As dialog box shown in Figure 13-7.**

Figure 13-7:
Use the
familiar
Save As
dialog box
to save a
drawing in
HTML
format.

3. **In the Save In box, choose the folder where you want to save the file.**

4. **In the File Name box, type a name for the file, including the *.htm* file extension.**

5. **In the Save As Type box, choose HTML files (*.htm, *.html).**

6. **Click Save.**

   The Save As HTML dialog box, shown in Figure 13-8, appears.

7. **Click the Filter Settings button if you want to specify zoom percentage, dots per inch (dpi), or screen resolution on the web page; then click OK.**

Figure 13-8:
Click the
Filter
Settings
button in the
Save As
HTML dialog
box.

8. **If your drawing includes hyperlinks that you don't want to appear in the Web page, click the Options button.**

   In the Export Options dialog box that appears, uncheck the Enable Image Maps check box; then click OK.

9. **Click OK again to close the Save As HTML dialog box.**

   Visio displays a message asking if you want to view the HTML page. Click Yes to view the page using your Web browser.

Part V
The Part of Tens

The 5th Wave   By Rich Tennant

"Correction, Dad—Mom goes at the top of the organizational chart."

In this part . . .

The Part of Tens — a mysterious name that indicates you're going to learn at least ten things about *something!* In this Part of Tens, you discover answers to the ten most frequently asked questions from Visio's top trainers, survey ten of Visio's interesting stencils and wizards, find out ten terrific tips for using Visio, and see ten sample drawings.

Chapter 14

Answers to Ten (Or So) Burning Questions about Visio

- -

In This Chapter

▶ Using other file types and saving files where you want them

▶ Choosing the right template

▶ Finding a shape

▶ Customizing your drawing environment

▶ Viewing multiple pages and copying formatting

▶ Using undo repeatedly

▶ Counting shapes on layers

- -

*T*he questions in this chapter come directly from Visio Corporation's top trainers. They say these are the top ten (well, thirteen, actually) most frequently asked questions by new users.

Can I Work with Other File Types inside of Visio?

You can open, or import, other file types like AutoCAD drawings and Windows Metafiles with the Visio program. To see a list of file formats that you can open, click the Open button and then browse the Files of Type list in the Open dialog box.

How Do I Know Whether I'm Using the Right Template to Create My Drawing?

To get help on using a template, or if you're not quite sure why you'd use a particular template, choose Help➪Template Help.

Can I Customize My Visio Drawing Environment?

You can customize your Visio drawing environment so that it suits your needs. For example, you can hide the grid and rulers if you don't care about positioning your shapes precisely and you want more screen space (On the View menu, remove the check mark from the Ruler and Grid options.) Or you can change the stencil view to display icons and names, icons only, or names only. (To do this, right-click anywhere on the green background of the stencil, and then choose a view style.) You can also view page breaks while creating your drawing so that you can take care not to position shapes too close to the edge of the page, because shapes in the page-break areas don't print. (See Chapter 2 for more information on printing.)

How Many Times Can I Undo in Visio?

By default, Visio can undo the last ten actions you perform. To specify fewer or more levels, choose Tools➪Options, click the Advanced tab, and then, under User Settings, type a new number in the Undo Levels box.

How Do I Search for a Shape in Visio? I Don't Want to Open Every Stencil!

Use Shape Explorer to find the shape. Choose File➪Stencils➪Shape Explorer. In the Search For box, type what you are looking for and then click Find Now. For more information, see Chapter 10. (By the way, Shape Explorer isn't installed with a typical installation. You may have to reinstall Visio and choose the Custom/Complete option.)

How Do I Unlock a Shape?

If you select a shape and it has gray padlock selection handles, the shape is locked to prevent changes. To unlock a shape, select the shape and then choose Format⇨Protection. For more information, see Chapter 12.

How Do I Copy Formatting from One Shape to Another?

Use the Format Painter to copy formatting from one shape to another quickly. Select a shape that's already formatted, click the Format Painter tool (it looks like a paintbrush) on the Standard toolbar, and then click the shape that you want to format. For more information, see Chapter 7.

How Do I View Multiple Pages at the Same Time?

You can view multiple pages at the same time by opening pages in separate windows and then tiling the windows. Choose Edit⇨Go To⇨Page, which displays the Page dialog box. At the bottom of the dialog box, choose Open Page in New Window. To tile the windows, choose Window⇨Tile.

How Do I Check a Drawing for Page Breaks?

You can quickly check to see whether your drawing fits within the printable area by choosing View⇨Page Breaks. For more information, refer to Chapter 2.

I Always Save My Files in the Same Folder. How Can I Let Visio Know?

Choose Tools⇨Options, click the File Paths tab, and then type the path in the Drawings box. You can also set default file paths for other files, such as templates and stencils.

Okay, maybe just a few more favorite questions!

How Can I Draw Shapes Precisely?

When you're drawing irregular shapes using the Pencil or Freeform tools, the snap feature can make you crazy snapping shapes and lines everywhere! To turn off the snap feature, choose Tools⇨Snap & Glue and then uncheck the Snap check box under Currently Active. For more information, see Chapter 7.

Can I Count Shapes on a Layer?

Yes. To see how many shapes are assigned to a layer, choose View⇨Layer Properties and then click the # column in the Layer Properties dialog box. The numbers tell only how many shapes are on each layer; they don't provide an accurate count of how many shapes are in your drawing because a single shape may be assigned to two or more layers. For more information, see Chapter 9.

How Do I Rotate Shapes to a Specific Angle?

You can use the Size & Position dialog box to specify the angle of rotation to a precision of 0.01 degree. To specify a precise angle, select a shape and then choose Shape⇨Size & Position. For more information, see Chapter 7.

Chapter 15

Ten of Visio's Coolest Stencils and Wizards

In This Chapter

▶ Getting a closer look at some of the greatest Visio wizards

▶ Investigating some of the most interesting Visio stencils

*W*hen you have a specific job to do — that is, creating a particular type of drawing and doing it quickly — you're probably not going to spend a whole lot of time snooping around in Visio just to "see what's there." This section on stencils is designed to show you what *is* there that you may have missed. Remember that regardless of the template you're using, you can open any stencil any time and use its shapes in the current drawing. Don't ever let the name of a stencil pigeonhole you; you can find all sorts of shapes to use on seemingly "unrelated" stencils. For a quick view of the myriad of shapes included in many of the Visio stencils, see Appendix A.

Check Out These Stencils

Many of the shapes that you see in the stencils in this chapter have more than one control point. To find out what a control point is for, float the mouse pointer over the control point without clicking the mouse. A tip pops up to tell you what the control point is for. You can also see Chapter 3 for more detailed information on control points.

When you're completely stumped as to what a particular shape is for or how it works, don't forget to use Shape Help. Get help by right-clicking the shape and then choosing Shape Help from the shortcut menu. An information box pops up to tell you about the shape and shows you how to work with it.

Geographical maps

Visio has a bunch of stencils for drawing geographical maps; just pick the part of the world that you want to draw:

- ✔ Africa
- ✔ Asia
- ✔ Europe
- ✔ North and South America
- ✔ Middle East
- ✔ U.S. and Canada
- ✔ Maps of the World

The first six stencils listed above contain shapes for the countries, states, or provinces that make up a region; the last stencil, Maps of the World, contains world and continental maps (see Figure 15-1). For a large corporation (or even a small company), these stencils are great for creating drawings that show sales or branch offices, service centers, carrier routes (for airlines or transport companies), wide area network locations, video conferencing facilities, weather patterns, temperature zones — the possibilities are really endless. In the "Build Region Wizard" section later in this chapter, you see how to use this wizard to create regions automatically from a selection of state, province, or country shapes.

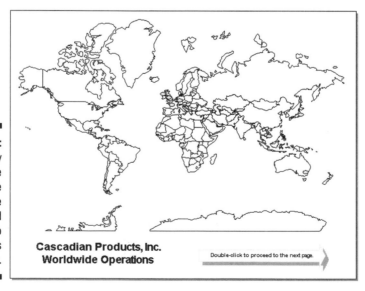

Figure 15-1: It takes only one shape from the Maps of the World stencil to create this map.

Cascadian Products, Inc.
Worldwide Operations

Double-click to proceed to the next page.

Directional Maps stencil

The Directional Maps stencil contains every shape you can imagine for creating roads, bridges, 3-way and 4-way intersections, cloverleafs, railroad tracks, metro lines, traffic signs, emergency services (hospitals, fire departments), landmarks, and bodies of water. This stencil is the one that you want for creating sightseeing maps, directional maps, area maps, tour maps, public transit maps, and so on (see Figure 15-2). If you're creating a city map in which streets run at odd angles, be sure to refer to Chapter 8 to see how you can rotate the page to make these streets easier to draw.

Marketing Diagrams stencil

Ever notice how marketeers are experts at illustrating data? They come up with some pretty snazzy-looking charts, graphs, and diagrams. If you're not a marketing-type person, though, you may never think to look at the Marketing Diagrams stencil. But you should — this stencil has shapes you may find useful even outside of marketing because they have a generic structure. Take, for example, a matrix, a classic marketer's tool. This stencil has several of them (see Figure 15-3), but you don't have to use them to present marketing information only. You can use any of these matrices to present growth/development data, dict/nutrition data, sales training data, academic requirements, or a hundred other types of information.

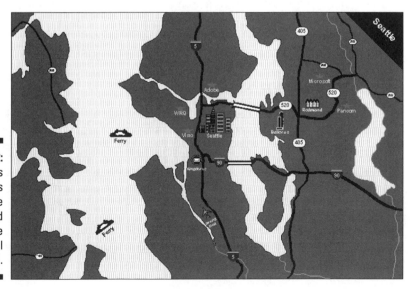

Figure 15-2: All shapes used in this map are created using the Directional Map stencil.

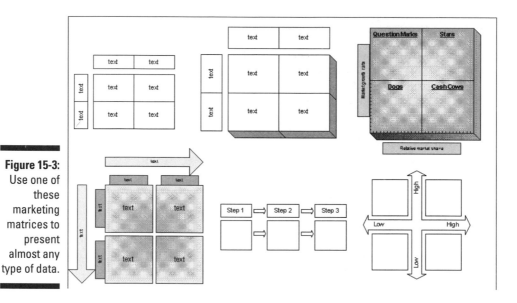

In Figure 15-4, you see examples of other shapes from the Marketing Diagrams stencil. Although these stencils were designed for marketing purposes, they can be used for any type of data. Think about the relationships they represent: The circle/spoke diagram can represent parts that contribute to a whole; the pyramid can represent building blocks or a hierarchical relationship; the arrows represent a continuous cycle. Use your imagination with these shapes. Each one is customizable; when you drag them into the drawing, Visio prompts you for the number of circles, pyramid levels, or arrows.

Form Design stencil

Have you ever tried to create a form using a word processor? You know, the kind with boxes of all different shapes and sizes, borders, grids, horizontal and vertical lines, and check boxes? If you have, then you know — it's a *nightmare*. Word processors are decidedly *text oriented* rather than *object oriented,* which means that they understand only how to move text from left to right and wrap text to the next line when you get to the end of a line. They don't understand anything else, and they beg you not to make them try! (If you do, you're only asking for major frustration.)

When you need to create a form, the Visio Form Design stencil is just what you're looking for. It contains all sorts of useful shapes like:

✔ Arrows

✔ Borders

✔ Data boxes (you know, those silly little boxes that are always too small to write just one character in — but not in Visio)

✔ Date/time/page number box

✔ Grids

✔ Logo placeholder

✔ Text boxes (plain, shaded, or with a black background and white characters)

✔ Title box

✔ Vertical lines

✔ Work order forms (see Figure 15-5)

Because Visio is object-oriented, moving all those little shapes into place wherever you want them is easy. Use the form design stencil to create purchase orders, invoices, fax cover sheets, packing slips, application forms, warranty cards, customer surveys — any kind of a form that is difficult to create with a word processor.

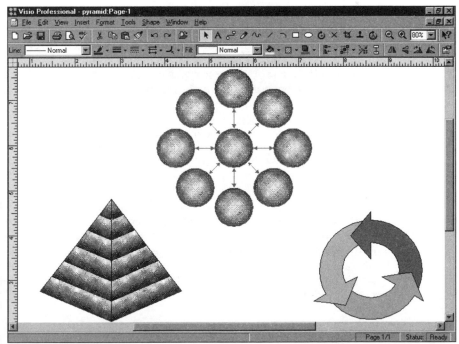

Figure 15-4: Use these marketing shapes to present other types of information.

Logo　　Check box　　Reverse text box　　¹/₁₆-inch border box

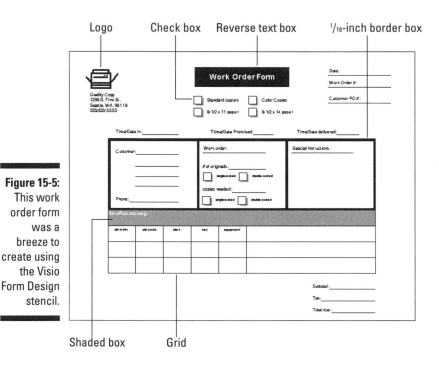

Figure 15-5:
This work
order form
was a
breeze to
create using
the Visio
Form Design
stencil.

Shaded box　　　Grid

Charting Shapes stencil

The Charting Shapes stencil is designed to help you create just about any type of business chart — pie chart, bar graph, line graph, row/column matrix — and do it quickly. Granted, these types of shapes aren't all that exciting, but I show them here because Visio makes it so easy to create and modify them for your needs.

Figure 15-6 shows an ordinary bar graph, but you don't have to create the pieces of this graph yourself. Just use the bar graph shape from the Charting Shapes stencil; then use the control points on the graph to change the number of bars and the bar height, width, color, and text.

You can create an impressive 3-D bar chart like the one shown in Figure 15-7 using the 3-D Axis shape and the 3-D Bar shape. Drag the axis onto your drawing page and then use control points on the 3-D Axis to vary the box depth and the number of gridlines. Now drag as many 3-D bars as you want on top of the axis. Use the control point on each bar to change the bar depth. To change bar color, click the bar and then choose a fill color from the Fill tool on the Standard toolbar.

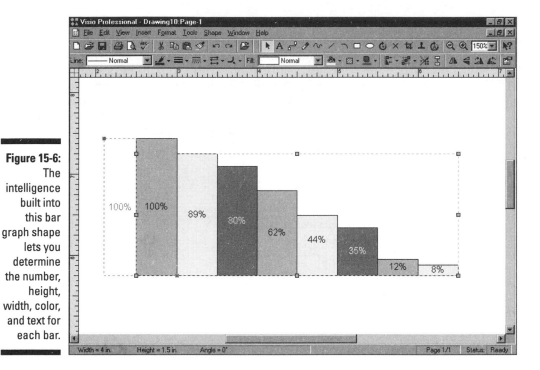

Figure 15-6:
The intelligence built into this bar graph shape lets you determine the number, height, width, color, and text for each bar.

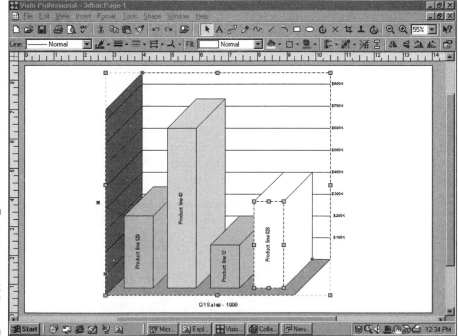

Figure 15-7:
3-D charts have more visual impact because of their depth.

Blocks with Perspective stencil

Like 3-D shapes, block diagrams have a lot of visual impact; they're a lot more interesting when you use shapes from the Blocks with Perspective stencil. Each shape in this stencil is three-dimensional with a *vanishing point* (the imaginary point where the lines of a three-dimensional shape converge). When you open the stencil on its own, you can adjust the vanishing point of any shape to any direction or depth just by moving the control point (see Figure 15-8).

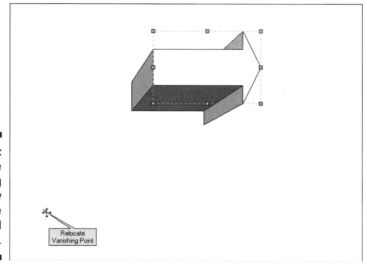

Figure 15-8:
Adjust the
vanishing
point by
moving the
control
point.

To coordinate the vanishing points of all shapes in your drawing, drag the vanishing point shape onto the drawing before dragging any other shapes. This shape represents a vanishing point for the entire page and is marked by a crosshair that covers the width and length of the page. Place the vanishing point shape anywhere on the drawing page. When you drag other shapes into the drawing, Visio automatically glues their vanishing points to the page vanishing point. This makes each shape appear to be "pointing to" the page vanishing point (see Figure 15-9). You can change an individual shape's vanishing point by dragging its control handle away from the page vanishing point. (By the way, the page vanishing point crosshair doesn't print with the drawing.)

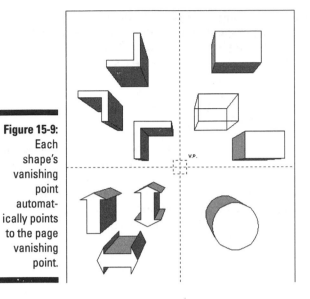

Figure 15-9:
Each shape's vanishing point automatically points to the page vanishing point.

In Figure 15-10, the vanishing point has been moved. Can you tell where it is now?

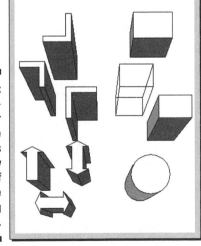

Figure 15-10:
The vanishing point for each shape now points to the new location of the page vanishing point.

Another way to use the page vanishing point is to create a new drawing using the block diagrams with a perspective *template* (which automatically opens the stencil). When you use the template, rather than just opening the stencil, the drawing page automatically contains a *page* vanishing point.

Some Great Wizards to Try . . .

Visio has lots of great wizards that are designed to help you accomplish tasks easily and quickly. Two great Visio wizards are the Organization Chart Wizard and the Project Timeline Wizard. You won't see these two wizards listed in this chapter because they're detailed in Chapter 13, where you find out how to use external data to create organizational charts and timelines. You see some other interesting — and very different — wizards in this chapter.

To use any of the Visio wizards, choose <u>T</u>ools⇨<u>M</u>acro. Choose a wizard from one of the categories on the submenu or click Macros to choose from an alphabetic list of wizards and macros.

Web Diagram Wizard

The Web Diagram Wizard is a very clever tool that completes two tasks for you automatically:

- ✔ Creates a Web site map in an organizational chart format
- ✔ Creates a text file of the Web site links in a tab-delimited (fields separated by tabs) format.

The Web Diagram Wizard does its job by "surveying," or analyzing, any Web site that you choose. The wizard lets you choose exactly how much of the Web site you want to survey (local links only, remote links, or both), and the type of links (pages on the same site, pages on other sites, links to files). You can explore up to four levels in the Web structure and include up to 1,000 links.

The Web Diagram Wizard is useful in a couple of ways. If you're designing a site of your own and see a Web site that you particularly like, you can use the wizard to map that site and then build your own site in a similar way. (Be aware, however, that some Web site designs and pages are copyrighted.) After your Web site is created, you can use the wizard to check out, manage, and reorganize the structure of your own Web site.

In Figure 15-11, you see a map that Visio Corporation created using the Web Diagram Wizard. Each box represents a page on the Visio Web site.

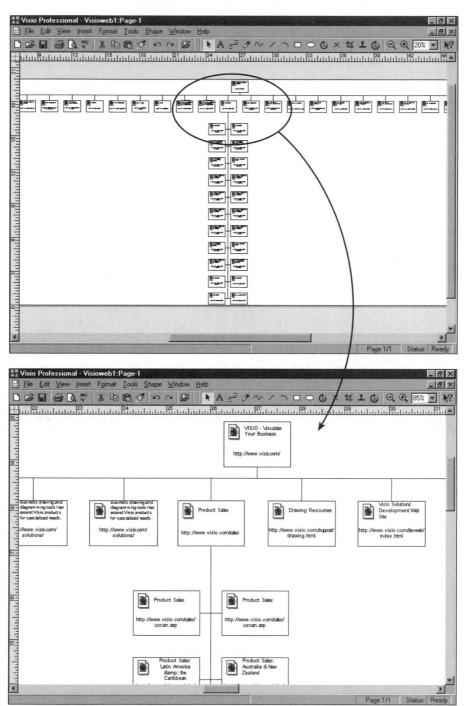

Figure 15-11:
Visio Corporation's Web site contains many first-level pages and several second-level pages under the Sales organization.

In Figure 15-12, you see the elements of Visio Corporation's Web site in a text file. Notice the column headings are ID, Parent_ID, Title URL, Link_Type, and Error. The Web Diagram Wizard creates and stores this .txt file automatically and stores it in the C:\Visio\Solutions\Internet Diagram\folder.

Chart Shape Wizard

Ever get tired of typical business bar charts that represent quantity with, what else, bars? Well you can jazz up your "bar" charts by creating *extendable* or *stackable* shapes using the Chart Shape Wizard. Visually, your charts are more interesting because the boring bars are replaced with shapes — whatever shape you choose or create.

- **An *extendable* shape is one that stretches when you resize it without distorting the shape itself.** It's usually made up of two or three sections because only one of the sections stretches; the other sections don't stretch to keep the shape from being distorted (see Figure 15-13). Visio contains some shapes that are already extendable, such as the pencil, flower, extend-o-hand, people, person, and umbrella shapes on the Marketing Clipart stencil. You can use these, or you can create your own using the Chart Shape Wizard. Shapes that make good extendable shapes are those that have straight-line elements without a lot of complexity or detail. Extendable shapes that you create can run horizontally or vertically.

- **A *stackable* shape is one that duplicates itself when you stretch the shape.** For example, if your chart depicts numbers of users who own a personal computer, you may make the PC shape from the Office Layout stencil a stackable shape. The larger the quantity shown in your chart, the more PC shapes are stacked on top of one another. Like extendable shapes, stackable shapes that you create can run horizontally or vertically (see Figure 15-14).

To create an extendable or stackable shape, use the Chart Shape Wizard:

1. **Open a new Visio file and drag the shape that you want to use into the drawing area.**

   If you're creating a stackable shape, you can use just about any shape. If you're creating an extendable shape, drag onto the drawing page the two or three shapes that will make up the extendable shape.

2. **Choose Tools⇨Macro⇨Business Diagram⇨Chart Shape Wizard to start the wizard. Click Next to move to the second screen.**

3. **Choose either Extendable or Stackable, and then click Next.**

4. **Follow the remaining wizard screens to finish your shape.**

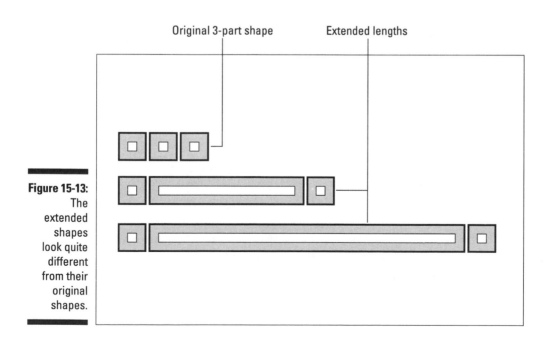

```
VISIO - Visualize Your Business. - Notepad                              _ 8 X
File  Edit  Search  Help
'Starting URL:          http://www.visio.com/
'Maximum Depth:         4
'Maximum Documents:     50
'Follow Method:         Follow All Links
'Diagram Links:         All Links
'Surf Algorithm:        Breadth First
'
'ID    Parent_ID       Title    URL     Link_Type       Error
'------------------------------------------------------------------
1                      VISIO - Visualize Your Business.        http://www.visio.com/   HTML document    N
2      1               Product Sales    http://www.visio.com/sales      HTML document   None
3      1               Contact Visio    http://www.visio.com/contact    HTML document   None
4      1               Support &amp; Service   http://www.visio.com/support    HTML document   None
5      1               Visio Search     http://www.visio.com/search     HTML document   None
6      1               VISIO - Visualize Your Business.        http://www.visio.com/index.html HTML docu
7      1               Company Background       http://www.visio.com/company/indepth/index.html HTML docu
8      1               Visio Enterprise Product Information    http://www.visio.com/products/enterprise/
9      1               Visio News       http://www.visio.com/news/      HTML document   None
10     1               Year-2000 Readiness      http://www.visio.com/yr2000.html        HTML document   N
11     1               SPA Anti-Piracy http://www.spa.org/piracy/report.htm    HTML document   None
12     1               Freeware        http://www.bsa.org/freeware     HTML document   None
13     1               Business drawing and diagramming tools that extend Visio products for specialized
14     1               Business drawing and diagramming tools that extend Visio products for specialized
15     1               Drawing Resources       http://www.visio.com/support/drawing.html       HTML docu
16     1               Visio Solutions Development Web Site     http://www.visio.com/devweb/index.html  H
17     1               Career Opportunities    http://www.visio.com/company/hr/        HTML document   N
18     1               Visio Investor Relations        http://www.visio.com/company/investors/ HTML docu
19     1               Important Legal Information      http://www.visio.com/legal/     HTML document   N
20     1               Visio: Protecting Your Privacy Online   http://www.visio.com/privacy/   HTML docu
21     1               Visio Solutions Development Web Site     http://www.visio.com/devweb     HTML docu
22     1               Partnering With Visio Corporation       http://www.visio.com/partnering HTML docu
23     1               Channel Resources       http://www.visio.com/channel    HTML document   None
24     1               Visio Corporation       http://www.visio.com/company    HTML document   None
25     1               Visio Products  http://www.visio.com/products   HTML document   None
26     1               Visio Standard  http://www.visio.com/products/standard/ HTML document   None
27     1               Visio Technical Product Information      http://www.visio.com/products/technical/
```

Figure 15-12: The components of Visio Corporation's Web site are listed in this .txt file that the Web Diagram Wizard creates.

Original 3-part shape   Extended lengths

Figure 15-13: The extended shapes look quite different from their original shapes.

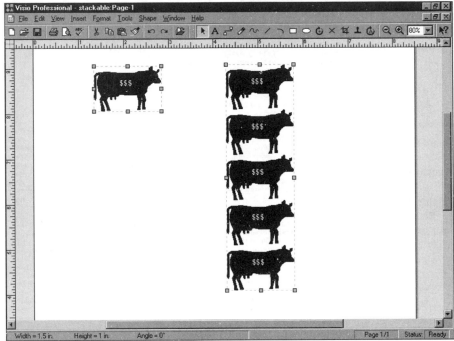

Figure 15-14:
How about a
stackable
"cash
cow"?

After you create an extendable or stackable shape, you extend or stack it by dragging a selection handle. If the shape runs horizontally, drag any of the right resize handles to the right or left. For shapes that run vertically, drag any top handle up or down.

Build Region Wizard

The Build Region Wizard is a nifty little tool that helps you create a geographic map. If you're creating a map of adjoining states or countries, it can save you the time of aligning each piece of the jigsaw puzzle. If you're creating a map of non-adjoining states or countries, it can make a nearly impossible task a breeze.

The Build Region Wizard works with any of the following stencils. (For more information on these stencils, take a look at the earlier section "Geographical maps.")

✔ Maps of Europe

✔ Maps of Asia

✔ Maps of North America and South America

- ✔ Maps of Africa
- ✔ Maps of U.S. and Canada
- ✔ Maps of the Middle East

To create a map, use any of the stencils and drag the shapes that you want into the drawing area. As you can see from Figure 15-15, you don't need to waste any time arranging the shapes; the wizard does it for you automatically.

To use the Build Region Wizard, follow these steps:

1. **Open one or more of the geographic maps stencils or use the geographic maps template to create a new drawing.**

2. **Drag all the shapes that you want into the drawing.**

3. **Select all the shapes that are part of the region you're building.**

4. **Choose Tools⇨Macro⇨Maps⇨Build Region.**

   The wizard creates the map for you from the shapes you selected.

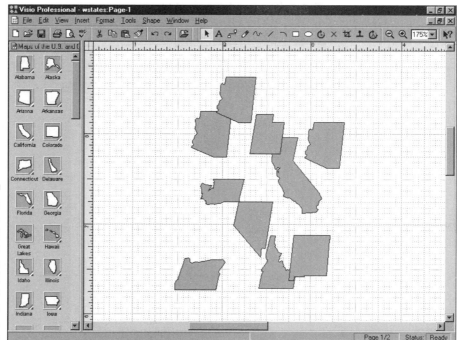

Figure 15-15:
This mixed-up mess of western states looks like a pile of jigsaw puzzle pieces.

If you want to add more states, countries, or provinces to the drawing, just drag them in and place them anywhere in the drawing area. Select all the new shapes along with the old and then run the wizard again. The wizard arranges the new shapes into the existing drawing. The drawing shown in Figure 15-16 is the result after running the Build Region Wizard on the drawing shown earlier in Figure 15-15.

Stencil Report Wizard

Think of the Stencil Report Wizard as a useful tool for creating a stencil reference sheet. Suppose that you manage a group of network engineers who are just learning to use Visio to create drawings and network diagrams. You could have your engineers study each stencil on the screen, but it would make much more sense to create a reference sheet that includes descriptions of all the shapes included in the network equipment stencils (see Figure 15-17). You choose the stencil, and the Stencil Report Wizard creates a drawing that shows an example of each shape, its name, and a description of the prompt shown on the status bar when you select the shape in the stencil.

To use the Stencil Report Wizard, choose Tools➪Macro➪Visio Extras➪ Stencil Report Wizard and then follow the prompts on the screen.

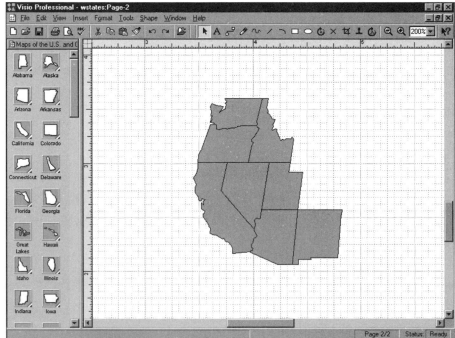

Figure 15-16: Each piece of the jigsaw is now neatly in place, thanks to the Build Region Wizard.

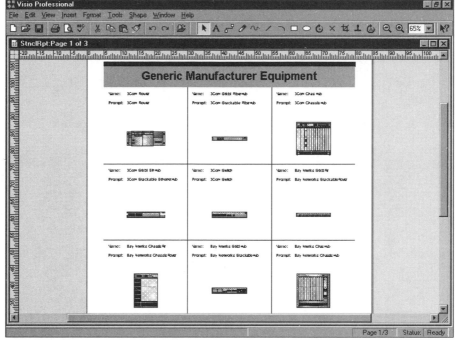

Figure 15-17:
The Stencil Report Wizard creates a nice, printable drawing showing all shapes on the selected stencil.

Adding more flair to Visio

Want to add even more flair to your Visio documents than a stencil or wizard can provide? Check out the following pages in the Visio Corporation Web site to find out more about other products you can use with Visio.

✔ **For information about add-on products:** Select Help⇨Visio on the Web⇨Visio Solutions Library or go directly to www.visio.com/solutions. Click the Product Directory for a list of add-on products that you can purchase on the spot.

✔ **For free add-on products:** Go directly to www.visio.com/support/downloads/visio.html for free add-on products, wizards, and other utilities from the Visio Development Team.

Chapter 16

Ten of the Best Visio Tips

In This Chapter

▶ Handy tips from the makers of Visio

▶ Features that you should play around with

*T*ips can be some of your greatest assets when you figure out how to use a new application. These are ten valuable tips from the pros at Visio.

Use Your Pasteboard

"Pasteboard? What's that?" you ask. You may not have noticed the blue area surrounding the drawing page when you create a new drawing. (In fact, you don't see the pasteboard if you zoom in on the drawing page.) When it's visible, you can drag shapes onto the pasteboard and use it as a sort of holding area for shapes that you're not ready to use yet. This is a great way to store shapes when you're opening a lot of additional stencils. You can drag the shapes onto the pasteboard and then close the stencils that you're not using anymore. The shapes are stored with the drawing, but they don't print. When you're ready to use the shapes, just drag them into the drawing area.

Preview Your Drawings in Windows Explorer

A fast way to view a drawing before opening it in Visio is to use the Quick View feature in Windows, available in Windows Explorer (**Note:** Before you get frustrated, you may not have Quick View installed on your computer.) Go to the directory where your Visio file is located, right-click the file, and choose Quick View from the drop-down menu that appears. Windows displays the file in a Quick View window so that you can identify the file quickly. To open the file in Visio, just click the Visio tool (it looks like the Visio company logo: dark blue with bright green shapes) on the Quick View toolbar. To close the Quick View window, click the window's close button.

Group Shapes

The more adept that you become at creating shapes, the more you realize that a good shape is often a combination of many shapes. When you spend a lot of time creating the various components, you don't want to lose any of the pieces and parts when you start dragging and copying them. The best way to avoid losing anything is to group the pieces. Remember, too, that you can group groups. If it makes sense to group five pieces of a shape, and then create and group five more — by all means, do it! Then you can group the two groups together. Refer to Chapter 7 for details on grouping shapes.

Use Shape Help!

When you're not sure what a shape is for or how to use it, right-click the shape and choose Shape Help. (You can right-click a shape in the stencil or in a drawing.) The help that pops up on the screen describes the shape and how it works, shows all the shape's control points, and tells you what each control point is for. Often with a more complex shape, a picture of the shape is included.

Use Guides to Position and Move Shapes

A guide is sort of like a Visio clothesline — or maybe *shapeline* is more appropriate! Use a guide when you want to "hang" shapes from the same line — horizontal, vertical, or diagonal. It's a great way to position and align shapes, but you can also move them easily using a guide. Just drag the guide, and all the attached shapes move along with it. To review using guides, see Chapter 6.

Work with Drawing Layers

Drawing layers are one of the most useful features of Visio. Think of them as transparent pages on which to place your drawing shapes. Layers help you organize your work, particularly with complex, detailed drawings. Group similar or related shapes onto the same layer. Duplicate shapes that you want to appear on multiple layers. Stack the layers together to see your complete drawing. You can print or view layers selectively, and you can lock layers to protect them from change. See Chapter 9 for details on creating and using layers.

Fool Around with Snap and Glue Until You Figure Them Out!

Snap and glue are two of the of most powerful features of Visio; they make creating drawings a whole lot easier. But when you're first checking them out, they can be confusing. So many choices: Dynamic or static? Snap and glue to what? Connection points? Handles? Grid? Guides? All or none? Set snap and glue strength? Yikes!

Don't worry. The best way to figure out snap and glue is to *play with them*. Create a drawing that you don't care anything about, and then go wild! Try every combination of snap and glue options that you can think of. Drag some shapes in. Move them around. Reset the snap and glue strength. Turn off some of the snap and glue options. Move shapes around. Turn *all* the options off. Now move shapes around again. You get the idea. Just play around with snap and glue to see what happens. The more you experiment, the more comfortable you'll feel.

Set Undo Levels

Many computer programs have only one level of the Undo command. That means if you want to take back a mistake, you better do it right away before you do anything else, or you lose your chance! Other programs have *levels* of the Undo command, which means that you can choose Edit➪Undo repeatedly and the command can undo the last few actions that you took. Visio defaults to ten levels of undo, but you can set the level if you want. If you think you'll never want to undo more than the last five actions, set the level at 5. If you want to be able to undo the last *50* commands, Visio lets you set the level at 50. To set this option, choose Tools➪Options and click the Advanced tab. Type a number — up to 99 — in the Undo Levels box. (Be aware that the higher the number you enter, the more memory resources you use on your computer.)

Quickly Edit the Text in Your Document

Press F7 to quickly run the spell checker, or choose Tools➪Spelling. Choose Edit➪Find to find text in a drawing; choose Edit➪Replace to search for and replace text in a drawing.

Use Keyboard Shortcuts

You can significantly speed up your work if you take the time to memorize some of the Visio keyboard shortcuts for menu commands. They are listed on every menu, just to the right of the command name (some commands have none). You also find other keyboard shortcuts that aren't really listed in any one place where you can find them easily. You just sort of pick them up as you go. See the Cheat Sheet for a list of helpful shortcuts.

Chapter 17

Ten Really Slick Drawings from the Makers of Visio

*T*he drawings in this chapter are samples intended to inspire, inform, moti- vate, and impress you! All of them are created by experts at Visio Corporation; who better to show off the capabilities of Visio than the makers of Visio themselves? Each drawing has a brief description of the product and stencils used to create the drawing. Sample drawings are from Visio Standard, Visio Professional, and Visio Technical.

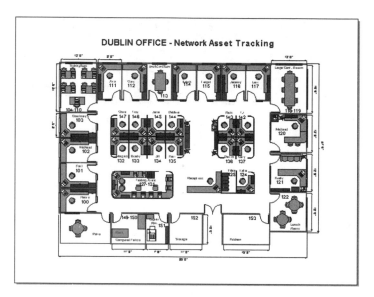

Visio Product: Visio Standard

Stencils Used: Business Diagram/Office Layout Shapes; Network Diagram/Basic Network Shapes; Visio Extras/Callouts

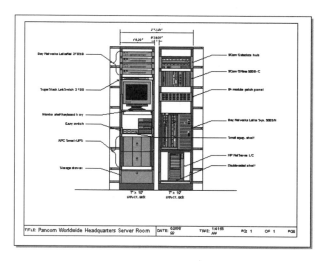

Visio Product: Visio Professional

Stencils Used: Network Diagram/Basic Network Shapes; 3Com Equipment; Bay Networks Equipment; Cabletron Equipment; Cisco Equipment; HP Equipment

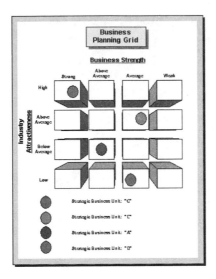

Visio Product: Visio Standard

Stencils Used: Block Diagram/Blocks with Perspective; Business Diagram/Marketing Diagrams

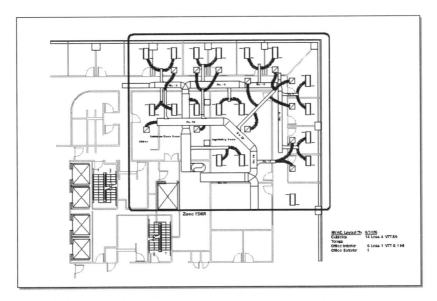

Visio Product: Visio Technical

Stencils Used: AEC/HVAC Controls; AEC/HVAC Equipment; AEC/HVAC Single Line; AEC/HVAC Double Line; AEC/Building Core; AEC/Walls; Shell and Structure

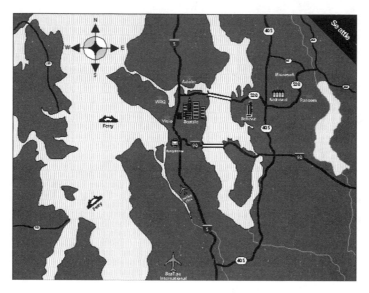

Visio Product: Visio Standard

Stencils Used: Maps/Directional Map Shapes

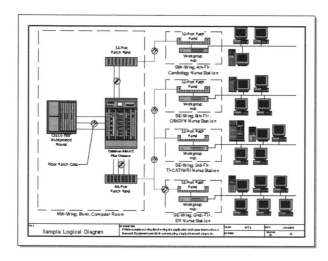

Visio Product: Visio Professional

Stencils Used: Network Diagram/General Equipment; Network Diagram/General Manufacturer Equipment; Network Diagram/Logical Symbols 1; Network Diagram/Logical Symbols 2

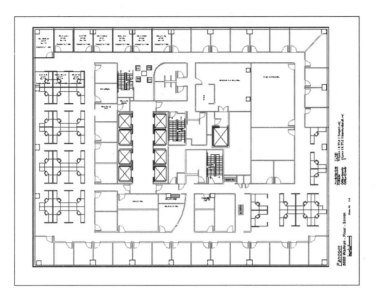

Visio Product: Visio Technical

Stencils Used: Facilities Management/Building Core; AEC/Electrical and Telecom; Annotations/General – Annotations; Annotations/General – Dimensioning; Architectural Facilities Management/Office Equipment – Electronic; Facilities Management/Office Equipment – Accessories; Facilities Management/Office Equipment – Services; Facilities Management/Office Furniture; Facilities Management/Resources; Equipment/Office Furniture/Steelcase; AEC/Walls; Shell and Structure; Facilities Management/Modular Office Furniture

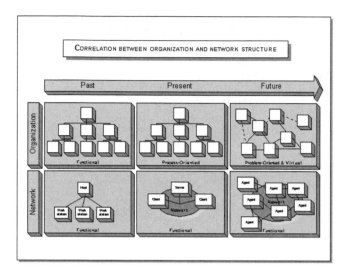

Visio Product: Visio Standard

Stencils Used: Block Diagram/Blocks; Block Diagram/Block with Perspective; Block Diagram/Blocks

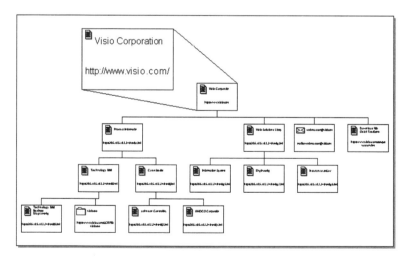

Visio Product: Visio Professional

Stencils Used: Internet Diagram/Web Diagram Shapes; Flowchart/Basic Flowchart Shapes 1; Flowchart/Basic Flowchart Shapes 2

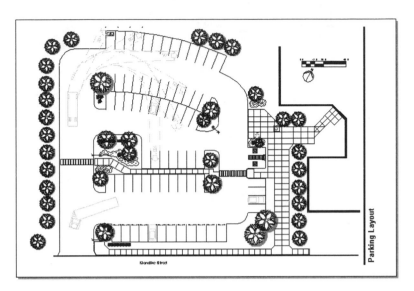

Visio Product: Visio Technical

Stencils Used: Facilities Management/Site – Parking and Roads; Facilities Management/Site Accessories; Facilities Management/Landscape Watering; Facilities Management/Landscape Plants; Annotation/Dimensioning – Engineering; Annotation/General – Annotations; Facilities Management/Vehicles

Appendix

Stencil Gallery

● ●

*V*isio organizes stencils into categories to make them easier to find. In this gallery, stencils are arranged by Visio product and then by category. Under the first heading, you see stencils that are available in all three Visio products: Visio Standard, Visio Professional, and Visio Technical. Subsequent headings show stencils that are available only in Visio Professional or Visio Technical.

Visio contains literally thousands of shapes on nearly 200 stencils. It isn't possible to show every stencil in this gallery. The stencils I included are the most commonly used or most representative of the category. The names of stencils that aren't shown are listed under each category.

Stencils in Visio Standard, Visio Professional, and Visio Technical

Category: Block Diagram

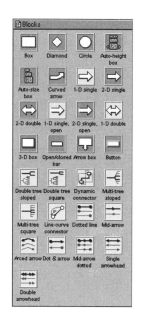

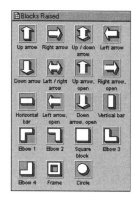

Category: Business Bonus Pack

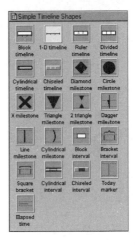

Stencils in the Business Bonus Pack category not shown: Cross-Functional Flowchart Shapes, Supersystem Map, Organization Chart 98 Shapes

Category: Business Diagram

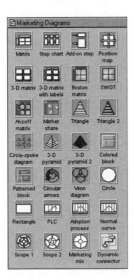

(continued)

(Business Diagram Continued)

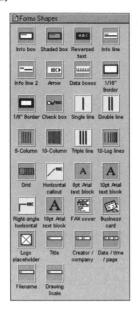

Category: Flowchart

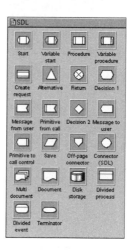

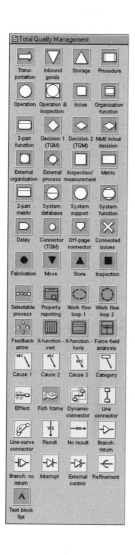

(continued)

(Flowchart Continued)

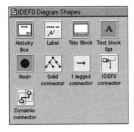

Stencils in the Flowchart category not shown: Basic Flowchart Shapes 2, Work Flow Diagram Shapes

Category: Maps

(continued)

(Maps Continued)

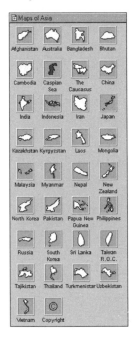

Maps of Asia: Afghanistan, Australia, Bangladesh, Bhutan, Cambodia, Caspian Sea, The Caucasus, China, India, Indonesia, Iran, Japan, Kazakhstan, Kyrgyzstan, Laos, Mongolia, Malaysia, Myanmar, Nepal, New Zealand, North Korea, Pakistan, Papua New Guinea, Philippines, Russia, South Korea, Sri Lanka, Taiwan R.O.C., Tajikistan, Thailand, Turkmenistan, Uzbekistan, Vietnam, Copyright

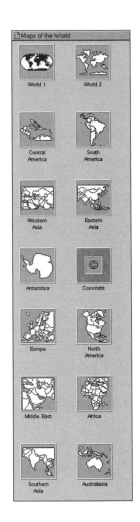

Maps of the World: World 1, World 2, Central America, South America, Western Asia, Eastern Asia, Antarctica, Copyright, Europe, North America, Middle East, Africa, Southern Asia, Australasia

Maps of Europe: Albania, Austria, Belarus, Benelux Countries, Bosnia-Herzegovina, Bulgaria, Croatia, Czech Republic, Denmark, Estonia, Finland, France, Germany, Greece, Hungary, Iceland, Ireland, Italy, Latvia, Lithuania, Macedonia, Moldova, Norway, Poland, Portugal, Romania, Russia, Slovakia, Slovenia, Spain, Sweden, Switzerland, United Kingdom, Ukraine, Yugoslavia (Serbia-Montenegro), Copyright, Europe

Maps of N. and S. America: Alaska, Canada, Greenland, USA, Mexico, Caribbean, Central America, Colombia, Venezuela, Guyana, Suriname, French Guiana, Ecuador, Peru, Brazil, Bolivia, Paraguay, Uruguay, Chile, Argentina, Copyright

Maps of the Middle East: Iran, Iraq, Israel, Jordan, Kuwait, Lebanon, Oman, Qatar, Saudi Arabia, Syria, Turkey, United Arab Emirates, Yemen, Copyright

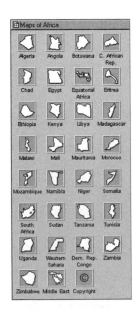

Maps of Africa: Algeria, Angola, Botswana, C. African Rep., Chad, Egypt, Equatorial Africa, Eritrea, Ethiopia, Kenya, Libya, Madagascar, Malawi, Mali, Mauritania, Morocco, Mozambique, Namibia, Niger, Somalia, South Africa, Sudan, Tanzania, Tunisia, Uganda, Western Sahara, Dem. Rep. Congo, Zambia, Zimbabwe, Middle East, Copyright

Category: Network Diagram

Category: Visio Extras

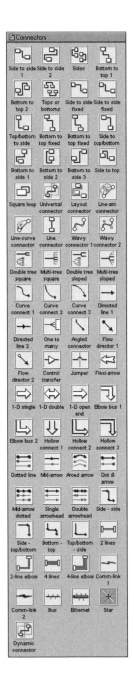

Stencils in Visio Professional

Category: Database

Category: Internet Diagram

Category: Network Diagram

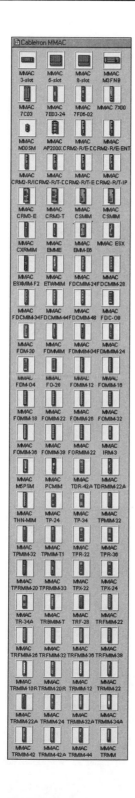

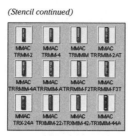

(Stencil continued)

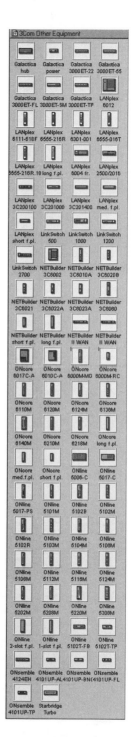

(continued)

(Network Diagram Continued)

Hewlett Packard

Adv. Stack 200/400 fr. · Adv. Stack 230 · Adv. Stack 240 · Adv. Stack 430
Adv. Stack 440/445 · Adv. Stack 470 · Adv. Stack 470/480 fr. · Adv. Stack 480
Adv. Stack 650 · Adv. Stack J2410A · Adv. Stack J2434A · Adv. Stack J2435A
Adv. Stack J2436A · Adv. Stack J2437A · Adv. Stack J2600A · Adv. Stack J2601A
Adv. Stack J2602A · Adv. Stack J2606A · Adv. Stack J2607A · Adv. Stack J2608A
Adv. Stack J2609A · Adv. Stack rt. eng. · Advance Stz 228662A · Advance Stack 228682A
Advance Stz 228688B · Advance Stz J2413A · Advance Stz J2414B · Advance Stack J2601B
Advance Stz J2602B · Advance Stz J2610B · Advance Stz J2611B · Advance Stack J2962A
Advance Stz J3027A · Advance Stz J3028A · Advance Stz J3030A · Advance Stack J3100A
Advance Stz J3102A · Advance Stz J3103A · Advance Stz J3108A · Advance Stack J3128A
Advance Stz J3133A · Advance Stz J3136A · Advance Stz J3137A · DesignJet 650c
DeskJet 540 · DeskJet 650/560c · EtherTwist 28641B · EtherTwist 28683A
EtherTwist 28685B · HP 14" monitor · HP 15" monitor · HP 3000 9X7 fr.
HP 3000 9X3 fr. · HP 9000 17" monitor · HP 9000 20" monitor · HP 9000 712 fr.
HP 9000 715 fr. · HP 9000 725 fr. · HP 9000 735 fr. · HP 9000 755 fr.
HP 9000 827+ fr. · HP 9000 8X7 fr. · Keyboard · LaserJet 4+/4M+
LaserJet 4L · LaserJet 4P/4MP · LaserJet 5P · NetServer LC fr.
NetServer LF / LM fr. · NetServer LH fr. · Vectra M2 fr. · Vectra N2 fr.
Vectra VE fr. · Vectra VL2 fr. · Vectra VL3 fr. · Vectra XM2 fr.
Vectra XU fr.

Bay Networks Other Equipment

Lattis Sys. 800 · Lattis Cell 10114R · Lattis Sys. 810M · Lattis Cell 10115A
Lattis Cell 10114A · Lattis Hub 2804 · Lattis Hub 2813-04 · Lattis Hub 2803
Lattis Hub 2814-04 · Lattis Hub 2814-SA · Lattis Hub 2813-SA · Lattis Net 2705B
Lattis Net 2712 · Lattis Net 2702B-C · Lattis Sw. 28115 · Lattis Sw. 514
Lattis Net 2712/15B04 · Model 800 · Model 810M · Lattis Sw. 515
Model CH2011002 · Model CH3133001 · Model CH2004001 · Model CH3133003
BCN 72000 fr. · Model CH3133002 · BLN-2 71000 fr. · BLN-2 71000
BCN 72000 · BCN 73000 · BCN/BLN 75020 · BCN 73000 fr.
Bay Stack RPSU · EtherCell 10328-F

Cisco Other Equipment

C/ FDDI WS-C1400 · C/ FDDI WS-X1431 · C/ FDDI WS-X1444 · C/ FDDI WS-X1483
C/FDDI WS-C1400 · E-Switch 1-slot f.pl. · E-Switch 2015-RS · E-Switch 2115M
E-Switch 500 · E-Switch EPP-253 · E-Switch EPP-254 · E-Switch EPP-255
E-Switch F100 · Light Stream HS-100 · Pro Stack 1-slot f.pl. · Pro Stack Matrix
Pro Stack Pro16 · Pro Stack PSP-100T · Pro Stack PSP-155AF · Pro Stack PSP-310F
Pro Stack PSP-373 · Pro Stack PSP-410T

Miscellaneous Equipment

10pt Arial text block · 24pt Arial text block · 12pt Arial text block · 8pt Arial text block
36pt Arial text block · Bracket connector · Arcnet · Building 1
Break line · Bus · Building 2 · Callout - bracket 2
Callout - bent · Callout - straight · Callout - curved · Circle callout
Callout - bracket 1 · Cloud · City · Comm-link
Coaxial line tag · Database · Curved bus · FDDI ring
Ethernet · Flow director · Fiber optic line tag · Horizontal - outside
Horizontal · Line connector · Horizontal baseline · Radio comm.
Microwave tower · Room · Radio tower · Satellite dish
Satellite · Star · Dynamic connector · Twisted pair line tag
Token-ring · Vertical - outside · Vertical · Word balloon
Vertical baseline

Cisco 7000 Family

Cisco Access Products

Acc. Prod. 2500 fr. · Acc. Prod. 2501 /2 · Acc. Prod. 2503 /4 · Acc. Prod. 2507
Acc. Prod. 2513 /15 · Acc. Prod. 4000 fr. · Acc. Prod. 4000M · AP-4000 NP-2E
AP-4000 NP-2T · AP-4000 NP-1F-D-MM · AP-4000 NP-2R

Bay Networks Distributed 5000

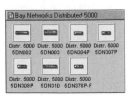

Distr. 5000 5DN002 · Distr. 5000 5DN003 · Distr. 5000 5DN304P · Distr. 5000 5DN307P
Distr. 5000 5DN308P · Distr. 5000 5DN310 · Distr. 5000 5DN378P-F

Accessories

APC Smart-UPS · Eazy switch · Eazy switch fr. · Generic 15" monitor
Generic equip. · Generic keyboard · Generic PC · Generic tower PC

 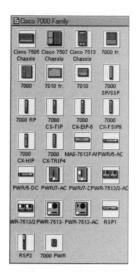 

Stencils in the Network Diagram category not shown: 3Com Linkbuilder, Bay
Networks Centillion, Bay Networks BayStack, Bay Networks Accessories,
Cabletron Micro MMAC, Cabletron MMAC Plus, Cisco Catalyst Switches,
Structured Racks

Category: Software Diagram

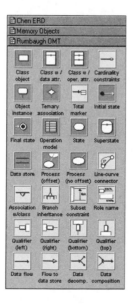  

(Software Diagram Continued)

Stencils in the Software Diagram category not shown: Express-G, Gane-Sarson DFD, Jacobson Use Cases, Language Level Shapes, Martin ERD, Nassi-Schneiderman, Shlaer-Mellor OOA, UML- Static Structure Shapes

Category: Visio Extras

Stencils in Visio Technical

Category: AEC

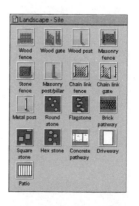

(continued)

(AEC Continued)

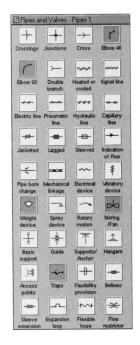

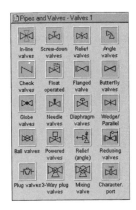

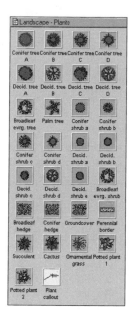

Stencils in AEC category not shown: Home - Appliance, Home - Cabinets, Home - Furniture, HVAC - Single Line and HVAC - Double Line, Initiation and Annunciation, Landscape - Watering, Pipes and Valves - Pipes 2, Pipes and Valves - Valves 2, Video Surveillance

Category: Annotation

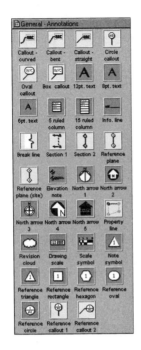

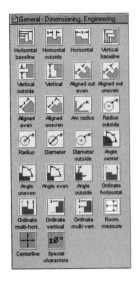

Stencils in the Annotation category not shown: General - Title Blocks, General - Drawing Tool Shapes

Category: Electrical & Electronic

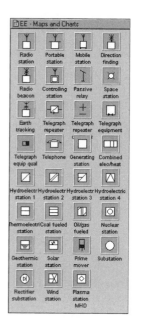

EE - Maps and Charts

Radio station	Portable station	Mobile station	Direction finding
Radio beacon	Controlling station	Passive relay	Space station
Earth tracking	Telegraph repeater	Telegraph repeater	Telegraph equipment
Telegraph equip qual	Telephone	Generating station	Combined elec/heat
Hydroelectr station 1	Hydroelectr station 2	Hydroelectric station 3	Hydroelectric station 4
Thermoelectri station	Coal fueled station	Oil/gas fueled	Nuclear station
Geothermic station	Solar station	Prime mover	Substation
Rectifier substation	Wind station	Plasma station MHD	

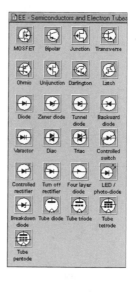

EE - Semiconductors and Electron Tubes

MOSFET	Bipolar	Junction	Transverse
Ohmic	Unijunction	Darlington	Latch
Diode	Zener diode	Tunnel diode	Backward diode
Varactor	Diac	Triac	Controlled switch
Controlled rectifier	Turn off rectifier	Four layer diode	LED / photo-diode
Breakdown diode	Tube diode	Tube triode	Tube tetrode
Tube pentode			

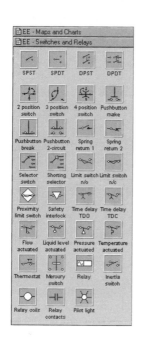

EE - Maps and Charts
EE - Switches and Relays

SPST	SPDT	DPST	DPDT
2 position switch	3 position switch	4 position switch	Pushbutton make
Pushbutton break	Pushbutton 2-circuit	Spring return 1	Spring return 2
Selector switch	Shorting selector	Limit switch n/o	Limit switch n/c
Proximity limit switch	Safety interlock	Time delay TDO	Time delay TDC
Flow actuated	Liquid level actuated	Pressure actuated	Temperature actuated
Thermostat	Mercury switch	Relay	Inertia switch
Relay coils	Relay contacts	Pilot light	

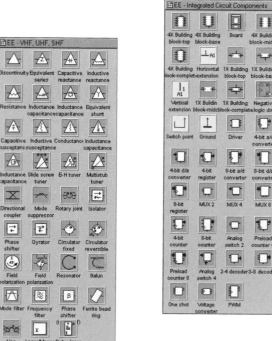

EE - VHF, UHF, SHF

Discontinuity	Equivalent series	Capacitive reactance	Inductive reactance
Resistance	Inductance capacitance	Inductance capacitance	Equivalent shunt
Capacitive susceptance	Inductive susceptance	Conductance	Inductance capacitance
Inductance capacitance	Slide screw tuner	E-H tuner	Multistub tuner
Directional coupler	Mode suppressor	Rotary joint	Isolator
Phase shifter	Gyrator	Circulator fixed	Circulator reversible
Field polarization	Field polarization	Resonator	Balun
Mode filter	Frequency filter	Phase shifter	Ferrite bead ring
Line stretcher	Laser/Maser	Ruby laser	

EE - Integrated Circuit Components

4X Building block-top	4X Building block-base	Board	4X Building block-middle
4X Building block-complete	Horizontal extension	1X Building block-top	1X Building block-base
Vertical extension	1X Buildin block-mid	1X Building block-complete	Negative logic dot
Switch point	Ground	Driver	4-bit a/d converter
4-bit d/a converter	4-bit register	8-bit a/d converter	8-bit d/a converter
8-bit register	MUX 2	MUX 4	MUX 8
4-bit counter	8-bit counter	Analog switch 2	Preload counter 4
Preload counter 8	Analog switch 4	2-4 decoder	3-8 decoder
One shot	Voltage converter	PWM	

EE - Analog and Digital Logic

Inverter	Buffer	Clock	Function generator
Amplifier	Converter	Logic gates 1	Logic gates 2
Flip-flops	Analog symbol	Digital symbol	Negative logic dot
Potentiometer	Positional servo	Crystal	Delay element
I/O port	Signal waveforms	Dimension line	Three-state buffer
Integrator	Summing amplifier	Multiplier	Divider
Function generator 2	Generalized integrator	Operational amplifier	Operational amplifier 2

(continued)

(Electrical & Electronic Continued)

Stencils in the Electrical & Electronic category not shown: Composite Assemblies, Fundamental Items, Maintenance Symbols, Qualifying Symbols, Rotating Equipment and Mechanical Functions, Transformers and Wingdings, Transmission Paths

Category: Equipment

Category: Facilities Management

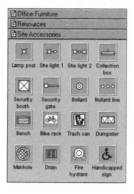

(continued)

(Facilities Management Continued)

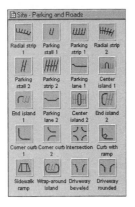

Category: Industrial Process

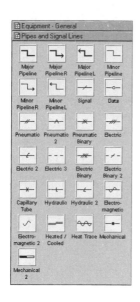

Stencils in the Industrial Process category not shown: Annotations, Vessels, Warehouse - Shipping and Receiving

Category: Mechanical Engineering

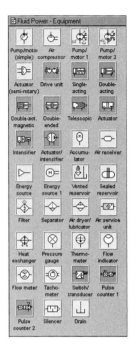

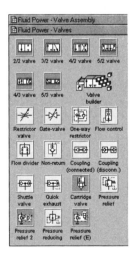

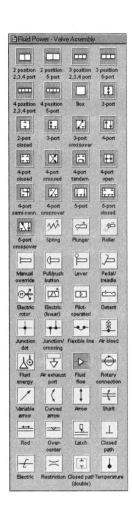

Stencils in the Mechanical Engineering Category not shown: Fasteners 2, General, Welding, Seals

Index

• *U* •

Notes

Notes

From PCs
to Personal Finance,
We Make it Fun and Easy!

For more information, or to order, please call 800.762.2974.

www.idgbooks.com
www.dummies.com

Dummies Books™
Bestsellers on Every Topic!

TECHNOLOGY TITLES

INTERNET

America Online® For Dummies®, 5th Edition	John Kaufeld	0-7645-0502-5	$19.99 US/$26.99 CAN
E-Mail For Dummies®, 2nd Edition	John R. Levine, Carol Baroudi, Margaret Levine Young, & Arnold Reinhold	0-7645-0131-3	$24.99 US/$34.99 CAN
Genealogy Online For Dummies®	Matthew L. Helm & April Leah Helm	0-7645-0377-4	$24.99 US/$35.99 CAN
Internet Directory For Dummies®, 2nd Edition	Brad Hill	0-7645-0436-3	$24.99 US/$35.99 CAN
The Internet For Dummies®, 6th Edition	John R. Levine, Carol Baroudi, & Margaret Levine Young	0-7645-0506-8	$19.99 US/$28.99 CAN
Investing Online For Dummies®, 2nd Edition	Kathleen Sindell, Ph.D.	0-7645-0509-2	$24.99 US/$35.99 CAN
World Wide Web Searching For Dummies®, 2nd Edition	Brad Hill	0-7645-0264-6	$24.99 US/$34.99 CAN

OPERATING SYSTEMS

DOS For Dummies®, 3rd Edition	Dan Gookin	0-7645-0361-8	$19.99 US/$28.99 CAN
LINUX® For Dummies®, 2nd Edition	John Hall, Craig Witherspoon, & Coletta Witherspoon	0-7645-0421-5	$24.99 US/$35.99 CAN
Mac® OS 8 For Dummies®	Bob LeVitus	0-7645-0271-9	$19.99 US/$26.99 CAN
Small Business Windows® 98 For Dummies®	Stephen Nelson	0-7645-0425-8	$24.99 US/$35.99 CAN
UNIX® For Dummies®, 4th Edition	John R. Levine & Margaret Levine Young	0-7645-0419-3	$19.99 US/$28.99 CAN
Windows® 95 For Dummies®, 2nd Edition	Andy Rathbone	0-7645-0180-1	$19.99 US/$26.99 CAN
Windows® 98 For Dummies®	Andy Rathbone	0-7645-0261-1	$19.99 US/$28.99 CAN

PC/GENERAL COMPUTING

Buying a Computer For Dummies®	Dan Gookin	0-7645-0313-8	$19.99 US/$28.99 CAN
Illustrated Computer Dictionary For Dummies®, 3rd Edition	Dan Gookin & Sandra Hardin Gookin	0-7645-0143-7	$19.99 US/$26.99 CAN
Modems For Dummies®, 3rd Edition	Tina Rathbone	0-7645-0069-4	$19.99 US/$26.99 CAN
Small Business Computing For Dummies®	Brian Underdahl	0-7645-0287-5	$24.99 US/$35.99 CAN
Upgrading & Fixing PCs For Dummies®, 4th Edition	Andy Rathbone	0-7645-0418-5	$19.99 US/$28.99CAN

GENERAL INTEREST TITLES

FOOD & BEVERAGE/ENTERTAINING

Entertaining For Dummies®	Suzanne Williamson with Linda Smith	0-7645-5027-6	$19.99 US/$26.99 CAN
Gourmet Cooking For Dummies®	Charlie Trotter	0-7645-5029-2	$19.99 US/$26.99 CAN
Grilling For Dummies®	Marie Rama & John Mariani	0-7645-5076-4	$19.99 US/$26.99 CAN
Italian Cooking For Dummies®	Cesare Casella & Jack Bishop	0-7645-5098-5	$19.99 US/$26.99 CAN
Wine For Dummies®, 2nd Edition	Ed McCarthy & Mary Ewing-Mulligan	0-7645-5114-0	$19.99 US/$26.99 CAN

SPORTS

Baseball For Dummies®	Joe Morgan with Richard Lally	0-7645-5085-3	$19.99 US/$26.99 CAN
Fly Fishing For Dummies®	Peter Kaminsky	0-7645-5073-X	$19.99 US/$26.99 CAN
Football For Dummies®	Howie Long with John Czarnecki	0-7645-5054-3	$19.99 US/$26.99 CAN
Hockey For Dummies®	John Davidson with John Steinbreder	0-7645-5045-4	$19.99 US/$26.99 CAN
Tennis For Dummies®	Patrick McEnroe with Peter Bodo	0-7645-5087-X	$19.99 US/$26.99 CAN

HOME & GARDEN

Decks & Patios For Dummies®	Robert J. Beckstrom & National Gardening Association	0-7645-5075-6	$16.99 US/$24.99 CAN
Flowering Bulbs For Dummies®	Judy Glattstein & National Gardening Association	0-7645-5103-5	$16.99 US/$24.99 CAN
Home Improvement For Dummies®	Gene & Katie Hamilton & the Editors of HouseNet, Inc.	0-7645-5005-5	$19.99 US/$26.99 CAN
Lawn Care For Dummies®	Lance Walheim & National Gardening Association	0-7645-5077-2	$16.99 US/$24.99 CAN

IDG BOOKS WORLDWIDE™

For more information, or to order, call (800)762-2974

FOR DUMMIES™
BESTSELLING BOOK SERIES

Discover Dummies™ Online!

The *Dummies* Web Site is your fun and friendly online resource for the latest information about *...For Dummies*® books on all your favorite topics. From cars to computers, wine to Windows, and investing to the Internet, we've got a shelf full of *...For Dummies* books waiting for you!

Ten Fun and Useful Things You Can Do at www.dummies.com

1. Register this book and win!
2. Find and buy the *...For Dummies* books you want online.
3. Get ten great *Dummies Tips*™ every week.
4. Chat with your favorite *...For Dummies* authors.
5. Subscribe free to *The Dummies Dispatch*™ newsletter.
6. Enter our sweepstakes and win cool stuff.
7. Send a free cartoon postcard to a friend.
8. Download free software.
9. Sample a book before you buy.
10. Talk to us. Make comments, ask questions, and get answers!

Jump online to these ten fun and useful things at
http://www.dummies.com/10useful

For other technology titles from IDG Books Worldwide, go to
www.idgbooks.com

Not online yet? It's easy to get started with *The Internet For Dummies*®, 5th Edition, or *Dummies 101*®: *The Internet For Windows*® *98*, available at local retailers everywhere.

Find other *...For Dummies* books on these topics:

Business • Careers • Databases • Food & Beverages • Games • Gardening • Graphics • Hardware
Health & Fitness • Internet and the World Wide Web • Networking • Office Suites
Operating Systems • Personal Finance • Pets • Programming • Recreation • Sports
Spreadsheets • Teacher Resources • Test Prep • Word Processing

IDG BOOKS WORLDWIDE BOOK REGISTRATION

Register This Book and Win!

We want to hear from you!

Visit **http://my2cents.dummies.com** to register this book and tell us how you liked it!

- ✔ Get entered in our monthly prize giveaway.

- ✔ Give us feedback about this book — tell us what you like best, what you like least, or maybe what you'd like to ask the author and us to change!

- ✔ Let us know any other ...*For Dummies*® topics that interest you.

Your feedback helps us determine what books to publish, tells us what coverage to add as we revise our books, and lets us know whether we're meeting your needs as a ...*For Dummies* reader. You're our most valuable resource, and what you have to say is important to us!

Not on the Web yet? It's easy to get started with *Dummies 101*®: *The Internet For Windows*® *98* or *The Internet For Dummies*®, 5th Edition, at local retailers everywhere.

Or let us know what you think by sending us a letter at the following address:

...*For Dummies* Book Registration
Dummies Press
7260 Shadeland Station, Suite 100
Indianapolis, IN 46256-3917
Fax 317-596-5498

™
FOR DUMMIES

BESTSELLING
BOOK SERIES